When AA Doesn't Work for You

Rational Steps to Quitting Alcohol

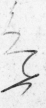

When AA Doesn't Work for You

Rational Steps
to Quitting Alcohol

by Albert Ellis Ph.D. and Emmett Velten, Ph.D.

Barricade Books Inc.
Fort Lee, New Jersey

Published by Barricade Books Inc., 150 Fifth Avenue, New York, NY 10011

Printed in the United States of America.

Library of Congress Cataloging-in-Publication Data

Ellis, Albert.
    When AA doesn't work for you : rational steps to quitting
alcohol / Albert Ellis and Emmett Velten.
        p.   cm.
    ISBN 0-942637-53-4 (pbk.) : $14.95
    1. Alcoholics—Rehabilitation.   I. Velten, Emmett Charlton.
II. Title.
HV5278.E45   1992
362.29'286—dc20   91-38539
                                                                      CIP

9   8   7   6   5   4   3

Contents

1

How Do You Know When Alcohol Is a Problem?

Ever since human beings discovered alcohol thousands of years ago, some have drunk too much of it. They've sabotaged themselves and others. Many have killed themselves with it. Alcohol is deadlier than all the "hard" drugs put together. It kills ten times more Americans than heroin does, and twenty times more than cocaine and crack. (Only tobacco is deadlier.)[1] The death toll is a small part of the story, because alcohol abuse also leads to appalling suffering and expense for us, the living. Its worst effects are child and spouse abuse, other violence, incest, broken families, accidents, injuries, absence at work and at home, ill health, and higher insurance rates for us all. In addition, hundreds of thousands of people feel scarred by having been raised with alcohol-addicted family members.

And the heavy drinkers themselves? Not only do many die, but so do the hopes, loves, and dreams of many others. Every day we see on television and in the movies, in magazines and grocery store tabloids the stories of degradation and recovery from the powers and perils of alcohol. Every neighborhood—almost every block!—has its own "meeting." The more we think we know about demon

1

rum and "the disease of alcoholism," the more its dangers seem to grow. And it isn't just alcohol. Other addictions, unheard-of mere years ago, pop up everywhere and seem to run our lives.

Has the number of addictions increased? If so, why? Is it the stress of modern life? Is it because our parents (and their parents!) had alcohol problems? What about the idea that addictions are caused by our genes?

You may have questions that hit closer to home. People you care about—loved ones, friends, relatives, neighbors—may drink too much. You'd like to help, but you wonder; "If I try to, will I contribute to their problems? Will I 'enable' them?" "*Did* I contribute to their problems?" Maybe someone *told* you so. And even showed you one of the many books that point the finger! But how valid is that line of thinking?

Then there's you, the reader, who may ask: "Do *I* have a problem? If my relatives have drinking problems, does that mean I have the wrong genes? Must I develop a drinking (or drug) problem some day? *Do* I drink too much? Should I (or *could* I) cut down on my drinking? Why is it so hard to do so? Will *I* become an alcoholic? What on earth *is* an alcoholic?"

Now that you think about it, with just about everybody claiming to be "in recovery" from familiar addictions, like alcohol and drugs, as well as from new ones now in vogue, like "codependency," *could* you be an addict and *not even know it*? Or maybe you *do* know it. Do you count yourself among the recover*ing* (but never the recover*ed*)? It can give you a good, warm, fuzzy feeling—and a safety net—to be part of the "in" group. But here, too, you may have nagging questions:

"Am I addicted to recovery meetings?"

"Even if I'm not addicted to the meetings, do I have to go to them the rest of my life?"

"Will I always want to drink, and if I do have a drop, will I develop raging alcoholism?"

"If *all* psychoactive, mood-altering substances are so bad, why do so many old-timers at recovery meetings—with all their years of 'sobriety'—chain-smoke and drink huge quantities of coffee?" —*"trading down" in addictions*

"Why *do* people cause themselves problems when they 'know' better?"

"Can I combine sobriety with growth? Can I ever leave behind my identity of 'substance abuser, in recovery' and close that chapter in my life?"

"Are my only choices: Self-help meetings forever, whether I am 'dry' or 'sober'? Relapse? Or abstinence with white knuckles?"

Well, wonder no more! We have written *When AA Doesn't Work for You* for people who want to work on themselves individually or who want to supplement their therapy or recovery meetings. It will provide answers to the above questions. We base this self-help guide on practical forms of psychotherapy designed to empower you and increase your self-acceptance and freedom. We have concentrated on showing you proven relapse prevention techniques. We will teach you how to direct your own therapy and become an effective self-helper. Specifically, we will demonstrate the ABCs of overcoming addictions, as made famous in Rational-Emotive Therapy (RET).[2]

The ABCs of Recovery

RET uses an ABC model to enable people to get a handle on their own self-defeating thinking, emotional reactions, and behavior. Let's begin with G, for Goal.

You pick a Goal, such as being happier and suffering less. Almost everyone shares that goal. (Even suicidal people have the goal of being happier and suffering less, for they nearly always believe they will be better off dead.) Once you choose a Goal, you can rate the value of your actions according to how they help—or hinder—your pursuit of that Goal. Your Goal gives meaning to your actions.

The main Goal we shall try to help you achieve in this book is that of giving up problem drinking. Why? Because you have decided that it interferes with your happiness and causes you needless suffering. Too much alcohol makes you fail at important tasks, lose important people's love, harm others, and create health hazards. You need it like you need rat poison.

Why, though, do you still drink too much? Because of your self-abusive ABCs. Your Goal, we said, is to stop your problem drinking. But your ABCs often lead you to sabotage this G and to drink excessively.

A stands for Activating Events in your life that precede your drinking.

B stands for your Beliefs or what you tell yourself about your A's.

C stands for the Consequences—your feelings and actions that stem from A's and Bs.

Suppose that your Goal is to refrain from drinking, even when you have an urge to do so and circumstances tempt you to drink. What are your ABCs when you actually refrain? Something like this:

A *(Activating Events):* You have had a hard day. You are at a party and friends keep urging you to have a drink. You know that they will be pleased if you do drink and that you will feel relaxed and will enjoy drinking.

B (Beliefs About A): "I would like to have a few drinks, *but* that will help me continue to be a problem drinker. I would enjoy drinking, *but* I will later regret it. I would prefer to please my friends, *but* I'd much rather please myself and my family by refraining. I often crave alcohol, *but* I never have to cater to my craving."

C (Consequences): Drinking only ginger ale and club soda. Remaining sober. Feeling sorry that you can't indulge and enjoy drinking like some of your friends are doing, but feeling good about your self-control and the approval of your family.

Notice that these ABCs of nondrinking include, at B, only Beliefs that are *preferences* and *dislikes,* but no real *demands* and *commands.* Notice, too, that *preferences* tend to yield successful results.

Now suppose that your Goal, again, is to refrain from drinking but that you actually sabotage it and take several drinks. Your ABCs then may go something like this:

A (Activating Events): You have had a hard day. You are at a party and friends keep urging you to have a drink. You know that they will be pleased if you do drink and that you will feel relaxed and will enjoy drinking.

B (Beliefs About A): "I'd like to have a few drinks to relax, and I *must* have what I want and *can't stand* being deprived! Even if I might later regret drinking, it's *awful* if I can't enjoy it right now! Whenever I have a *real* craving for alcohol, I *have to* give in to it. Screw it! I'll drink and be happy right now!"

C (Consequences): Having several drinks. Feeling angry and depressed about drinking. Making up excuses for drinking. Putting yourself down the next morning for having foolishly indulged. Becoming more depressed. Having more of an urge to drink to "treat" your self-downing and depression. Further damage to your body.

Notice that in this case your ABCs include, at point B, strong *shoulds, musts, demands,* and *commands,* as well as *awfuls* and *I-can't-stand-its* that accompany these rigid demands. The *musts* tend to yield poor results.

According to the ABC theory of Rational-Emotive Therapy (RET) that I (AE) originated in 1955, and according to the other cognitive-behavioral therapies that followed RET, this is what usually occurs when you make yourself neurotic. That is, when you make yourself anxious, depressed, enraged, self-hating, phobic, or addicted. You take your *preferences* and *desires* for healthy Goals (such as success, approval, comfort, and pleasure) and you turn them into strong, rigid *shoulds, oughts, musts,* and *commands.* Like the rest of us, you are fallible and imperfect. Because others and world conditions often thwart your grandiose *musts,* you *make yourself* needlessly miserable when you devoutly believe a must. In RET we coined the term *musturbation* to highlight humorously this unhumorous process by which you make yourself miserable. An old saying in RET is "Musturbation leads to self-abuse."

A *preferred* Belief has obvious or implied *buts* attached to it. "I'd very much *like* money (love, success, or alcohol), *but* I don't absolutely *need* it. I can be reasonably (though maybe less) happy without it!" Just try to get disturbed if you really and truly believe this self-statement!

A *mus*turbatory Belief is very different, and it tends to yield worse results! "Because I very much like money or booze, I absolutely *must* have it. If I don't get what I completely *must* have, life is *awful,* I *can't stand* it, I'm *worthless,* and I'll *never* get what I really *need!*" Just try on *that* self-statement and see if you can remain *un*disturbed.

Let's look at the ABCs of a common emotional problem, like anxiety:

> *G (Goal):* To feel good and enjoy oneself. To succeed at projects and relationships.

> *A (Activating Events):* You fail at work, school, or a relationship.

> *rB (rational Belief):* "I don't like failing, *but* it's not the end of the world. I'll try again. Even if I never succeed, that's too bad, but I can still lead a fairly happy life."

> *aC (appropriate Consequences):* Feelings of disappointment and regret. Determination to keep trying to succeed. Criticizing your inadequate *behaviors* but not downing *yourself* for failing.

If you stopped at this point, you would feel appropriately concerned about your behavior. You wanted to do better, but you failed. You would feel motivated to try to change your behavior so that you'd have a better chance of success. When, however, you feel anxious and depressed *in addition to* feeling disappointed and concerned, you went beyond a *preference* to a *must:*

> *iB (irrational Beliefs):* "I absolutely *should* not have failed! I'm no good for failing. It's *awful* to be the kind of *rotten person* who will *always* fail!"

> *iC (inappropriate Consequences):* Feelings of anxiety, depression, and self-hatred. Avoiding trying again. Indulging in alcohol or drugs to avoid thinking about what a rotten person you are and to dull your emotional pain.

How the ABCs Can Set You Free

Whenever you have a Goal (G) of becoming happier and suffering less in life by *not* drinking compulsively, alcohol is often available to you at point A (the Activating Event). When at point C (Consequences) you self-defeatingly drink to excess, the theory of Rational-Emotive Therapy (RET) says that A *contributes to* but does not directly *cause* C, your self-defeating drinking. According to RET the much more important and *direct* cause of C (your overdrinking) is B (your Belief System or your attitudes, ideas, opinions, expectations, memories, and images). The B is *you:* a thinking, feeling, acting, creating human being. The key question then is, "Are my Beliefs— that is, am I—for me or against me?"

The fact that your mind is complex and creative provides great strength, but often contributes to your downfall. You can easily hold contradictory opinions. You can believe one thing one minute, another a minute later, and both of them quite firmly. You, for instance, are very much against discomfort. Like most people, you probably have deeply believed and felt about some specific discomfort, "This really stinks!" This strong negative opinion about discomfort motivates you to try to change, escape, or avoid it. If you did not detest discomfort, you (and the human race) would have died out long ago. Why? Because you would not have avoided your enemies. You would not have invented ways to earn money, eat, and stay warm. You would not drink to quench your thirst. Your ability to feel pain, deprivation, and fear (and to ward off those feelings) *helps* you stay alive.

But too much of a good thing can lead to trouble. Like most humans, you *also* tend to say, "It's *awful!* I *can't stand* it" when faced with stress, hassles, and minor deprivations. You then create whining, depression, tantrums, avoidance, jealousy, or other, unhelpful emotions. You may bring on more trouble when you choose long-term goals, such as getting a college degree or maintaining a relationship. Because if you focus too strongly on the discomforts and hassles you then experience, and if you *demand* that they not exist, you disturb yourself.

If you avoid such frustrations, you feel better in the *short* run, but over the years you will feel worse, because you won't realize your important goals. Thus, Beliefs may help you in some situations but defeat you in other ways. How can you unravel your self-helping from your self-hurting, your rational from your irrational Beliefs?

Our approach is first to empower you to see the big picture in your self-help projects (and in life). The second step is to show you how to develop good reasons for your choices and actions. Then we will show you how to choose to get more of what you want and less that you don't want out of life by working and practicing your own self-help program.

If your Goal is to stop problem drinking, you can help yourself by changing many situations (A's, in the ABC model) *related* to your boozing (Cs, in the ABC model). Later we will discuss such changes and show you how to make them. Now, however, we will focus chiefly on how you can make changes in B, the Belief System that *you bring to* the various situations (A's) you encounter. It is your Belief System—*you*—that gives meaning to the situations and adversities (A's) of your life—present, past, or future. And it is your Belief System that gives meaning and power to alcohol.

Your Bs—Belief System or attitudes—largely create your Cs (Consequences), namely your feelings and actions. These include problem drinking, anxiety, compulsions, depression, anger, self-hatred, and shame. It is your Cs, of course, that you strive to change when you start a self-help project. Your A's (Activating experiences) can be a second choice target. But changes in your Beliefs (Bs) are deeper and more lasting and will usually help you *get better*, not just temporarily *feel better*.

The comic strip character Pogo summed it all up years

ago. Oliver Hazard Perry, the famous naval commander in the War of 1812, sent a message back to General William Henry Harrison after Perry's forces had won the Battle of Lake Erie: "We have met the enemy, and they are ours." Pogo applied it to human nature and said, "We have met the enemy and they are *us!*"

On the field of battle against addictions, *we* defeat ourselves. We often don't realize that the most important enemy lies within. Until we do realize it—and do something about it—we lose battle after battle. Like Don Quixote (but not so funny), we tilt at windmills, thinking they are the opponent.

Stinking Thinking

The world of self-help meetings has given us many useful ideas and commonsense slogans to help us keep those ideas in mind and stay on track. "Stinking thinking" is one of them. It refers to the kinds of thoughts, attitudes, and expectations that move us *back* into substance abuse and *out* of recovery. Stinking thinking is the irrational, or self-defeating, part of our Belief System (B). It is the most direct cause of our disturbances, lapses, relapses, and wrecked recovery at C (Consequences).

In this self-help book we teach the most widely useful methods for seeking out, discovering, and Disputing (at point D) your *stinking thinking* Beliefs (RET calls them irrational Beliefs or iBs) until you rarely create them. Then you can achieve a more durable recovery. We also will show how *chains* of ABCs lead to a maze of thoughts, feelings, and actions that constitute neurotic personality. And we will demonstrate how to break those chains and get better results (Cs).

Is stinking thinking or irrational Beliefs (iBs) *always* the cause of your drinking problems? No, not the *only* cause. When you have just about any problem you can find a number of reasons why you have it. Your family upbringing, for example. Your early life experiences. The neighborhood you were raised in. Your economic circumstances. Your friends. Your taste buds. And purely chance factors. Et cetera!

Okay. But why do *you* drink too much while your friends and relatives, many of them raised under similar conditions, do not? Or why did your brother and sister, raised just the way you were, drink heavily for a couple of years, then become abstinent or cut back to mild social drinking? After they changed, why did *you* continue to drink six-packs of beer all day long? "Well," you say, "I'm just different from them." Different, you are. But where'd you get the "*just* different"? Mainly from your thinking.

"That may be true for some people," said Craig, one of our clients whose series of blackouts and decaying liver still didn't deter him from polishing off a whole bottle of wine every night. "But that's not me. I start with a single glass at dinner, which even my doctor said I could have once in a while, and then I *just* finish the bottle. Maybe other people have stinking thinking. Not me! I don't think *anything*. I just have that first drink, and then it automatically goes on from there. I don't even *know* that I'm taking the second, third, and fourth glasses. It just happens. How can you say that I *think* my way into doing so?"

"Very easily!" I (AE) replied. "Let's just look at a few of your thoughts before you get soused every night. First of all, you decide to bring home a bottle of wine. Nobody *forced* you to stop at the liquor store, and the clerk didn't *make* you carry the bottle out of the store. So you *chose* to buy it, *chose* to reach into your pocket for the money, *chose* to carry the wine home, *chose* to open it, and *chose* to have "just one glass" even though you know you never stop at that. Right?"

"Well, in a way, yes."

"'In a way'? In what way did you *not* make all these choices? How come, at any one of these deciding points, you did not say to yourself, 'I'd better decide to avoid the liquor store, to buy only nonalcoholic beverages, to have only one drink and immediately put the bottle away,' or something like that? How come you keep deciding to go on and on and on?"

"Hm. I see what you mean. But that's because I merely wanted a drink or two. And with my family history of drinking and enjoying it, why shouldn't I automatically want some wine every evening?"

"Right. Why not? But you forget that a want is, first, a thought, second a feeling, and third, an action tendency. To have a want or a desire for wine and to *give in* to it, you first have to *know* that you have the desire, *realize* that you will feel good by indulging in it, *see* that it is possible to fulfill it, *decide* to gratify it, *plan* how to get the wine, *figure* out a reason for drinking it even when you have previously discovered that it leads to bad results, *argue against* the reasons for not drinking, *make up excuses* for indulging *this time*, and later *evaluate* the 'good' and 'bad' results of your having imbibed."

"Ouch! As you say, I guess I do have many thoughts along the way as I buy the wine, take it home, and start drinking too much. But do I really have all those irrational musts and demands that you keep looking for in RET?"

"You damned well do! For let's suppose that you only—yes, only—had desires and preferences. Considering what your dismal history of drinking has been, the series of thoughts we just mentioned that now drive you to drink would go something like this:

"One: 'I am passing the liquor store and I remember that drinking relaxes me, makes me forget my troubles, and gives me a buzz. But it also gets me into many difficulties and health problems.'

"Two: 'Now that I've broken my vow not to buy a bottle of wine, I could take only one glass tonight and not harm myself. But that's too dangerous. So I'd better not drink at all. No, to hell with it! One glass won't hurt anything.'

"Three: 'I've already had one drink, which I promised myself not to have, and I could go on, very easily go on, to finish the bottle. But that's what I've done so many times before and really screwed myself by doing. That's exactly what got me to be the problem drinker I am today. But it's too hard to stop this time. I'll stop tomorrow!'

"Four—"

Craig broke in, "Okay, I get it! You're saying that instead of sticking to my preferences for the pleasure of wine, on the one hand, and the good effects of my *not* drinking, on the other hand, I'm sneaking in some demands for alcohol. And my demands overcome my preferences?"

"Exactly! I can see that you're learning the RET pamphlets that we gave you for homework when you first came to the Institute. Your *demands*, your *musts* about drinking are overwhelming your *desires* to stay sober. Let's clarify some of these right now. When you pass the liquor store and decide to enter it, what's your must?"

"Mm. 'Even though I know it will be wrong to go into the store, I *shouldn't* have to do without?'"

"Right! And what's your *must* when you have the bottle at home and decide to take the first drink?"

"Oh, yes. I see. Something like 'I *should* be able to have it if I want it. I know I could refuse to have any alcohol tonight, but I *can't stand* the frustration. I *need* to get immediate relief.'"

"Right again! And when you keep drinking and drinking till you finish the bottle, what's your continuing demand?"

"You're right. 'I *can't stand* stopping, now that I'm feeling so good. I *have to* get the most out of this bottle. I *have* to have it *all* no matter what happens to me later!'"

"See? One *must* after another. No wonder your preferences—your Goal of helping yourself by not drinking—get dissolved."

Craig asked, "You mean, get dissolved in alcohol?"

"No, dissolved in your devout, rigid, not-to-be-stopped *musts.*"

"Yes. What do you know? And just a few minutes ago I was swearing that I *just* drank. That I didn't have any thoughts at all before I bought the stuff and started drinking. I can see now that's BS!"

"What kind of homework can we devise that will help you *keep* seeing that, *keep* finding those self-defeating musts, and *keep* Disputing them?" I asked.

Craig thought for a moment. "Every time I feel upset or overworked and start thinking that I deserve some wine, I could write down my thoughts. I could look for the musts. Then I could Dispute them and write down why I *don't* have to drink wine to relax. How does that sound?"

We worked out details of when Craig would do the homework, how he would remind himself to do it, and how he might reward or penalize himself for doing it or not doing it. I reminded him, "You may never become perfect at doing homework or at not drinking. You can look at a slip as information about how you are doing, not a disaster. A slip is not your whole worth. A slip gives you ideas about how to fine-tune your efforts. As you listen to your tape of this session, you may pick up more ideas about how to design your homework."

Craig did keep doing his homework of detecting and Disputing his drink-encouraging musts. After three months, he had little trouble passing up liquor stores. Even when his wife or son brought home some wine and had a glass or two at dinner, he strongly realized that he didn't *have to* join them. And he rarely did.

In this book we also will teach the less widely useful but still sometimes lifesaving methods by which you can *(a) change* A by, for instance, staying out of bars or not having any liquor at home; *(b) temporarily change B* by, for instance, learning to stop obsessive negative thoughts, or by making positive affirmations; and *(c)* directly *change* C (Consequences, such as compulsive drinking) by, for instance, getting someone to lock you in a room to prevent you from drinking.

But we are getting ahead of ourselves. Let's begin at the beginning and take "first things first." The first step is to figure out whether you have a true problem.

2

How *Do* I Know When My Drinking Is a Problem?

Lots of people ask that question. You'd think the natural next question is "How much do you drink?" But it isn't. People can drink like troopers and be very little if any the worse for it. Some can rarely drink and have a major problem with it. The early American colonials, for instance, drank morning, noon, and night and consumed much more liquor per capita than do Americans today. A typical breakfast menu included hard liquor. Yet the only ill effects of alcohol back then seemed to be idleness and drunkenness. The colonials saw that drinking caused drunkenness, of course, but they did not view it as an uncontrollable disease. The idea of being "out of control" was virtually unknown to them, and they did not believe alcohol caused aggression, violence, or crime. Cotton Mather, the famous Puritan fire-and-brimstone preacher, called alcohol "the good creature of God"![1]

"What? Doesn't drinking cause alcoholism?"

Well, it helps, but it doesn't do so directly. Most people who drink, no matter how regularly, never have any problems from it. Even if you drink daily, it does not necessarily "spread" and take over your life. You could, however, rarely drink but have major problems when you do. The chemical effects of the alcohol have surprisingly little to do with it.

What does alcohol mean to you? Much of alcohol's power depends on its meaning in your culture and especially its meaning to you. Its power depends on what you use alcohol for and what you expect it to do for you. You could, for example, come from a family that had wine at most meals, thought of it as quite normal and ordinary, and included no one who had a problem related to it. Whole cultures—the American colonials, for instance, and traditional Jewish, Italian, Greek, and Chinese cultures—tend to hold that viewpoint. They show much less problem drinking than does mainstream American culture.[2]

Or you could come from a family that thought of alcohol as sinful and powerful, as leading to "tying one on," to rowdy times, to the expression of anger, sexuality, or other unseemly emotions, or as _necessary_ for relaxation. Your family could have emphasized that it was against the law to drink a drop till you were twenty-one and warned "Be careful! Don't drink too much!" The authorities in church or school might have cited examples of people who were good and responsible _until_ they fell into the clutches of demon rum. They thought (and taught) that drinking alcohol is a direct cause of out-of-character behavior. Modern Americans generally see it that way. Women, for example, who are battered by problem drinkers tend to blame the alcohol. So do people who are caught for child molesting (if they claimed they had been drinking at the time and "lost control").[3]

The mainstream of American culture sees alcohol as causing _uninhibited_ behavior: anger, confrontations, aggression, violence, crime, and unrestrained sexuality. Where alcohol consumption takes place largely outside the family or is reserved for unruly (mostly male) occasions—such as was true on the American frontier—there tend to be more problems with alcohol. Even in melting pot

America certain cultures and subcultures tend to show more than average alcohol abuse: the poor; the working class; males and various male-oriented environments such as the military and fraternities; Southerners; Protestants; gays and lesbians; the Irish; many Native American cultures; and students.

Even among the groups with the lowest rates of problem drinking, however—such as Italians, Chinese, Greeks, and Jews—there are drinkers with blatant alcohol-related problems. Similarly, among the groups tending to have the highest rates of problem drinking, most people have no problem with it. What are these problems and why do some people have more than their share?

What Makes a Problem a Problem?

If you drink alcohol so that it interferes *directly or indirectly* with achieving your goals, you have a problem with it. You can make drinking a problem when you give it excessive power to enable you to cope better, to feel good, or to help you reduce emotional distress. It's a problem when you believe you need it for those or other purposes. Problem behavior is *defined by how much it hinders you in reaching your goals.* Because different people have different goals, your problem in one situation may not be a problem for other people in a different setting. If, for instance, you go out every night with your crowd and drink, and then fail a big test, your drinking is a problem *if* you believe it is more important in the long run to pass the test.

In Rational-Emotive Therapy (RET) we *define* stinking thinking that leads you to act *against* your own interest as *irrational.* In the example above, one of my (EV's) clients, Chad, had self-defeating or irrational Beliefs (iBs, stinking thinking) that led him to drink too much before an exam. It was, "I *can't stand* the hassle of studying and knowing that everybody is having fun but me. I've *got to* pass the test tomorrow, but also _must_ not miss the fun that everybody is having tonight! How _awful_ if I lose out!" He also thought, "They _mustn't_ think I'm a nerd. It would be _too_ embarrassing if I said I couldn't go out because I had to stay home and study." Chad's irrational, stinking thinking harmed him because he really wanted to pass the test.

If Chad had felt that how he did on the test didn't matter much, or if he wanted a good reason to quit school, then his going out drinking could be _rational or self-helping_.

RET defines thinking as _rational_ if it tends to help you feel happier and achieve your goals in the long run. Self-helping behavior usually stems from _rational_ Beliefs (rBs) that express your preferences, wishes, wants, or desires, _not_ your unrealistic demands.

In your own case, staying in and studying every night and _not_ ever going out with people to drink _could_ be _irrational_. Let's say that you were at college, were very shy, and had crummy social skills and that one of the more social people in your dorm invited you out with the group. You might _irrationally_ (against your long-term interests) turn down the invitation, if your studies would not suffer too much by your accepting it. Here your self-defeating or irrational Beliefs (iBs, stinking thinking) might be: "I _must_ not show them how socially anxious I am. I _can't stand_ going out with them and showing them what a nerd I am!" "If I failed socially, that would show that I'm a hopeless loser! I don't really have to study tonight, but that's a good excuse to avoid going out."

At times in this self-help book we use the term "inappropriate." In RET "inappropriate" feelings or actions are _those that hinder you in reaching your goals and in feeling happier_. RET is highly individualistic. Its purpose is to help you solve _your_ problems, feel happier in _your_ own way, and reach _your_ goals. At the same time, because you are a social creature and choose to live with others, you _also_ want to get along with other people and to help your social group. An urge to have fun by yelling, "Fire!" when there is no fire in a crowded theater would be antisocial and therefore irrational. You will sanely or "appropriately" avoid harming yourself *and* your social group.

If, let's say, you want to advocate an unpopular opinion or dress in a way that is comfortable for you but distressing to other people, go for it! Unless, of course, other people would be likely to be *so much* against your view or your way of dressing that they might harm you. In that case, voicing your opinion or wearing the unpopular garb could be irrational and inappropriate *to your goals* of staying free and alive. It might be, however, that you would consider your goal so very important—for instance, throwing off the chains of tyranny or bigotry—that you would still voice and battle for your view, even at great personal risk. Doing so could be rational and appropriate to your goals and purposes. It all depends on what your goals are and what consequences you are willing to risk.

It's time for an exercise to show the differences between thinking that is rational versus irrational, self-helping versus stinking. For each of the following statements, decide whether it is rational or irrational, and why. Be definite about your answers and write them down. Respond to all these statements before looking at our comments. Then you will profit more from our feedback. Our answers are on the following page.

1. "People who fail are failures."

2. "I hate the anxiety and shakes that may come if I stop drinking."

3. "I have to succeed!"

4. "The 49ers have to win!"

5. "I went out drinking last night because you yelled at the kids."

6. "Dealing with my drinking problems is very hard. It takes too much time and energy."

7. "After our child died, I felt so much grief. I fought against it, but I couldn't help going back to drinking."

8. "Joe didn't get the love he needed as a child. That's why he's so hostile now."

Possible Answers to the Quiz

1. Irrational. Why? Because to call *oneself* a failure is an overgeneralization. It implies that you will *always* fail, which means you know the future. Also, if you see yourself as a failure, then you don't try to change and you may consciously or unconsciously make yourself keep failing.

2. This one is harder. If you mean that you hate the bad feelings of anxiety but are willing to go through them in order to get better, the statement is *rational*. It is rational because it would *help* you to believe it. If you mean "I *can't stand* feeling anxious!" the statement is *irrational*. It is irrational because it leads you away from facing your anxiety, from seeing what you do to create it, and from working at overcoming it.

3. This one's irrational. The reason? You *don't* have to succeed. You could fail. If you believe you *have to* succeed, you may make yourself so anxious that you drink to temporarily reduce or cover up your anxiety. Or you may procrastinate at working to succeed because you fear that you will fail. If you do fail, you will call it a disaster and may call yourself a worm. The rational, self-helping statement would be "I prefer to succeed, and I will work hard to do so. But if I fail, I fail. It's not the end of the world. Maybe I can learn something from it."

4. Aha! Trick question. No, of course the 49ers don't have to win even if you say so. The statement is therefore illogical. But is it also irrational, that is, self-defeating? Probably not. Though you may actually upset yourself if the 49ers don't win—particularly if a game official made a bad call that made the difference—you may not do anything self-defeating. For instance, you may not get drunk over it, try to attack the referee, or start arguments or fights with anyone who says the team played lousy and deserved to lose. If you did do those things, statement number 4 *would* be irrational. If you don't do those things, the statement—for you—is not truly irrational since it may not lead you to self-defeat.

5. If you are admitting you *decided* to go out drinking, that's good. If your drinking is self-defeating, then your decision—whatever it is based on—is still *irrational*. If you imply that your mate's yelling at the kids *made* you decide to go out drinking, that's additional stinking thinking.

6. The first sentence could easily be true and rational. Dealing with a drinking problem usually *is* difficult. That's why it's good to work at it with a plan. But does dealing with the problem take "*too* much time and energy"? No. You really mean that dealing with it *must* not be so difficult and that therefore it is *too hard* to tackle. No. It may be *very* hard but hardly *too* hard.

7. The first sentence is quite rational. It is normal and appropriate to feel very much grief when a loved one dies. When your child dies, the resulting emotional pain would normally be severe. If you did not care, that would be *irrational*. Why? Because you might be a person who does not care about other people. And if that were so, you would probably get into trouble with people because you have no feelings for them.

The second part of the statement, however, is *irrational*. Grief and the pain did not *make* you drink. You *chose* to deal with the pain that way. If you have a drinking problem, the choice to drink would cover up your pain and grief, but it might keep you from working through it. And the drinking could give you other kinds of problems. No one, we hope, would damn you as a person for drinking, but many people would rightly put down your self-defeating *behavior*. Even if you have no good reason for drinking, *you* are not blameworthy. Your stinking thinking and your drinking are foolish, but you are not a *rotten fool*.

8. The speaker may not actually know whether Joe got love as a child. But let's assume he didn't get it. If Joe now thinks "My blasted parents didn't give me love! I deserved it and it makes me furious just thinking of how they loved my brother more than me," *that thought* would cause his hostility, not the lack of love. The lack of love would be a sad, unfortunate event from his past. If he gives it power over himself now, that is self-defeating and irrational. And it hardly makes him very lovable right now! Nobody loves a human porcupine! If you want love, you had better act lovingly to others and stop thinking that they *must* love you first because someone else didn't love you years ago.

Obvious Problems of Drinking

Alcohol's obvious interferences with your goals include health, legal, social, and financial problems. We have listed some examples below. There are also signs of *upcoming* problems, and we've listed some of those, too. If you experience and hate to suffer from any of the following difficulties, *then you do have a problem with alcohol*. Choosing self-help is wise. If, on the other hand, you suffer poor results from drinking alcohol but do *not* think you have a problem, well, it's a free country! You still can wisely keep reading and think about this old Alcoholics Anonymous (AA) saying: "If ten people say you're drunk, you'd better lie down!"

- *Health problems.* Abnormal liver function, cirrhosis, pancreatitis, certain heart diseases, high blood pressure, ulcers, gastritis, malabsorption, atrophy of the testicles, sexual impotence and frigidity, osteoporosis, blackouts, and brain damage.

- *Legal problems.* Arrests for driving under the influence (DUI; also known as DWI, driving while intoxicated); getting stopped by the police; legal charges resulting from accidents and damage you did; loss of driver's license; child abuse and child neglect.

- *Social problems.* Your friends, relatives, and associates say you have a problem; missed work; absences from important meetings and affairs; arguments or fights with loved ones; loss of important relationships; divorce; arguments or fights in public with strangers.

- *Financial Problems.* Insurance premiums raised, insurance canceled because of accidents; overspending; losing money; getting "rolled" or mugged while under the influence; breaking or losing things; cigarette burns, fires; extra health and medical costs; considerable money spent on drinking; low-paying jobs, failure to get promoted, unemployment.

- *Other signs.* If you gulp alcohol to speed up its effects, drink the first thing in the morning, feel you have to make sure your supply doesn't run out, or have a hard time imagining a life without being able to drink, you will probably achieve drinking problems like those listed above. It's just a matter of time. You can save yourself much time and trouble by not waiting to "hit bottom." You are close enough to it already!

We would appreciate your feedback and suggestions about additional items for our list of drinking-related problems. If you live east of the Rockies, write Albert Ellis, Ph.D., Institute for Rational-Emotive Therapy, 45 East Sixty-fifth Street, New York, N.Y. 10021. If you live in the West, write Emmett Velten, Ph.D., Box 14523, San Francisco, Cal. 94114.

My Name Is _____?

Not all ill effects from boozing are so obvious. You don't have to nurse a bottle of cheap wine in a paper bag or wake up in the drunk tank to show problem drinking. Your pattern may include the problems listed above (and the potential for more of them!), but you may be far from the stereotype of the "alcoholic." Consider these examples of people who have more subtle or sporadic drinking problems.

1. Karen does not drink much—anymore! Her doctor told her, "Your liver is on its very last legs. When it goes, you go." Karen's liver tests had been shocking. Her doctor had continued, "And, Karen, I must be brutally frank here. The Transplant Committee has a very hard time approving a transplant for someone who isn't firmly sober. You aren't." This had frightened Karen badly for six months. But by the time her birthday rolled around, she had been "a good person" for so long she thought, "Just one tiny glass of brandy won't hurt." And it hadn't seemed to. Now Karen is up to a large glass of wine several times a week and thinks, "I need it to relax and get my mind off my health problems."

2. John recently was promoted to supervisor at his plant. He sure missed going out with his crew and seeing all the regulars at the local tavern (where he was a great favorite), but it just didn't seem right anymore. His boss had predicted, "You really can't socialize with men you supervise."

This was okay at first, but John began to feel alone, deprived, and overwhelmed at work and sorry for himself. One night he drove to his sister's place in a distant part of town and got plastered with his brother-in-law at a beer joint. Somebody said something John didn't like, and John took a swing at him.

3. Not long after she'd given birth to the twins, Kate really began to feel the strain. Dave worked so hard and was so supportive, she could hardly fault him for asking her to get a part-time job to help with their money problems. The first panic attack happened on the way to an important interview. "It's bad enough," she thought, "that I'm a failure as a mother, but I can't even look for work!" After the third Xanax prescription ran out and the panic attacks got worse, her physician suggested that she seek therapy. Kate couldn't stand having Dave know how "weak" she was, so she didn't go for therapy. If she drank vodka, she could manage.

4. Sean had never been drunk in his whole life. He was quite a cautious person, shy really, and drinking too much would never do. When he got home from work, though, he was so stressed out and lonely that he would have a beer or two. Maybe three or four after a hard day. While he felt better after the beers, and that was good, he also felt lethargic. "Oh, well," he thought as he went to check the refrigerator, "I should really go out tonight and make some friends," but he was too scared of rejection. "Maybe I'll be up for it tomorrow."

5. Stephanie had a weight problem and was afraid of turning off men because she was "fat." She went on a liquid diet, took off all but twenty pounds of the excess weight, and then she began to date. To her shock, she found she got terribly nervous on dates. Before dates, too. It helped to have a few drinks before going out. Drinking during the date didn't hurt. "It would be awful if I looked anxious," she told herself. "And if I don't like the guy it would be terrible to reject him and to hurt his feelings."

She woke up with men she didn't even like. Worse, she kept going out with some of them. And she kept regaining weight. Alcohol is not exactly low-cal.

6. Angela was a successful manager and destined for promotion. She had gone back to school, owned a small business, edited a newsletter, was wife and mother—you name it, she did whatever she "should." Her appointment book was full of obligations and duties. When friends told her to take time for herself, she couldn't grasp their meaning. Wasn't she doing so? She didn't have time to waste goofing off. "There's so many things I've got to get done." Every five or six weeks, however, her tensions would build up, so much so that Angela would spend most of Friday and the whole weekend under the influence of alcohol. After her hangover wore off on Monday, she would redouble her efforts to catch up in her duties. When her therapist asked her what she was telling herself during those weekends or what she thought the drinking might mean, she said, "Nothing."

7. Bill had hated arguments with people, female type people in particular, for as long as he could remember. His wife, Beth, was no exception. He wanted more sex with her, but didn't want to offend her by asking. Besides, "I shouldn't have to ask!" He made himself furious about asking for sex. "Don't I deserve better? After all, I don't run around! I always bring home a paycheck!" Each evening he parked himself in front of the TV set and got silently, completely drunk. "I can't let her know I'm pissed," he vowed. "One day she's going to push me too far, and I'm going to take the sex I deserve. To hell with her!"

8. Ramon drove the ninety miles and hit the streets and gay clubs of Big City on weekends, where he mingled, danced, drank, and partied in the fast lane. Safely. Or at least he meant to. A couple of times recently he'd noticed when he got back home that his package of condoms was unopened! "I guess the other guy used protection," Ramon said hopefully.

9. Janice felt depressed and hopeless. A high school dropout with two children and living on welfare in a public housing project—who wouldn't be depressed? After a bout with cocaine, she steered clear of other users. To cover her depression and her anger, she drank. When she got the chance to go get her high school diploma, she thought, "What if I fail? I couldn't face it," and didn't show up for her first class. That night, after she had drunk four beers, Janice said, "Screw it," and headed for the nearest corner and a kid selling crack.

Each person described above had a problem with alcohol. More accurately, they experienced poor results, or Consequences (Cs in the ABC model of disturbance). Did alcohol itself lead to the poor results? We say it *contributed*. The *real* culprit in each case was their *stinking thinking:* their irrational Beliefs (demands) about themselves, others, and conditions and their Beliefs about alcohol and its chemical effects. That is why even after you stop drinking, you'd better still combat and quit your stinking thinking. If stinking thinking keeps pushing your drinking buttons, your recovery is never secure.

You can stop your stinking thinking, but you can't just run and hide. It follows you. It's wherever you are. If you move to a new city, a new job, a new apartment, or a new mate, stinking thinking is there with you. Waiting.

Problems With Alcohol and Problems With "Alcoholic"

If drinking contributes to your self-defeat, you have a problem with alcohol. But you may also have a problem with the word *alcoholic*. In a typical scenario, you may admit to drinking too much and begin to look at what changes to make. Then a would-be helper asks, "Do you think you're an alcoholic?" Or says, "The first thing you have to do is admit you are an alcoholic. You won't get anywhere till you do that."

You may retort, "Well, I have a problem from drinking, but how do I know I'm a *true* alcoholic?" Or, "I know I'm not an alcoholic because [fill in the blank]." The would-be helper then points out, "You're in denial." Sound familiar?

What is an alcoholic? What is a true alcoholic? Most books on "alcoholism" say or imply that there is one pattern to overdrinking. They also say that you must admit that you are "an alcoholic" as the first step in getting better. Yet research shows there are many patterns of heavy drinking, many kinds of heavy drinkers, and many scenarios for developing "alcoholism." Large numbers of people go through times in which they drank too much, took stock of the poor results they were getting, and reduced or eliminated their drinking. The biographies, autobiographies, and public statements of numerous celebrities such as Bing (once known as "Binge") Crosby, Johnny Carson, Robert Redford, Frank Sinatra, Mickey Mantle, Nick Nolte, Steve Martin, and John Phillips (of the Mamas and the Papas) clearly show that many people "mature out" or give up substance abuse. They curtail their drinking when new goals and changed situations in their lives—like stardom—collide with it. As Bing Crosby, for example, became a superstar, he didn't become an angel. But he did reduce his drinking.[4]

College students, for instance, who drank so heavily that they had blackouts, were followed up as middle-agers. There was no correlation between the amount they drank in college and the amount they drank in middle age. They had severe alcohol problems as youngsters, but still did not go downhill the way "everybody knows" they should. Why not? No doubt many reasons, but our point is that "alcoholism" takes no single course.[5]

People can and do transform themselves in many ways over their lifetimes. They change careers, professions, partners, nationalities, interests, residences, sexual practices, and so on. A few people even change sex. "Alcoholism" is only a part of a whole human being, and often is given up as people confront it. Forcing those people with alcohol problems to "admit" they are permanently "alcoholics" may work with some drinkers, but it misses the mark with just as many others.

The original members of Alcoholics Anonymous were heavy-duty drinkers who had major, life-threatening problems with alcohol. It would surprise them to learn that every one of the nine people we described above has "an alcohol problem." The AA old-timers formed theories about "alcoholism" based on their own patterns. They adopted a treatment approach that worked for them. Yet their ideas about alcohol problems have become the gospel and have been applied to all drinkers, as if all people had the same problem.

The word _alcoholic_, like many nouns, is an _over-_generalization. It gives a _name_ to a group of behaviors accompanying problem drinking. It is also a theory about why those behaviors happen. It says, "Because you show _some_ actions characteristic of 'alcoholism,' that proves that you _have_ 'alcoholism.' And if you _have_ 'alcoholism,' that shows you _are_ an 'alcoholic.'" It also says, "You show actions characteristic of 'alcoholism' _because_ you are an 'alcoholic.'" This "explains" your actions on the basis of the _name_ (an overgeneralization) _it gave_ to your actions! This is like saying "You _are_ a neurotic" when you have some neurotic _traits_ and then saying "And your neurotic traits are _caused by_ your neurosis."

Calling yourself "an alcoholic" also leads to the myth, "Once an 'alcoholic,' always 'an alcoholic.'" As we will be teaching in this self-help guide, a major part of _rational_ self-help is learning to think clearly about _problem behavior_ and not rigidly to define it as your _self_. Rational-Emotive Therapy (RET) discourages overgeneralizations because they are often muddled. They ignore important aspects of you and push you to admit to "facts" about yourself that are not true. As Alfred Korzybski noted, a _word_ or a _name_ or a _behavior_ is not you. _You_ are not what you do or what group you join. You are a living, creative, self-creating _process_. If you label yourself _an_ alcoholic or an _anything_, and see it as unchangeable, _you_ will restrict your growth.[6]

Also, don't overgeneralize about the "stages of alcoholism." You may hear, for instance, that Anna and Mike are "middle stage alcoholics." This makes it sound as if their "alcoholism" itself developed from an early to a middle-stage. A more accurate statement would be "In my opinion, Anna and Mike have trained themselves to a midway point between a mild drinker and someone who is close to dying of alcohol abuse."

As a human being, you frequently accept or create labels and adopt a rating system that produces self-hatred. To admit you _have_ a problem is good. To identify your_self_ with the problem is bad—because it can lead to demoralization ("I'm hopeless. Who am I fooling?"); to denial ("I'm not _an_ alcoholic, so I don't have a problem"); and to defensiveness ("It's your fault that I'm a drunk. You drove me to it!"). Self-labeling is bad because it can keep you locked into a _battle_ and into an identity from which you may never escape. It can also keep you locked into the _bottle_. One alternative to AA, Women For Sobriety, has a saying, "I have a problem that once had me."[7] It captures the idea that we emphasize: _You_ do not equal your _problems_.

Using the word _alcoholic_ can sidetrack you from working on your alcohol-related problems. Not only stubborn, resistant people balk at "surrendering" and being classified "alcoholic." You may correctly admit that you have a problem but know _you_ are not the same as the problem or its label. You may see the term _alcoholic_ as an overgeneralization and realize that "alcoholism" describes only part of your _current_ behavior. You may have heard too, that a label like _alcoholic_ means perpetual attendance at twelve-step meetings, and—for better or for worse—

you may recoil from that idea and may stay away from recovery groups.

Most *self*-labels, or *self*-concepts, give you a plus or minus rating *as a person*. Once you buy into rating yourself as a person, you can get into trouble even with a positive rating. How so? Let's say you are a young woman who is extremely proud of her*self* for being gorgeous and sexy. Or a young man who prides him*self* on nonstop sex performance. How will you feel about those characteristics *and yourself* in fifty years? Probably negative if you still buy into our culture's crazy rating system for "good" people rather than of "good" deeds and traits.

Self-rating often supports the Establishment and your present culture, because you tend to rate yourself in terms of the culture's values. But what about *your* values? What about your own individual hopes and goals in life? Have you the right to seek what *you* want and live as *you* like? We think you do. However, if you rate *yourself* at all, even in terms of your own values, you may *hinder your* going after what *you* want. Why? Because you will tend to put your self down for your shortcomings. And when you do well, you will take false pride in your *self* rather than in what you *do*. Why false pride? Because "pride goeth before a fall." You are never really a *good or bad person*, but only a person with *good or bad acts or traits*.

What if you are proud of your*self* for being "in recovery"? If so, how will you feel about your*self* when you have a slip? Chances are, not very good. In the literature on relapse prevention there is a term for it, *abstinence violation effect*.[8] It refers to an *attitude* toward your*self* for having slipped, an attitude that converts a slip into a full-scale relapse. "Oh, God, I slipped! I've ruined everything and thrown away all my progress. I knew a failure like me would never make it. I might as well drink myself into an early grave." This kind of attitude helps you believe the old saying, "One drink, one drunk." That saying tells you what to expect and how to keep acting when you slip even once.

Even if you stay in recovery forever and therefore never put yourself down for slipping and never view yourself as less of a person, you _will_ show many flaws in other areas. _Then_ you will curse your_self_ for those! You make this happen because you buy into _self_-rating rather than into merely rating your _behavior_. Some AA sayings are pertinent at this point, "Salute your progress," and "Cherish your recovery." Notice they do not say, "Salute and cherish _yourself_ for your progress and your recovery."

Like everybody else we, too, deplore slips back into self-defeating behavior. It's great to have goals, such as becoming healthier and happier in recovery, and to work persistently toward them. Commitments and purposes are vital to happiness and health. Once, however, you rate your_self_ according to how you achieve such goals, you have a strong tendency to rate yourself _down_ for less than great progress. Then you may demoralize yourself (by labeling yourself a "loser"). Or you may deny you have a problem. Or you may defensively accuse others of being the real problem.

If, however, you stick with rating your _behavior_, in terms of its helping or blocking your _goals_, you are on better footing. When you see that certain actions, thoughts, and feelings are handicapping you, you will be better able to correct and change them.[9] If the new behaviors don't work, you will be able to try again, rather than thinking "Nothing I do is right. It'll never work out. I'm just a failure."

When we use the word _alcoholic_ in this book, we will enclose it in quotation marks to show that the word itself is an overgeneralization. Though it is difficult precisely to define "alcoholism," you can more easily show yourself (and others) that heavy drinking can lead to problems you largely cause _yourself_. We will use terms such as problem drinker, heavy drinker, and alcohol abuser, though these terms, too, can be overgeneralizations. Not all "problem drinkers" are alike, nor do their problems start, develop, and end the same way.[10] Let us also keep in mind that many bona fide heavy drinkers with major problems consider themselves "different" from similar heavy drinkers and deny that they have a problem. Getting rid of the word *alcoholic* removes only part of the motivation to deny problems.

Denial

Denial may be the most used word in the whole chemical dependency industry. Like the weather, everybody talks about it. But can they do anything to change it? What is it? What causes it?

Denial has many different meanings. When people use the word they think that they have *explained* something by naming it. At best, they have only *named* some specific behaviors. The word tells little about why those behaviors are happening.

To say that someone is "in denial" expresses an *opinion* about that person's behavior. For instance, "in denial" can mean "does not agree with me." Someone may say she does not have a problem, but you think she does. Therefore, you say, she is "in denial." (Another possibility is that *you* are "in error"!) When correctly used, *denial* means that the denier does not see self-defeating behaviors or *actively refuses* to admit to them. People "in denial" may not see any connection between their choices and the poor results they get from them. Sometimes they do not even admit they are getting poor results. They do not see the connection, but everybody else can.

The question, "How much do you drink?" often gets denying answers. Reasons for denial are many:

Sometimes the denier's memory is genuinely poor. Heavy drinking does your brain no favor!

If you drink much of the time, your drinking truly does not stand out in your memory. You don't notice how much you drink because you do it so often that you no longer really pay much attention to it. If someone asked you how many breaths of air you took each day, could you give an accurate answer?

We humans are great wishful thinkers. Looking back into the past, we tend to see what we *expect* to see and what we *want* to see. This means you genuinely remember inaccurately because you *want* to remember it that way. Obese people, for instance, often swear on stacks of Bibles that they only consume, say, 800 calories a day, and are not losing weight because of their "metabolism." Put them in a controlled environment, such as a hospital, give them 800 calories a day, no more, no less, and what happens? Yes, the pounds melt off! They do not count all sorts of calories they habitually take in, and therefore believe they are reporting accurately. This is normal, wishful thinking. It is not a disease. But it can contribute to problems and lead to early death.

Some heavy drinkers who do not agree that they have a problem simply *lie* about the amount they drink. They may think they are getting away with something and pat themselves on the back.

People also deny their alcohol abuse because they *want* to keep the *positive* aspects of drinking. They believe they *need* its pleasures. It also takes work and practice to stop drinking, and that prospect does not thrill most peo-ple. They therefore resort to wishful thinking: "I *have to* have the positives of alcohol and *not* have the negatives. If I really did have a problem, I would have to give up the positives. Therefore, I *don't* have a problem!"

Problem drinkers in denial may be shocked that *they* (of all people) get poor results from drinking. Like every-one else, they *want to believe* that their habits are okay, not self-destroying. They often worry, "If I couldn't stop, then I'd be an alcoholic! But since I'm *not* an alcoholic, that proves it's okay if I drink."

For example, Rocky, a client referred from a homeless shelter, complained to me (EV), "Yes, I've seen plenty of people end up on the street, but I never thought it would happen to me!"

"Why not?" I asked. "You said you were drinking and using drugs almost around the clock."

"I always thought I was better than that, but I'm a bum, just like them."

Rocky's comment shows the major reason people deny (fail to admit) their responsibility for their poor behavior. Because the only alternative they see (if they do admit responsibility) is to condemn *themselves*, not just their poor *behavior*. So it was with Rocky—after he could no longer ignore the crummy results of his daily substance abuse.

To behave self-defeatingly *is* stupid. When you admit a foolish *act*, it is very easy to jump to "That makes me a *stupid person*." Self-reproach makes you feel depressed and guilty. It wrongly implies that a "weakling" like you *can't* change. But you *can*—if you admit that you are *behaving* poorly, are *choosing* to do so, and can always *decide* to change. A person who *acts* weakly has the inner resources to show more strength later. A *weak person* is stuck forever!

The Disease Theory Spreads

AA adopted the Disease Theory of "alcoholism" to stop "alcoholics" from self-blame. In 1935, at the height of the Great Depression, AA started as part of the Oxford Group Movement, an evangelical religious organization whose purpose was to revitalize religion. The movement was founded and led by Frank Buchman, an unusual but dynamic man who was much more for stamping out *self-*

abuse (masturbation) than alcohol abuse. Buchman believed that all the world's problems were moral, not economic, social, or political, and that the world could be saved by a "God-controlled democracy," a "theocracy," or a "God-controlled Fascist dictatorship." He created a major public flap with pro-Hitler statements in 1936. [1]

Bill W. and Dr. Bob, AA's founders, were enthusiastic members of the Oxford Group Movement, and each had extreme drinking problems. In 1935 Bill W. visited Akron, Ohio, on a business trip and there met Dr. Bob, a proctologist and rectal surgeon. They teamed up and changed their lives and helped the lives of untold thousands of other people.

Bill W. and Dr. Bob remained part of the Oxford Group Movement (also known as the Oxford Group, and unrelated to the Oxford Movement of the 19th century) until they branched off in late 1937 to specialize in alcoholics. (The name, AA, came from the title of "the Big Book," published in 1939; the first group to call itself "AA" formed in Cleveland after that). Bill W. and Dr. Bob applied the principles of the Oxford Groups to problem drinking. They urged "alcoholics" to admit defeat, take a personal inventory, confess their defects to another person, make restitution to those they harmed, help others selflessly, and pray to God for the power to put these ideas into practice.

At the time AA started, people mainly saw alcohol problems as moral weakness and sin. Some physicians, however, viewed drinking as a medical problem. AA's Bill W. dried out several times at Towns Hospital in New York City, which was run by Dr. William Duncan Silkworth, who viewed problem drinking as an "allergy." As Bill W. reported in his book on AA's origins, he was drying out in Dr. Silkworth's hospital, taking the belladonna cure (morphine and belladonna, which in high doses causes hallucinations), when he had his "spiritual awakening" and God appeared to him. [2] The rest is history.

One advantage of the Disease Theory is that it brings medical science into the picture. The Disease Theory's main advantage, however, is that it gets people off the self-blame hook: "*I* am not responsible for my behavior, but my Disease *makes me* act that way." You will not, of course, damn yourself (and others) for having a Disease (particularly an allergy) if you thought *it* made you (and them) misbehave. This is one reason many people so ferociously hang on to the Disease Theory: They sensibly fear the self-damning that easily (though falsely) ties itself to self-responsibility for poor behavior. They know that freedom from blame opens the door to self-help. But they fail to realize a flaw in the Disease Theory: *If* your disease is responsible, then it may seem a bit odd to say, "My Disease was responsible up to this minute, but from this minute forth I am responsible." How, exactly, would that work?

If a Disease caused your poor behavior in the past, why *would* a Disease decide to stop doing so now? "Well, because now, knowing that I have a Disease, I can take responsibility for my own behavior from here on out." Or "I first have to admit I am powerless over my Disease, and that gives me the power to take responsibility and control it now." These arguments seem illogical to many people. What *kind* of Disease could make you drink until you find out you have it, and then (if only you accept your powerlessness and a Higher Power) will *let you* take responsibility and control? What Disease knows that you have now made a pact with the Higher Power and that it had damned well better surrender its power to make you powerless and submit to you and the Higher Power?

The answer is that it is a special Disease made up for the occasion and useful in reducing self-blame. In 1935 when AA adopted the idea, it was distinctly better than the idea that heavy drinkers were morally defective. In this book, however, we will describe a much more honest and useful method to ward off self-damning. It does not lead to the (unintended) abuses of the Disease Theory that shock us these days: seeing mayors, college presidents, and Watergate conspirators get caught doing crimes and discovering that little or nothing happens to them when they get caught. Why not? Because their Disease "makes" them do drugs or drink and act illegally. Dangerous, violent criminals who get caught and have the right lawyers have jumped on the Disease bandwagon with "I had a bad childhood" and "I was abused." Maybe so, but what of the millions of people of similar backgrounds who behave responsibly?

This attitude—it's not my fault *or* my responsibility—often *causes* more misbehavior. It damages the fabric of our society because it helps people avoid answering for their poor behavior. If "the Devil made me do it!" as comedian Flip Wilson was fond of claiming, then you are not to blame and you are not responsible. But you're stuck—because you don't learn to behave more responsibly.[3]

Blaming Outside Conditions

If you see yourself as having *internal* control, you assume responsibility for your behavior—good, bad, or indifferent. If you see yourself as being *externally* controlled, you find—yes, *actively* find—something outside yourself to account for your behavior. Then you don't put yourself down for it. The problem with this "solution" is that your fate depends on the whims of outside forces. If the external situation gets better, you get better; if it stays the same, you stay the same; if it gets worse, it's not your fault. Good luck!

Your desire to avoid self-blame fuels not only the Disease Theory but also three other extremely important theories that lead you to believe that external causes are responsible for your addictions and other disturbances. However, the irrational Belief that something *outside of* you is responsible for your behavior *encourages your natu-*

ral tendency to addict yourself. It is STINKING THINK-ING in capital letters. Three popular cop-outs for your problem drinking are:

1. Your family, your past, and your environment.

2. Your genes.

3. Alcohol and other drugs themselves.

The Family Disease of "Alcoholism"

A variation on the Disease Theory that "explains" your current disturbances and addictions is "the Family Disease of Alcoholism" and similar notions that your past and your family *make you* do the bad things you do today. The Adult Child, codependency, and Inner Child movements have now invented an all-purpose "cause" of anything you do badly, namely, "I come from a Dysfunctional Family." This supposedly *makes you* a near-hopeless addict.

What about these Diseases? Do real diseases need to remind us that they are diseases? Obviously not. No one says, for instance, "the disease of tuberculosis." Tuberculosis *is* a disease. It is a real one, and it does show some tendency to run in families. To say "The disease of . . ." or "The family disease of . . ." is a *theory* about the origins of heavy drinking that was a way to avoid self-downing in 1935 but that always had its limitations. Not that your family environment is not important. It is.

If a heavy drinker raised you, that can *help* you become a heavy drinker yourself. But it does not *make* you take on and carry out your parent's attitudes about imbibing. If your family upbringing *entirely* dictated your behavior, you could never change because you could never have a new upbringing. Yes, it can feel nice to hold a teddy bear at a codependency meeting, but that will not create a new childhood. It isn't your crummy past that makes you disturbed but some of your *attitudes about* this past. Codependency meetings can easily help you increase rather than *uproot* those neurotic attitudes.

So, *is* "alcoholism" a family disease? We think it's unuseful to think of it that way. True, your family members often behaved poorly and treated you shabbily. (They probably say the same thing about you!) That is unfortunate, but not a disease. It is the common crummy way that people act. Calling it a disease gives it powers that it does not in itself have.

Thousands of people have learned to see themselves as "alcoholics" because they have heavy drinkers in their family, sometimes even their distant family, although they themselves do not even drink! They go for lengthy (and expensive) codependency, Adult Child, or Inner Child therapy to cure various Diseases their upbringings supposedly gave them. Disturbances, including addictions, of course, *do* run in families, because *people run in families!* Yes, your parents may have set lousy examples for you, but who followed their examples back then, *and*, especially, who follows them now? You. True, you may not have known any better back then, but do you know better *now?*

Even when, as sometimes happens, you inherited tendencies to addict or disturb yourself, remember that they are only *tendencies*, not *behaviors*. You do not *have to* indulge yourself in them. I (AE) had a mother who indulged in sweets all her life and was caught, at the age of ninety-three, stealing candy from other residents of her nursing home! I have such a sweet tooth myself that up to the age of forty I always put four spoons of sugar and half a cup of cream in my coffee. "You call that coffee!" the *real* caffeine drinkers would exclaim. "How disgusting!" I paid them no heed.

At forty, I became diabetic. Since that time, I have taken *no* sugar in my coffee and very little cream. Does my inherited tendency to easily addict myself to sugar *make me* indulge in it? Of course not. Nor does your genetic *tendency*—if you are one of those who really have this tendency—to drink too much *make you* indulge. *You*, and only *you*, can make yourself indulge in that tendency.

The Walking Wounded Inner Child and Adult Child believers often firmly claim to see that they are responsible for their own behavior. Do they then take charge of their addictions? Often not, because they believe, "I have to work through my 'issues' and my 'stuff' *first*," or "I have to finish my 'grief work' and my 'pain work' *first*," or, "I have to really get in touch with my anger at my parents *first*" (that is, "*before* I change my behavior").

These ideas are modern incarnations by John Bradshaw and other codependency writers of Sigmund Freud's psychoanalysis and Arthur Janov's Primal Scream Therapy. Such codependency writers are caring people, and their books have valid and useful ideas. But they have gone right down the garden path to psychoanalysis. With their ideas, you can (and probably will!) spend forever chasing after the *right* insights about your gruesome, deprived past, getting your anger out to the *proper* degree, finishing off that *last little bit* of grief and pain work, and draining off the *dregs* of your "issues" and your "stuff."[4] It can be satisfying and fun to indulge in that form of "therapy," and quite dramatic. If you choose to spend your time looking backward, however, you may never change what you *can* change: your current behavior. In this book we will show you ways to change what you *can* change, namely your current disturbances and addictions, and to accept what you *cannot* change, including your past, your family, and your genes.

If you say, "I have to complete my Dysfunctional Family of Origin work" (before I can change my current behavior), you may be slipping dangerously close to copping out. Parent-bashing and past-blaming may give you a feeling of vindication, but do they really help? By blaming others, you still avoid making real changes in your behavior now. Why so?

Our guess is that there are two likely reasons why you

(and millions of others) may take your Inner Child of the Past much too seriously:

1. When you bash your parents and your past (and what normal person hasn't?), you believe that people who (you think) *behave badly*, your parents for instance, are therefore *bad people*. If you overgeneralize in this way, you *make* yourself hostile and self-pitying. Because your Belief System *generates* the hostility and poor-me feelings, there is no end to those feelings. You can never get the bad emotions "all out" because you yourself, though unknowingly, recreate more of them by focusing on the damning ideas behind them. Blaming your parents or your past experiences promotes the idea that external people, places, events, and conditions "caused" your (past and present) disturbed feelings and actions. Moreover, damning others also encourages you to damn *yourself* for your past, present, and future failings.

2. When you bash your parents, your past, and your present environment, you tend to believe that it is *easier* to blame others and outside forces than to change yourself. We would all like to believe that if we achieve the great insight, namely, that our parents were mean to us and gave us our screwed-up, "wounded" Inner Child, it will cure us. Most people like to believe that if they have a good cry, and wail and thump with their foam rubber bats and cling to teddy bears as we've seen them do on public television, all their hurt will go away, they will be healed and mended, and they won't have to work one day at a time. Lots of luck with that one! Refusal to work and be uncomfortable *drives* addictions. Screaming about past, present, or future discomfort *feeds* addictions.

You probably will *feel* better, at least spent and exhausted (just as after any physical exercise), after a blame session. You very likely will not *get* better because you do not Dispute, challenge, and change the *core, crazy-*

making ideas contained in your stinking thinking and irrational Beliefs. The Freudian Inner Child therapy approach is extremely inefficient and time-consuming when it works at all. Further, blame sessions may make you *worse* over the long-term, because they give you still more *practice at* the crazy-making stinking thinking. Haven't you practiced it enough already? It's time to Dispute, challenge, and change those irrational Beliefs (iBs) and self-defeating behavior, and get on with your life.

Even if your family members helped you behave badly, do they *need* to be in treatment or even to change *at all* before you can change? No. Family therapy is important—we do a great deal of RET couples and family therapy ourselves. Most people were reared in a family, and most adults still live as part of a family, though often a nontraditional family. It can be quite important to learn to listen better, communicate better, negotiate better, and assert oneself better with one's family members.[5] At times, too, it helps you to try to motivate family members to change. But, alas, some of them refuse to or are unable to do so.

It may, of course, help you if your family members are in treatment or in self-help groups with you. Their obnoxious behavior at A (the Activating Events or Adversities of your life) may often be the *occasion* for your *decision* (B) to destructively drink (C). If your family members did straighten up and fly right it wouldn't hurt. However, it is not *necessary* for them to do so for you to work on yourself. Your family members also may show you times that they did try to influence you constructively and you warded off their efforts. Just how responsible were they for your behavior then? They may frequently claim that your drinking caused *them* to behave obnoxiously, and that *you* should change first. However, it is not necessary for *you* to change for *them* to be happy. They are responsible for their choices and their feelings.

The Search for Genetic Causes of "Alcoholism"

How successful has been the search for genetic causes of "alcoholism"? You probably have seen newspaper articles and heard experts on TV talk shows firmly stating that "alcoholism" is inherited. Writers in the popular press and in the "alcoholism" treatment industry, not biologists or geneticists, advance the extreme biological theory that certain genes cause you to become "alcoholic."

Biologists and geneticists, however, tend to see the evidence for biological contributions as slim.[6]

Some studies of adopted children and twins suggest that people may have underlying biological reasons for developing at least *some kinds* of alcohol problems. Even in these studies, however, only a minority of the "alcoholics" had an "alcoholic" for *either* parent. In fact, most "alcoholics" had *neither* parent a problem drinker. In addition, most people with alcoholic parents did *not* become "alcoholic" themselves. Further, people who come from the same basic gene pool, for example, Native Americans and Eskimos, on the one hand, and Chinese-Americans, on the other hand, differ widely in their rates of "alcoholism."[7]

Marian, a forty-two-year-old teacher, came to my (AE's) therapy group after twelve years of psychoanalysis, three years of recovery meetings, and eight months in an Adult Child of an Alcoholic group. Although she had indeed stopped her daily drinking pattern at about age forty, she still had a weekend binge about once a month and never lost the thirty extra pounds of stomach and hip fat she kept planning to lose.

In group, Marian kept whining and wailing about her "dysfunctional family upbringing" because her mother and father were both "serious alcoholics" and her two older brothers took everything from pot to heroin. Seeing them continually under the influence, she insisted, "naturally made me feel unloved and abandoned, and drove me to alcohol and Quaaludes when I was a sophomore in high school. How can I ever be expected to completely stop drinking with a family background like that? I have a lot of stuff to process."

For the first several sessions of RET group therapy, the other group members were patient with Marian and tried to get her to stop her incessant whining. No dice. Finally, Kyle, who hadn't drunk in the two years after he got into alcohol-related trouble, became a little impatient. "Look! I've been listening to this cop-out complaining of yours for a couple of weeks. Frankly I'm sick of it! So what if your stupid family drank like fish and used every drug under the sun? Well, mine didn't, so I can admit that I *chose* to drink. I don't have to blame others. My parents were both Seventh-Day Adventists, pillars of the church. The most respectable people in town. So were all my aunts, uncles, grandparents, and my brothers and sisters. I always hated being square like them. I couldn't stand it! I did everything I could to rebel and be different. So what did I do? Started drinking when I was fourteen, got in with the drinking crowd at school. I kept it up through college. I never stopped till I had the accident and crippled someone. How come my highly *functional* family upbringing didn't keep me from drinking?"

"Yes," chimed in Jo, a thirty-two-year-old attorney. "Kyle's right. You think your family was dysfunctional! Mine was Irish Catholic on both sides, but hardly any of them went to church. No pot, no coke, nothing like that. Just good old Irish whisky. If a single day passed without a drunken brawl or some episode, I don't remember it. Some times when I'd get home from school, I'd find two or three of them passed out or at least nursing a hangover. My mother's brother and sister, who never married, lived with us, and my dad's parents and one of his brothers lived next door. They're all still alive and they're all still drinking! So, did I become a basket case who had to drink every time I had a problem? Exactly the opposite. I *hate* drinking. If I have one glass of eggnog at Christmas or a sip of champagne on New Year's Eve, that was a big drinking year for me. About the only good thing I got out of my childhood was to know better than to drink too much. So you should admit that you're responsible for being a drinker."

Three other members of Marian's RET group also showed her that their early childhood traumas had little to do with their present crooked thinking and emotional problems. They urged her to take responsibility for her own drinking and upsets. Within the next five months Marian made good progress in this respect. She decided to graduate from and quit her Adult Child of an Alcoholic group, stopped bingeing, and got on with her life.

Many thousands of chronic "alcoholics" and other dyed-in-the-wool addicts have *decided* to stop the addiction and have made that decision stick. This would not be possible if inborn tendencies were the only cause of the addictive behavior. Addiction comes from a thinking, feeling, planning, plotting, and scheming human being who *wants* and *insists* upon getting certain feelings, who steadfastly refuses to feel uncomfortable *without* alcohol and who may believe alcohol is *necessary* for him or her to function.

It is possible some day that a grouping of genes will be discovered that contributes significantly to one's tendency to develop "alcoholism." Such a finding could prove important for it might lead to new treatments. However, if brain chemicals "caused" your addictions, wouldn't it be quite a coincidence that the chemicals changed just at the time you joined an antiaddiction group like AA, Narcotics Anonymous, Rational Recovery, Women For Sobriety, Men For Sobriety, or Secular Organizations for Sobriety?

We take the position that it is likely that certain people have more of a talent than others for developing a heavy drinking problem.[8] Their talents may be inborn, but it is unlikely that it is anything simple, such as their rate of metabolizing alcohol or their blood alcohol levels.[9] It makes no practical difference what your particular inborn, nature-given talent is, however, so long as you assume that you have *some* responsibility for using or *not using* that talent.

A poor alternative to these biological explanations is blame and moralizing. People think they have to damn themselves if they admit that they *choose* to drink. The desire to avoid self-blame fuels their Belief that scientists have truly found genetic *causes* of "alcoholism." With RET, as we show below, you can choose to accept responsibility for what you do *without blaming yourself as a person.* When I (EV) encounter clients who are devoted to the idea that they inherited so many "alcoholic" genes that they therefore are unable to stop drinking, I confront them, using an example from their own history. For instance, "You mean to tell me a disease, or your genes, hid the liquor bottle under the car seat to keep the highway patrol officer from seeing it? Are you sure that wasn't *you?*"

Yes, we may indeed find genetic *contributors* to the tendency to persist at drinking heavily. But contributors contribute; they don't *make you* do anything. If they do, you are out of luck—aside from an *actual* miracle. AA may say, "Expect a miracle," but we say, "Don't *wait* for one. Set about helping *yourself.* Keep God in reserve to change the things that you *truly* cannot change. You do not need God to pull your hands and your mouth away from alcohol. You can do that job yourself."

Biological theories of "alcoholism" may contribute to your disempowerment, to your giving up the responsibility and power that you do have. You may wrongly think that if compulsive drinking has *any* biological, biochemical, or genetic basis, it proves you cannot possibly stop it. But all human behavior has a biological, biochemical, or genetic basis: Our bodies are nothing but chemicals. Every thought you think, every word you read on this page, every sound you hear, causes chemical changes in your body. This could not happen without a genetic basis. You also inherit, as a human, a strong tendency to *perceive* and to *think about* your problem drinking. And to change your destructive behavior. How about using *that* genetic tendency?

4

Alcohol and Drugs Addicted Me

Another very widespread Belief in external control may take away much of your power over your own life. It is the idea that the alcohol or drug *itself* addicted you. The *rational* idea that will bring *back* your power is that *you* addicted yourself to the alcohol or drugs (or, more accurately, to the feelings and powers you associate with them).

Your Belief in the addictive powers of substances may be a major cause of your potential for addicting yourself. Our very language reinforces the idea that chemicals addict you, poor you. Just the phrase, "got addicted," implies that something was done *to* you. Or "cocaine is very addicting" implies that if you take it (through some accident, presumably!), *it* addicts you. "The substance made me do it" is a cop-out and gives away your power to resist. But again, to believe that the substance addicted you, rather than that *you* addicted *yourself* to it, helps you avoid self-blame.

Substances such as alcohol and other drugs do produce some of the feelings and experiences to which people addict themselves. However, many people addict themselves to relationships ("love"), gambling, shopping, or work. With these addictions *there is no physical substance*. Substances do not addict. If you take some of them regularly, for example heroin or alcohol or Valium, your body does develop *tolerance*. As time goes by, it takes more chemical to produce an equal effect. You also develop *physical dependence* so that if you abruptly stopped taking the chemical, you would have *withdrawal symptoms*. But neither of these is addiction.

Many addicts take it for granted that if they should experience any significant withdrawal symptoms, they couldn't possibly stand them. The classic example of this is heroin addiction. Other substances, such as cocaine or speed, do not lead to the same kind of dramatic withdrawal symptoms, yet they are very difficult to give up. Whether continued use of certain substances leads to chemical changes in your brain and to withdrawal symptoms is a scientific question. However, it has almost nothing to do with addictability. That depends on what you believe the drug (or the activity) does for you.

If substances "caused" addiction, then all the service people who addicted themselves to heroin in Vietnam would have remained addicts upon their return to America. Instead, the vast majority of them stopped using heroin when they left Vietnam and never used it again. If "addicting" substances caused addiction, then all the surgical patients who take morphine for pain for a long time would go on to "be" addicts. They would seek out morphine (or heroin) after they no longer took it for pain. Very few of them do so, however. When they are withdrawn from the morphine, they have withdrawal symptoms and feel crummy. In time, the crummy feelings go away and are forgotten. *That's it—for them*, because they don't have strong addictive *attitudes*.

Methadone maintenance gives us another fine example of how physical dependence on a substance does not *cause* addiction. Methadone patients may take methadone for years and use no heroin at all. When they leave methadone-based treatment, some of them eventually relapse into drug use. What do they use? Heroin, almost every time—not "street" methadone. They had a strong *physical dependence* upon the methadone for years, but their *addiction* is almost always to the heroin. This is because heroin addicts *like* the feelings produced by heroin much better than they enjoy feelings produced by methadone. They *decide* to go back to heroin even though they could purchase methadone on the street.

You *give* alcohol or another chemical addictive power by weighing, first, what you expect its "high" to feel like and how long it will last. The second factor in addiction is your expectation about how much relief from hassles, pain, and worries the chemical or the activity will give you. The third factor is your expectation about the coping powers you "need" the chemical to give you.

There is a saying, "Different strokes for different folks." People differ in the sorts of feelings ("highs") they prefer and seek. How a chemical makes you feel is obviously a big factor in whether you seek that chemical. No matter how good a feeling is, you do not *have* to have it. To say that a certain substance is powerfully addicting *for you* means mainly, "Because I *like* the high or the relief it gives me, I continue to *choose* to use it, come hell or high water, and to kick up a fuss at the prospect of not having it." When you say, "I (she, he) *got* addicted to alcohol" it is more truthful, hopeful, and powerful to say, "I (she, he) addicted *myself* (her/himself) to alcohol." Let's say all your relatives are "alcoholics," so you may have lots of alcoholic genes. In that case, strongly tell yourself, "Okay, so I *easily* and *naturally* like alcohol. But I *chose* to addict myself to what I like. I did that myself, and I can stop doing it."

Sabrina, a twenty-eight-year-old woman who owned and worked in a "love connection" telephone and escort service, sought therapy because she was depressed. She drank heavily and snorted cocaine to deal with her depression. Though she understood that the alcohol and cocaine probably made her feel more depressed, she insisted she needed the drugs to deal with work. Besides, she disclosed to me (EV) in her third therapy session, "It feels so good that once I get started I just keep partying." She said that she would think back to how good it felt. Then at times when she wasn't even depressed, she couldn't keep from remembering that good feeling, and that made her say yes when her friends offered her coke.

By looking for a situation in her life in which she had refused to use drugs when offered them, I tried to show Sabrina that she could do so again. No dice. "Well, what if each time you used coke or alcohol you had to phone up your parents and describe in detail three or four typical phone calls from your customers? Would you then indulge?"

"Never!" Sabrina answered.

Accepting Responsibility Without Self-Blame

Your best bet for changing your self-defeating behavior is first to admit you are responsible for your behavior and for changing it. Second, accept yourself as a person who currently is defeating yourself. Third, refuse to label yourself as a loser or a victim. If you call yourself a victim, you focus on the unfortunate Activating Events or Adversities (A's) in your life. But in doing so you may give these A's too much and yourself too little power and control over you. If you adopt the role of "victim," you make yourself powerless to do anything about your Belief System (B) *concerning* the Adversities (A's). When you neglect changing *your* Belief System, you will fail to change your disturbances and addictions (Cs) *and* your Adversities (A's). Then you make yourself into a "helpless victim."

Unconditional Self-Acceptance vs. Conditional Self-Esteem

Most therapists, including the famous codependency, Inner Child, and Adult Child therapists, such as John Bradshaw and Melodie Beattie, imply that as a child you *must* be loved "for yourself." Further, you *must* be accepted, given your way, and not frustrated if you are to achieve self-esteem and live an unneurotic, productive, happy, and non-substance-abusing life. In therapy, they try to give you love and success experiences to build your self-esteem.

RET (Rational-Emotive Therapy), however, takes a quite different approach. We are all for love and success *experiences* because they help us reach our goals and enjoy ourselves. The Achilles heel of helping people have love and success experiences, however, is that they tend to rate *themselves* as worthy *because of* them. The problem comes when you inevitably *fail* at those experiences or at new ones. Then, back to shithood you go!

RET is one of the few therapies—and philosophies—that clearly distinguishes self-acceptance, which is fine, from self-esteem, which is perhaps the greatest sickness known to humans. Sickness? Yes, emotional and behavioral sickness. For self-esteem, when you accurately define it, is still a measurement of your entire "self," "being," or "personhood." But you cannot make such evaluations or measurements accurately. Why? Because your *self* is all of you: everything you've ever done, are now doing, or will do in the future. Your "self" is so complex and so constantly changing (as every life process is), that your giving it any kind of accurate global or general rating is really impossible. What you are today is different from what you were yesterday, and from what you will be tomorrow. You are therefore much too complicated and changeable to be given any *general* evaluation.

Self-ratings seem "naturally" and "automatically" to stem from measuring your deeds. They mainly do so because you arbitrarily *define* your estimation of your self in terms of how you measure (some of) your traits. The two are not *actually* related. If you want to evaluate your "self" or "essence" at all (which you really *don't* have to do), you can measure it in terms of almost anything. For example, you can rate yourself in relation to your aliveness, your upbringing, your nationality, your height, your appetite, your religion, your home, or almost anything. Moreover, the weights that you give to these measures of your worth can also easily be arbitrary. Thus, you can say, "I am a good person because I am short" or "I am a good person because I am tall." Or you can say, "I am a worthy individual because people like me," or "I am a worthy individual because only a few select people like me."

Moreover, when you measure or rate yourself, you almost immediately create emotional jeopardy. For you really have to measure you, an ongoing process, by what you have done and what you now do, which are limited aspects of you. In so doing you are then making what philosophers of logic, like Bertrand Russell and W. V. Quine, call category errors: "Because I do X well, I am a good person. Because I do Y badly, I am a rotten person." Quite an illogical and illegitimate overgeneralization, as Alfred Korzybski, the parent of general semantics, wisely pointed out.[1]

Again, you can rate or measure your acts only when you establish a goal or purpose. *Problem* drinking means that it creates problems for you. Thus, if your goal is to think clearly and act efficiently, taking several drinks of liquor is bad, because it defeats your goals. But if your goal is to relax (and you don't need to think clearly or operate machinery later that night), then taking several drinks of liquor might well be good. It would help you toward that goal of relaxing. So your acts and deeds, once you establish a purpose, can fairly easily be rated or measured as good, bad, or indifferent.

Once, however, you believe, "I *am* my good or bad act," you can't win. "Am," "are," or any other forms of the verb "to be" imply that you *always* are what you do today, or did yesterday, or may do tomorrow. And because you and your acts ceaselessly change, this is really impossible! How can you be a "good person" for doing well today, and also be a "bad person" for doing badly yesterday or tomorrow?

Self-esteem almost always means, "I am good for doing good things." This Belief leads to anxiety and depression. For even if you do very well today, how do you know how you will do in the future? When you esteem or rate yourself as a good person for doing good deeds, you remain likely to rate yourself as a bad person whenever—at any time in the future—you do *bad* deeds. (And you will!) Self-rating and self-esteem, then, simply will not work to keep you unanxious, undepressed, and happy. Evaluations of your *self* only work when, now and forever, you have a guarantee that you always will perform well and therefore consistently be worthy of self-esteem.

AA has folk sayings that advise, "Beware of phony pride," "Avoid self-righteousness," "Don't dwell on others' faults," and "Suspend judgment of yourself and others." We endorse those eminently sane ideas. Every reader knows, we suspect, at least one person who goes around saying, "I'm in recovery, I'm in recovery, I'm in recovery," and often *implying* "and that makes me a better person than all you nerds and schlemiels who *aren't* in recovery!" What happens to such people when they slip? Back to wormhood they go, with all the nerds and schlemiels they were lording it over!

Tim, after being off alcohol and pills for three months, told his RET therapy group that he had gotten a ninety-day "chip" (as a reward) at his Narcotics Anonymous group. "I really made it! Not a single drink or pill in three months. That's my all-time record. I really feel good about myself now!"

"You'd better not feel too good about yourself," said Marlene, another group member. "Feel good about how you're doing. But if you feel good right now about yourself for not drinking and using pills, what happens when you foul up, maybe not on the drinking and pills, but on something else?"

"Right," Tim responded. "I'd better say, 'If I'm doing well, that's good, but I will accept *myself* regardless.' " It's easy to *say*. But it's difficult to *believe*.

To summarize: Rating your self and giving yourself esteem:

- Lead to anxiety, depression, anger, guilt, shame, envy, greed, and waste of money on status.

- Contribute to procrastination and interfere with reaching goals (because your main goal becomes having self-esteem, rather than doing well or enjoying yourself).

- Keep you from doing new things you might enjoy because you know you may not do well at them.

- Often lead you to support the Establishment's values and goals, rather than *your* values and goals.

- Keep you from enjoying success, because even when you do well you think you "should" do still better.

- Lead you to feel threatened by feedback and criticism that might help you improve your behavior.

- Help you deny responsibility for your crummy actions and help you blame others and outside factors.

Rational-Emotive Therapy shows you how to achieve *unconditional self-acceptance* rather than highly conditional self-esteem. How do you gain self-acceptance? Simply by *choosing* to have it, instead of choosing, as you often do, to set yourself up for a fall by trying to achieve pride and self-esteem. More specifically, you can heed the following directions that I (AE) have distilled from some of my main writings and that I frequently give to my therapy clients during one of their early sessions. I have also included these directions in my Introduction to Paul Hauck's *Hold Your Head Up High*.[2]

As a person, you were born and reared with two strong tendencies: to rate or evaluate your acts, thoughts, feelings, and behaviors, to determine whether they are "good" or "effective"; and to rate or measure your "self," your "being," your "essence," your "totality." In RET, we encourage you to continue the first of these tendencies—performance ratings—but to be most cautious about the second tendency—self-ratings.

After giving much thought to the problem of self-evaluation, RET has come up with two fairly good—though still imperfect—solutions. The first is difficult but still do-able: Decide not to rate your "self," your "being," *at all*. If you want to assume that you have a "self" or an "essence," okay—even though you will have some difficulty, as scholars have had for ages, in clearly defining it. Anyway, stubbornly refuse to rate, measure, or evaluate this "self." Only—yes, *only*—rate what you *do* (so that you can discover how to do better and how to enjoy yourself more)—and not what you *are*. If you want to label yourself as "you," then acknowledge that *you* are responsible for what you do, and that you *act* irresponsibly when you do poorly (e.g., lie to yourself or others). But still don't rate your *youness* or *self*.

This is probably the most elegant RET solution to the problem of self-worth and will get you in practically no trouble. As a less elegant, but still viable option, you can rate your *self* or *being* but only in terms of some general, safe concept, which is never likely to change, at least during your lifetime, or can only change by your deciding to change it. Thus, you can say, "I am a good person because I exist, because I am alive." You then can't be "bad" or "no good" until you are dead!

Or you can say, "I am good because I am a fallible, imperfect human"—and then you can be pretty sure that this will, as long as you live, always be true! Or you can say, "I am good because God (or the Devil) loves me" and you can then decide that God (or the Devil) exists and always loves you.

Either of these solutions to the problem of self-worth will work. Take your choice. For rating your "self" is a *choice*, not a *necessity*. You can choose to rate or not rate your "self," as long as you (for practical purposes) rate your (and others') performances. And if you choose

to be a "good" person, you can strongly convince yourself, "I am good because I choose to see myself as good;
and I choose to see myself as good *whether or not* I
perform well and *whether or not* others approve of me.
Now that I have *decided* this, how can I more effectively
continue to live, to enjoy myself, and continue to aid the
social milieu in which I *choose* to live.

As one of the main rational self-help methods, you can
strongly decide to accept yourself *un*conditionally, *no matter what* you do or don't do. You can, as we have just
shown, *choose* to do this and learn it as a habit if you *work*
with determination to do so.

Why Do People Drink Too Much and Addict Themselves? And What Does It Take to Change?

The desire for intoxication is worldwide. Throughout history people have industriously tried to figure out ways to alter their consciousness and moods with chemicals. If it's not chemicals, it's chanting, drumming, fasting, meditation, exercise, and many other methods. Because chemicals quickly cause mood changes, they are favored by people who go overboard in striving to alter their consciousness. Humans have been creative in figuring out ways to addict themselves to various substances and behaviors. They have persisted in creating addictions, often against enormous odds. Many have given up their lives though they knew how dangerous indulgence might be.

The desire for altered consciousness and moods is at the bottom of addictability. That desire is probably part of human nature and stems from life-preserving instincts to avoid pain and seek pleasure. Family upbringing, social environment, and cultural values help promote the tendency towards addiction. It may be with us as long as humans exist, and so may people's tendency toward drug and alcohol problems.[1]

People prefer certain pleasurable feelings and relief from discomfort. *The tendency to prefer certain feelings to others, however, is different from the process of addiction.* A preference is just a *preference.* No matter how strong it is, you do not make it a *necessity,* an *addiction,* unless you believe you *must* have what you want.

A person, for instance, may have a marked preference for sweets, and have a well-established reputation as having a sweet tooth. However, later she or he gets diagnosed as diabetic and immediately and permanently stops consuming sweets—as I (AE) did when I became diabetic at the age of forty. Other people, however, with a weaker desire for sugar (or almost anything else) may insist that they must not be deprived of it *at all.* They may make themselves obsess about it and give it control over them.

Addiction is a mental state, a thought process, a purpose. It is a meaning we give to feelings and experiences (especially "high" and relaxed feelings). Addiction includes our pigheaded determination to seek certain feelings and experiences with little regard for later consequences. It includes rationalizations we make up about how it's okay to keep doing what we're doing. Sometimes, when addicted, we even go so far as to claim that we aren't doing what we are doing!

Addiction is a system of choices in which we may get some good results, but also get more and more *bad* results that unfortunately go along with the *good* results we insist we must have. Later, when the bad results have built up enough, we often stop. At that time we may *invent* "forces beyond our control" that "made" us choose our addictions. When the coast has been clear long enough, we may invent again that we can, too, choose to have the good results *without* suffering the bad results we got before.

And then back to the addiction we go!

This is not a disease. It's just human nature to think that we *should* be able to have exactly what we want and to ignore the costs of getting it. Humans tend to instinctively think that way. If we didn't, the race would have died out eons ago. Babies, for example, instinctively cry for what they want. It helps them to get it. Too much of the same attitude can hurt adults.

People, including you and us, are contradictory and can have many conflicting ideas. You may, for instance, have a spouse and a lovely family and strongly wish to live with them the rest of your life. They may literally be more important to you than life itself. You also may want some luxuries of the single life and like to fool around and may jeopardize your family life by doing so. If you abuse alcohol, you may like its positive and dislike its negative aspects. You may like the short-range relief and the buzz drinking gives, but dislike the long-term pains it can bring about. If you are, like so many humans, a short-range pleasure-seeker, immediate gains may easily influence you more than long-range pains.

What does cause problem drinking? Well, having unfortunate things happen to you and living in a crummy environment contribute. They help increase the chances that you'll decide to drink too much as a way of "dealing" with them. The more bad things in your life, the greater the chance you'll decide to drink. There are, however, droves of people with enormous handicaps and odds against them, and they never abuse substances. Others get a hangnail and turn to drink and drugs.

If, for instance, you live in poverty in a housing project surrounded by drugs, booze, and people who feel hopeless, it *will* be easier for you to decide to drug and drink away your cares. But *easier* does not equal *have to*. Or let us say that most of your blood relatives are "alcoholics." So, to whatever degree there is an inborn tendency to drink too heavily, you've got it. Tough. As we mentioned above, studies of twins and adoptees show that only a minority of "alcoholics" have an "alcoholic" parent. A large majority of the children of "alcoholics" do not themselves have alcohol problems. Let's say you served in Vietnam or were abused as a child or were an incest survivor. All very bad things, almost anyone would agree. Yet do *all* people who underwent those experiences have *identical* reactions? Why not? And if the bad experience did cause your reactions directly, how could you ever change? How *do* those who recover do it?

We *could* easily prove that how much you drink is a choice and that you don't *have* to drink too much. Ever. How? Simply hire someone to guard you and to chop off one of your toes every time you had a drink. Maybe you'd lose one toe, but not two! If your genes really "made" you drink and get "out of control," you'd lose all of your toes and your fingers, too!

Do you drink to punish yourself? Come now! Old-fashioned psychotherapy seriously offers such ideas as wishing to punish oneself as the "cause" of addiction. Nothing could be less likely for most substance abusers. We train ourselves into addictions because we believe we *have* to have positive feelings and relief from negative feelings, including guilt. Right now! In time, this leads to self-defeat and punishment, but that was hardly our purpose.

Then once we get dismal results—hurting ourselves or others—with our short-sighted, pigheaded insistence upon instant gratification and relief from bad feelings, we blame. Mostly we blame our "disease," our parents, our pasts, our families, our environments, our genes, and the chemicals we put into our bodies. We don't know how to accept responsibility without self-blame. Sometimes we blame ourselves, and when we do, we incorporate our poor behavior into our self-concepts. Because we rightly call *it*—our bad actions—bad, we wrongly call our *self* bad. That makes it still less likely that we can change.

If you have begun to accept yourself unconditionally despite your poor behavior (but dislike the poor behavior) you are ahead of the game. You are better off than (but not *a better person than*) most people. What else helps you change? Next, learn and practice the three insights of Rational-Emotive Therapy (RET). They can give you the power to change yourself in the here-and-now, not just "some day."

RET's Three Insights

Insight No. 1: Your current feelings and actions have *causes*. The most important causes of your addictions are your thoughts, attitudes, images, memories, and other cognitions. This is what RET calls B, your Belief System, especially your stinking thinking or irrational Beliefs (iBs).

Insight No. 2: Wherever your Belief Systems originated (parents, family, society, traumas, biology, self-inventions), you carry them on now and actively believe and follow them. *You* steadily reindoctrinate *yourself* in them today and sometimes actively fight off others' attempts to get you to change them.

Insight No. 3: You require hard, persistent work to change your Beliefs, actions, and feelings, to practice new ones, and to avoid returning to old ones. Further, your human condition tends to give new problems and stresses. So insight is not the main watchword. Eternal vigilance plus much work and practice is.

The message of RET's three insights is hopeful, because what you do, you can refuse to do. If you yourself largely cause your own drinking problems and emotional disturbances, that's good! It's the best-case scenario. There are many things in the external world you cannot change. Therefore, the larger the number of your problems caused by something you *can* change—you!—the better it is.

Where and how it all started (or you started it all) makes little practical difference, because *the past does not exist*. The past cannot make you do, think, or feel anything at all right now. You are doing that yourself, though you may be largely unaware of it. If you *are* aware of it, you still may be unaware of *how* you are doing it. Without realizing it, once you create many of your own problems, you actively maintain them. Actively.

Like many people, you may enjoy thinking about the past and probing it in great detail. You may believe that you have to understand it to be able to escape its hold. Fortunately, the past does not exist except in your head and in your present habits. You can escape its hold by focusing on the present and by detecting, challenging, and changing your own Beliefs. And by forcing yourself to change your here-and-now habits.

People who obsess about the past often feel a need to *justify* who they are before they feel qualified to move on. They are afraid to take action right now to change their lives because "What if I made a mistake?" And "It'll be easier to do once I have the right insights about how my Dysfunctional Family of Origin made me what I am today and gave me the disturbances and addictions I have now." Such ideas *sound* plausible. They will sound plausible ten years from now, too, but you won't have changed.

There is probably never one invariant "cause" of any human disturbance—including "alcoholism." Yes, problem drinkers more frequently do come from disruptive, economically poor, disturbed, abusive, too critical families and environments—but not always! All these "bad" Activating Events (A's), or influences, importantly *contribute to* but do not necessarily *cause* neurosis and compulsive drinking. Even if they did, what can you now do about changing your early environment? Nothing!

The main and most direct "cause" of your disturbed, problem drinking is your Belief System (B). It is your Belief System *about* the early, present, and possible future Activating Events or Adversities (A's) of your life. It is your Belief System *about* the negative emotions you create with your Belief System and how you *can't stand* those feelings. And it is your Belief System *about* pleasurable feelings and how you *must have* them and *can't stand* not having them. Addiction is strengthened by your Belief System about how you *must not get* and *can't stand* the poor results you cause yourself because you devoutly Believe you *must have* certain good feelings and *must not have* certain bad feelings. And, finally, addiction is strengthened by your tendency to *damn* yourself, others, or life because of their bad characteristics.

What is more, B is *your* choice, *your* philosophy, *your* outlook. So no matter what and how difficult your A's are, you can usually discover, understand, and *change* B. Whatever you believe, you can challenge and rethink. Not, of course, if you are in a coma or seriously brain damaged! Not very effectively if you are (temporarily) panicked, drugged, or intoxicated. But when you free yourself to stop and think, you can greatly change B. How? By using many Rational-Emotive Therapy (RET) methods that we shall describe in detail, and that we'll call *Self-help: RET style*.

What Will It Take for Me to Change?

Once you've got the three RET insights and are willing to use them, you can use a notebook. Yes, a notebook. To get the most out of this self-help guide, you will study your thoughts, feelings, and actions to see how you change them under different conditions. If you keep notes, you will much more easily see how they relate to each other and how to healthfully reconstruct them. You can alter your ways haphazardly, but why not be more efficient and systematic?

Self-help is a learning experience. You learn by doing. The more you work at it, the more you will get out of it. We can give you ideas and suggest assignments, but we can't make you do them. That is your job. Thomas Edison said genius is 1 percent inspiration and 99 percent perspiration! The playwright Noel Coward said, "Thousands of people have talent. I might as well congratulate you for having eyes in your head. The one and only thing that counts is: Do you have staying power?"

Reconstructing parts of your Belief System is a *big* project. So push yourself to take it seriously. How? By fashioning long-range and short-range goals, tools, and a timetable.

Your timetable had better be flexible, but your self-work had better be, well, not rigid, but no-nonsense. To improve your chances of getting more of what you want and less of what you don't want in life, does it make sense to work only when the mood strikes you? You had better *schedule actual appointments* with yourself to evaluate your progress, assign yourself homework, and choose new goals.

Your notebook will be your Daily Journal. In it you can keep your Activity and Reward Schedules. (We'll explain all of these terms and how to use them later). You can also use a small notepad or index cards and lots of "stickies" to remind yourself of assignments and to jot down your ideas when you don't have your notebook with you. Carry pens or pencils with you or have them immediately at hand. They are part of your basic self-help tool kit. Below, we will provide examples of forms you can use to note your self-defeating thoughts and to write down new, more useful ideas.

You will schedule a typical self-help session regularly. You can vary the frequency and length of sessions and still be effective. There is no one right way to do it. We can say that daily self-help sessions of, say, twenty minutes, will usually work more effectively than weekly sessions of, say, two hours. More frequent and shorter is usually better than occasional and longer.

There is nothing magical about any particular time of day for your sessions. Try to *schedule* each appointment with yourself, and then make that appointment a priority for that time. If, as you sit down at the appointed time for your self-help session, you notice that the plants need watering or the furniture needs dusting or whatever, let those things wait. First things first.

If you plan to do self-help homework only when you *feel* like it, your chances for improvement are not quite zero. Just very close to it! Schedule yourself to work on yourself at *regular times*. It does not have to be the same time each day, but it helps if it is regular. The more established you make it, the less effort you will require to remember it and the less you will have to push yourself to do it.

Fit your self-help work into your current daily schedule. That way it will be part of the natural flow of your day. It helps if you normally do your self-help homework before, not after, your favorite activities. First you work, and then you play; first you eat your vegetables, and then you get dessert. First you work on yourself, and then you grow.

If you are retired, unemployed, or disabled or work at home and have few fixed routines, we advise you to schedule self-help at specified times. You wake up, you eat, you take a shower, and you sleep. You can schedule your self-help sessions, say, before a meal or before bed or before a shower or before sex. If you schedule your self-help sessions in that way, you probably will find that it takes less memory and "willpower" to "get up the energy" to do the required work.

At a typical self-help session, you have your notebook, notepad, forms or charts, and other supplies and tools ready. Look at instances of strong urges to drink (whether resisted or carried out) that you have noted in your Daily Journal or on cards. Then look at your notes about what you were telling yourself just before you got the urge to (or actually did) drink. Then you strongly Dispute your self-defeating thinking and affirm your self-helping thoughts.

What was going on at a time when you had a big urge to drink? These were your A's—Activating Events or Adversities—that preceded your strong drinking impulses. Where were you? What time was it? What were you doing? Who was there? What were your thoughts? How were you feeling emotionally before the urges began to well up? Did you notice any reaction in your body? Write, for example: "At home, in the front room," "10:00 A.M.," "Looking out the window while doing chores," "Alone, but I saw a couple walking down the street hand in hand," "I thought about my ex," "Lonely," and "I felt my stomach tighten and my heart pound."

Be sure to record your Bs, your stinking thinking. What were you *telling* yourself to create the urges, heighten them, and indulge in them (if you did so)? If you fought your urges successfully, what was your self-helping, non–stinking thinking? Your next step is to interrupt and Dispute your stinking thinking and create or strengthen your realistic, helpful, alternative rational Beliefs. Finally, you will keep forcefully pushing yourself to *practice* your anti-drinking Beliefs.

Self-help, of course, aims to help you solve problems and reach your Goals. Your main Goal (G) usually is to find happiness, suffer less, and stay alive. But you also want to actualize yourself—be *happier*. So you ask yourself, "What would it take for me to feel happier and *more* fulfilled?" Think about this and write down what it would take for you to feel happier. For instance, you might say, "I'd be happier if I had more friends, felt less depressed, and stopped drinking." Once you identify those goals, make notes on what you can do to have more friends. Your answer might be "I'd have to push myself to overcome my shyness and take risks of being rejected. I could keep my *desire* for approval but had better give up my *dire need* for it."

Your next step might be to think of a recent occasion where your shyness stopped you from being as friendly as you wanted to be. Once you have that particular occasion firmly in mind, ask yourself, "What was I telling myself to *make* myself so shy and avoid the risk of rejection?" You can then look at the rationality of those Beliefs. You can challenge and change the self-defeating ones—like, "I *must* never get rejected. How *awful* it would be! That would show how worthless I am!" You can rationally answer, "It's tough if I get rejected, but it's never really *awful* or *more than* rough. No matter how many times I fail, rejection doesn't make me worthless—just a person who failed this time. Too bad. Now, what can I do to keep trying?"

We suggest you use a chart along the lines of Figure 5.1 to track your daily activities, to study your schedule, and to plan various rewarding activities.

Recording your observations and experiences in your notebook and on copies of the Daily Planned Activity Chart will help increase the accuracy of your self-observations. Make notes as soon as possible after an event that highlights your self-defeating and self-helping actions. You can record how often or how long or how strongly you thought, felt, or did something.

If you are monitoring your thoughts and learn that you have many self-defeating thoughts in so many settings that you would spend your whole life writing, then you can set a timer to ring, say, every half hour. Each time it goes off, you write down the last disturbing thought you had before the timer went off.

Simply monitoring your own behavior can be of great help. If you keep a count of specific "good" or "bad" behaviors, you may find that your behavior begins to change in the desired direction.

Figure 5.1
Daily Planned Activity Chart

Date: _____

Time/am/pm	Activity Planned	Done	Good	Bad[1]

---

[1] Done = degree on a 10 point scale to which you did the activity you had planned.

Good = degree on a 10 point scale to which you got good results.

Bad = degree on a 10 point scale to which you also got bad results.

In connection with doing your monitoring and filling out Daily Planned Activity Charts, we remember the story about Jascha Heifitz. Someone asked him, "Mr. Heifitz, you are known as the world's outstanding violinist. How come, then, you still keep practicing at least a few hours a day?" Heifitz replied, "Oh, that's an easy question to answer. If I fail to practice one day, I can hear the results and I know it. If I don't practice for two days, the critics know it. And if I fail to practice for three days, the whole world knows it!" Take heed! Even one day's failure to do self-help homework may let you, your critics, and if not the whole world, maybe the whole block, see how you give in to your low frustration tolerance!

What else can you do to become an effective self-helper? "Keep it simple" is a good idea, but self-improvement takes planning and work. If you can improve your efforts with equipment, do so. You can use a cassette recorder for noting your thoughts and for talking back to your negative ones. You can also keep a small library of notes, clippings, pamphlets, books, or other material you find helpful. Some people write reminders and ABCs on a white board. A small bulletin board can be handy for tacking up reminders, clippings, and messages.

You may want to keep a list of self-help meetings (Rational Recovery, Secular Organizations for Sobriety, Women For Sobriety, Men For Sobriety, Alcoholics Anonymous), telephone numbers, addresses, and meeting times.[2] If you don't have a physician, by all means get one, particularly if you think certain medications, like Antabuse, would be a help to you. You probably can locate a physician by calling your local medical association.

What about a therapist? Fine, *if* the therapist advocates your keeping a tight focus on the here-and-now, on what you can do today to make specific changes in your thoughts, feelings, and actions. If the therapist wants you to *dwell* on the past or on negative feelings, good luck! Run, don't walk to the nearest referral source for practical therapy. You can locate a more here-and-now therapist by calling or writing the Institute for Rational-Emotive Therapy or the Association for Advancement of Behavior Therapy (See Appendix A).

But Therapy
Doesn't Work!

How many times have you heard this said at recovery meetings? Chances are, a good many. It is an older bit of meeting lore formulated in the 1930s, '40s, and '50s, when it made much more sense than it does today. AA itself for the most part takes no position for or against anything other than "alcoholism." However, from the start some *people* at AA meetings were antitherapy and remain so (except for various brands of codependency, Adult Child, or Inner Child therapy). Had medicine and psychiatry known what to do with problem drinkers, this reaction (and AA!) might not have happened. Other than psychoanalysis, professional counseling and therapy were almost nonexistent when AA began in 1935.[1]

Traditional psychiatry erroneously views drinking as only a symptom that will go away if its root psychological causes are addressed. It doesn't care if it takes years (if not the rest of your life!) to get to these supposed roots. Mainstream psychotherapy in the 1930s (and unfortunately, even today) was very passive. Therapists listened, you talked. If you asked a question, the answer often was "Why are you asking that question?" According to therapists' passive theories, it would disrupt your therapy if they *told* you to do anything. For instance, to stop drinking! This therapist passivity led to very inefficient treatment of people who had never been told they had to stop drinking.

As we indicated above, most of today's psychotherapists (including the codependency, Adult Child, Inner Child therapists) strongly hold a crucial irrational Belief that has changed very little since Sigmund Freud voiced it nearly a century ago: The past made you what you are and you must fully understand it and keenly re-experience it to be able to change now. This Belief keeps you endlessly recycling "old stuff." Understanding the past can *feel* very satisfying, but it does not change your present behavior. To change, you now have to work and practice new ideas and new actions.

Sandra, a serious problem drinker with whom we (AE and EV) worked at an RET workshop, told us and the audience that she had gone to Al-Anon in her teens, attended AA and OA (Overeaters Anonymous) faithfully, and felt great after she had retold the stories about her "horrible" childhood. She had also been in "rebirthing" and "past lives" therapy for a year and a half. She felt she got a lot of good out of dramatically reliving her childhood and working through the many times her mother had punished and scolded her and told her she'd never amount to anything and was a "slut." Sandra said that she "relived" these horrible events, released her innermost feelings, and always felt cleansed and healed afterward.

"How many times have you done that?" I (EV) asked.

Sandra indicated that it had been many dozens of times. "But my rebirthing therapist says I'm getting close to a breakthrough."

"Lots of luck!" we (AE and EV) said in unison. We then focused Sandra on what her current irrational beliefs were that kept her drinking. The first one was her belief that reliving her admittedly painful memories would make her change her drinking habits. After discussion, Sandra agreed that, if anything, the reliving of her past made her feel more bitter and resentful. We suggested that she consider attending Rational Recovery meetings.

I (AE) later heard from Sandra after she had spent a month at the Rational Recovery Center in Diamond Springs, California. There she had learned to *prove* that she knew she was responsible for her own feelings by working actively against her own current stinking thinking. No more did she focus on how her mother drove her to drink and overeat.

AA's Answer

In AA's advocacy for alcoholics and its setting up a separate treatment system of them, for them, and by them, it outflanked medicine and psychiatry and beat them at their own game. AA adopted the no-fault Disease Theory to reduce condemnation of heavy drinkers. In so doing, however, it created the identity of always being "an alcoholic" that trips up so many people with drinking problems.

Medicine and psychiatry in 1935 got nowhere with most problem drinkers. Clinical psychology, clinical social work, and counseling hardly existed. What could Bill Wilson and Dr. Bob Smith call upon for help but religion? Problem drinkers were a minority group that banded together, adopted a creed, and began to organize. AA's answer for alcohol abusers was a simple form of spiritual healing through the Grace of God, but without the trappings of formal religion and churches. Many twelve-step program followers (who abide by the twelve steps used in AA and other "Anonymous" groups) today make a distinction between spiritual and religious, as if religion were automatically a bad thing. However, "the God part" is a big feature of AA and remains a major strength and attraction.

Many people, however, are unable to buy into the particular belief system of AA and related twelve-step approaches. That is no criticism of AA, for it was never meant to be a universal treatment. One of the traditions of AA is that it gains followers *by attraction*. If it were all things to all people, its philosophy would be too vague and indefinite to attract. Its offer of a fellowship of people in a setting of acceptance, informal religious or spiritual teachings, and its practical advice attracts large numbers of people. But definitely not everybody. AA's very appeal has led to diversity in the self-help sector. Secular Organizations for Sobriety, Women For Sobriety, Men For Sobriety, and Rational Recovery would probably not exist if many people did not perceive AA as religious.[2]

Religious conversion has gotten a bad press from the "conversions" of Watergate and other criminals. The exploits of Jimmy Swaggart, Jim and Tammi Bakker, and other televangelists haven't helped. However, religious conversion undoubtedly works for many people. It does so because it entails a major change in their Belief System that can *rule out* certain self-defeating behaviors (like heavy drinking) that sprang from their *previous* Belief System. Strong belief in *anything* that contradicts the addictive Belief System, the stinking thinking, can help you conquer an addiction. It doesn't matter whether the replacement Belief System is based on fact, faith, or fancy. If you believe it and if belief in it excludes substance abuse, then you will tend *not* to abuse substances.

The kind of the Belief System you adopt *does* have some importance to long-term sobriety, however. This is because we often start out gung ho with a new Belief System, but the fire dims as time passes. Farfetched Belief Systems with little general problem-solving, happiness-producing capacities frequently lose their hold on us. This often happens with cults, even powerful and dangerous ones. In time we see their limitations, learn that their leaders are only human, and realize that we do better when we put ourselves ahead of the cult leader.

We lose faith in faith-inspired Belief Systems unless

we continue to surround ourselves with other true believers. This is why you have to attend most kinds of churches pretty well forever. The same thing is true of some kinds of recovery meetings. If you don't attend, your faith may fade. People who adopt a faith-based Belief System and improve often think it *should* work for others also—if those others will just "work a good program." They may feel threatened and attacked if some people don't like that approach and prefer something different.

The Newer Psychotherapies

The field of psychotherapy has diversified in the last thirty-five years, so that "one size fits all" no longer. Many dozens of new forms of therapy have developed. Most still look for past "causes" of current problems, but other new therapies frankly operate in the here and now. Some of these practical newer therapies believe that people are responsible for their own thoughts and actions and that they largely learn and create their problem behavior and *persist* in it. These therapies believe that while people often may be born with *leanings* toward problems, they are not unable—with work and practice—to change. The first of these new therapies was Rational-Emotive Therapy (RET). After RET, quite a few other similar therapy brands have developed, but they are more similar to than different from each other. The general name for them is "cognitive-behavioral therapy."[3]

One main advantage of the method we teach in this self-help guidebook—Rational-Emotive Therapy (RET)—is that it helps you solve *your* problems and reach *your* goals. It teaches you to be skeptical, to think for yourself, and to guide yourself with evidence and facts, not faith. It shows you how to test out your ideas to see how they work for you. It encourages you to get answers *for yourself* rather than giving you *the* answers and asking you to have faith in them. It does not tell you what your goals should be; it helps you discover them. It also shows you ways to figure out how you block yourself from reaching your goals and then how to unblock yourself and start moving ahead.

Rational-Emotive Therapy (RET) sees humans as having important capacities to grow, actualize, and choose new directions. It views people as able to unlearn old habits and learn new ones to correct for their tendencies toward self-defeat. RET especially holds that individuals had better accept responsibility for their own behavior so as to have the best chance to change that behavior and transform themselves.

Before we get into more detail on teaching self-help methods, let's look at a few other questions and answers to help you start your self-help project.

Do You Need Inpatient Treatment?

Some heavy drinkers require hospitalization or brief residence in a detoxification center to prevent seizures and other possible severe consequences of withdrawal. While only a minority of heavy drinkers show "DTs," those who do are at great medical risk. People can and do die of alcohol withdrawal (not as many as die of *not* withdrawing from it, of course!).

In assessing your risk for such problems, look at your previous history. Have you stopped drinking before and had the shakes or DTs? Or experienced seizures or other serious symptoms while stopping? If so, then you had better consider undergoing withdrawal in a supervised medical or detoxification setting. If you have been drinking a lot over a long time, your chances of having seizures while withdrawing increase. If you have any doubts on this matter, discuss them with your doctor.

Hospitalization also may be worth considering if you have severe medical or psychiatric disorders that need to be treated. The same is true if your health is so iffy that you need to stop drinking entirely right now if you want to stay alive much longer.

If hospitalization proves necessary, it had better be long enough for you to recover some of your physical and mental health and for arrangements to be made for you to return to a changed environment. Inpatient treatment works best for those who are least able to afford it, namely people who are severely addicted, such as "skid row alcoholics." For the more middle-class "alcoholic," follow-up statistics after inpatient treatment are typically disappointing. Therefore, fewer insurance companies are eager to pay for inpatient treatment. Inpatient treatment is also at a disadvantage because it is not "the real world." On the other hand, if you had trouble quitting drinking in the real world, hospitalization or "detox" may be highly desirable.

Keep in mind that the getting-off-alcohol part of recovery is simple compared to the staying-quit part. Getting yourself through a few "dry" weeks is important, but it's just the beginning of what may be a long journey.

Let's say you do decide to help yourself. What now?

Self-Help Therapy, RET Style

The ABC Model

The ABC model helps you organize your thinking and get the most out of your efforts as you gather information about your actions, feelings, and thoughts. It helps you look honestly at them in the light of your goals and then act to make the changes you want. It gives you a new perspective and a new way to think, and it can unleash your personal power. Let's now go over it in more detail, as it is central to the Rational-Emotive Therapy (RET) approach to quitting problem drinking *and* stinking thinking. The ABC model is illustrated in Figure 6.1, on page 86. How can you zero in on the A's, Bs, and the Cs of your addiction and your recovery from it?

Understanding A (Activating Events or Adversities)

A stands for your Activating Events, Activating Experiences, or Adversities. A can include anything in your present, past, or future environment. As examples, some A's are situations, opportunities, peers, your family background and parents, your economic circumstances, and where you live. When you feel disturbed or drink too much (Cs), A's usually, though not always, are Adversities, such as stressors, fears, frustrations, or temptations. But when you feel good, your A's are usually "positive." Examples of positive A's might include winning the lottery, getting a promotion, finishing a tough job, or enjoying a birthday or holiday. Some A's are your own characteristics, such as your educational level, job skills, racial or ethnic group membership, or sexual orientation.

Some A's are thoughts. For instance, your *memory* of experiences with alcohol can be an important "reason" for you to decide to seek the experience again. Similarly, your plans and expectations about the future can be A's. If you believe, for instance, you "know" you will never be happy, it is only a thought in your head. But you may take it as a fact and may even kill yourself because of that "fact."

Some A's are emotions. For instance, depression, anger, anxiety, joy, or almost any other emotion can become a cue (an A) for you to decide (B) to drink (C).

When you change A's to combat your drinking, you often make changes in your environment. For instance, *moving away* from a well-established network of bars and drinking cronies is a change in your A. Such a move would be an effort at your trying an "A solution." Your own behavior is part of your environment. So you may think about yourself in a different way (at point B) if you learn assertiveness, more effective communication skills, or job skills. Your A may consist of planning to write a whole book, and your B (Belief) may be, "This task is horrendous. I must escape from it!" So at C (Consequences) you may run for a bottle. But if you change A to planning only to outline a single chapter of the same book, your B may be "That's not too hard. I can do it." You may then choose to stay sober. In this case, changing your A helped you change your B, which in turn helped you change your C, drinking.

Understanding B (Belief System)

B stands for Beliefs or Belief System. Your B is anything in your head that has to do with evaluating, perceiving, sensing, imagining, dreaming, or thinking about a past, present, or future situation (A). In this book we capitalize the word Belief when it refers to a group of attitudes you hold and that you can change. B includes attitudes, values, expectations, images, choices, decisions, meanings, assumptions, opinions, predictions, plans, memories, wishes, dreams, negative thinking, rationalizations, and judgments. All these are thoughts or cognitions.

When you change B, you make yourself think in a different way about your circumstances (A's), thoughts (Bs), and feelings and actions (Cs). B includes both self-helping or rational Beliefs (rBs) *as well as* self-defeating or irrational Beliefs (iBs). To recover from problem drinking, you try to change B so that you weaken your irrational Beliefs (iBs) and strengthen your rational Beliefs (rBs). For instance, you can learn to think about the long-term *displeasures* of alcohol use instead of focussing on the short-term *pleasures* of its use. Or, you can learn to view boredom as merely bad, not *awful*. Then you can choose to remove or tolerate it without deciding to "remedy" it with alcohol.

Figure 6.1
Rational-Emotive Therapy's
A-B-C Theory of Emotional Disturbance[4]

"Men are disturbed not by things, but by the views which they take of them."
— Epictetus, 1st century A.D.

It is not the event, but rather it is our interpretation of it, that causes our emotional reaction.

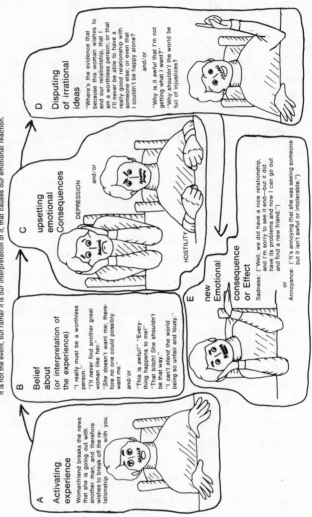

A
Activating experience

Womanfriend breaks the news that she is going out with another man, and therefore wishes to break off the relationship with you.

B
Belief about (or interpretation of the experience)

"I really must be a worthless person."

"I'll *never* find another great woman like her."

"*She* doesn't want me; therefore *no* one could possibly want me."

and/or

"This is *awful!*" "Everything happens to me!"

"That bitch! She *shouldn't* be that way."

"I can't *stand* the world being so unfair and lousy."

C
upsetting emotional Consequences

DEPRESSION

and/or

HOSTILITY

D
Disputing of irrational ideas

"Where's the evidence that because this woman wishes to end our relationship, that I am a worthless person; or that I'll *never* be able to have a really good relationship with someone else; or even that I couldn't be happy alone?

and/or

"Why is it *awful* that I'm not getting what I want?"

"Why *should* the world be full of injustices?"

E
new Emotional consequence or Effect

Sadness: ("Well, we did have a nice relationship, and I'm sorry to see it end—but it did have its problems and now I can go out and find a new friend.")

or

Annoyance: ("It's annoying that she was seeing someone but it isn't awful or intolerable.")

Understanding C (Consequences)

C stands for Consequences, such as your actions and feelings that usually accompany your A's (Activating Events, Adversities) and your Bs (Beliefs). Cs largely, though not completely, *stem from* your Bs *about* A's. When you are disturbed, Cs include drinking, lapsing and relapsing, depression, anxiety, anger, jealousy, procrastination, impulsivity, and shame.

One way to change C is to work on your body or emotions more or less directly. For instance, you can use antidepressants, tranquilizers, acupuncture, exercise, proper nutrition and sleep, relaxation exercises, massage, and herbal remedies and teas. Substance use and abuse itself *is* a C method of changing feelings *with chemicals*. Substance abusers easily lean in that direction. Your best bet for making lasting changes in your disturbed feelings (Cs) is to change your A's (Activating Events, Adversities) and, especially, your Bs (Beliefs). Changing your feelings by changing your attitudes (B) and environment (A), however, takes work and practice. That is the main reason why so many people choose the seemingly easier way of using chemicals.

When you intervene to make C changes, you also usually involve A and B. For example, massage can relax you, but may not if it is done too roughly (A) or by someone you dislike (B). Psychosurgery and direct brain stimulation may be the only "pure" C interventions, but even then you know (B) that they were done and that knowledge may affect you. Even very effective medicines work partly because of your expectations about taking them (placebo effect). The results you get with alcohol and drugs also considerably depend on your expectations. Some people act drunkenly when they *think* they drank alcohol, but they actually didn't. Others drink alcohol, but don't know it, and they are unfazed—it has no effect on them![5]

Medicines, such as tranquilizers and antidepressants, change you at point C. Since they are chemicals, and chemical "interventions" at C are the substance abuser's great stock in trade (and downfall), consider them carefully. Some medications, such as Valium and Xanax and other members of the benzodiazepine family, readily play into addiction. We suggest that you avoid them as part of your antiaddiction treatment. Antidepressants, on the other hand, rarely lead to addiction.

Your tendency to addict yourself depends mainly upon your immediate feelings when you take the medicine. Medications that make you feel good fast are most dangerous to abusers. Antidepressants are slow-acting (taking days if not weeks to have an effect) and do not usually give a "high." Abusing them is rare. If you are significantly depressed, you may find antidepressants useful. Many alcohol-related depressions do clear up when drinking stops, and the same is true of many cases of insomnia. There is no guarantee this will happen, however.

Several years ago, I (AE) had a series of RET sessions by telephone with Marty, a psychiatrist, who said his career and family life were going very nicely. Nevertheless, he felt quite depressed and suffered severe insomnia. Diagnosing himself as seriously depressed, he had taken antidepressants. We worked on his guilt related to the suicide of his mother. And we worked on his perfectionism that kept him from enjoying his career success. Nothing worked. I finally learned that Marty had three or four stiff drinks every night to "put me to sleep." He was sure that this amount of alcohol was more helpful than harmful. But I finally persuaded him—as an experiment—to abstain from the alcohol for six weeks. To his surprise, his insomnia completely evaporated, and much of his depression lifted. It was the turning point in his therapy.

In chapter 8 we include questions you can use to measure your degree of depression. We will provide guidelines for considering antidepressant medications.

ABC Chains and How to Break Them

The ABC method of RET will help you handle your disturbed reactions. Let's look at some examples.

At A (Activating Event, Adversity), let's say you failed a test. At B (Belief System), you think, "I should have done well! Nothing I do is right. I'm a failure in life." B then leads to the C (Consequence) of depression.

At A (Activating Event, Adversity), you have an important job interview coming up. At B (your Belief System), you think, "I have to impress my interviewer! Oh, God, what if I fail? My career would be over!" Then, at C (emotional consequences), you feel panic.

Another typical A is your wish to ask someone for a date. At B, you think, "I must get this date! It would be *awful* if I were rejected! That would show I really am the nothing that I know I am." And then, at C, you make yourself quite anxious and cop out.

At A, you encounter one of your old drinking cronies and he says, "Let's go have one for old times' sake. I've heard you've stopped drinking, but just one won't hurt." You say no, but at B (your Belief System), you think, "It sure would be good. I sure want to. I sure would like to have just one beer on a hot day like this. It's horrible having to do without!" Then, at C (Consequence), you give yourself strong cravings for alcohol.

At A, you feel very strong cravings for alcohol. At B, you think, "I can't stand it. I can't take this any longer! I've got to have a drink!" At C (Consequences), you drink.

At A, you got drunk and now have a hangover. At B, you think *irrationally*, "I must never do a stupid thing like that! This shows there's no hope for me. I wish I were dead." Then, at C, you depress yourself and drink more.

A second possible scenario, however, is that, at B, you challenge the depressed thinking. "Yes, I slipped again, because of my stinking thinking. I had better work harder against it and practice my rational thinking more vigorously. But even with one or a thousand and one slips, I am still just me, a fallible human being. Like all humans I can learn from my errors and construct a better life for myself." In this second scenario, the C (emotional and behavioral Consequences) are more likely to be *disappointment* and *determination* (not depression), and a return to abstinence (rather than continued drinking).

The examples above show a few ABCs and how they link together. Let's look at somewhat more complicated examples.

ABC No. 1. The first A is, let's say, the *possibility* of striking out (that is, rejection) when you go to a singles hangout. Rejection is *always* possible. You are right about that. It's a pain in the ass to get rejected. However, if you only *prefer* not to get rejected, you'll think, "Well, dammit, I'll go to the bar, start conversations, and if no one seems to like me, tough. I'll keep trying." That would be your *rational Belief* (rB). Why is it rational when it makes you have negative feelings like disappointment and frustration? Because disappointment and frustration, while unpleasant, help you *motivate* yourself to keep trying to reach your goals.

We humans, however, tend to go beyond *preferring* what we want and then feeling disappointment if we don't get it. We go to *demanding, requiring, and needing* what we want, and then feeling horror, depression, panic, or hostility if we don't get it. These are also negative emotions, like disappointment and frustration. But, unlike the latter, horror, depression, panic, and hostility are *inap*propriate Consequences (iCs) rather than appropriate Consequences (aCs). Why so? Because they make you miserable and don't help you get what you want. They stem from iBs (irrational, unrealistic Beliefs; stinking thinking).

ABC No. 2. Let's continue the above example. You still want to go out and meet someone, but you feel panic and dread the prospect of getting rejected. (You also feel natural, helpful *concern* when you go out looking for dates, mates, and friends). You know you will feel depressed and despairing (because of your Belief System) if you do get rejected. Drinking alcohol reduces or prevents all these feelings. Thus, this second ABC chain has as A your *prediction* that you will feel not merely concerned, but panicky and full of dread before going out. And that you will feel depressed and despairing—not just disappointed and frustrated—afterward if you *do* get rejected (as most people do).

If you then *irrationally* Believe, at B, that you must not feel panic or depression and that it would be awful and unbearable if you did, then you may drink or take drugs to deaden your distressed feelings. Drinking is an inappropriate Consequence for you because *(a)* you have a drinking problem, *(b)* drinking does not give you social successes (you just think it does), *(c)* you are training yourself more thoroughly to avoid facing your painful emotions, *(d)* you prevent yourself from learning to do something constructive about painful emotions, and *(e)* you reduce your chances of learning how to approach people more effectively. So at the social function you may say and do dumb things, still feel some discomfort, and then decide what you need is another drink!

ABC No. 3. Somewhere along the line you develop a self-concept of a loser who can't function and would be lucky to get any love at all. You then hook up with a partner who is not good for you and who treats you poorly. Had you not gotten yourself anxious and intoxicated and had you not come to think of yourself as a loser, you would leave this person. But your irrational, self-defeating Belief is "I *have* to have somebody! I'm a complete nothing if I'm alone." So you stay with your unsuitable partner.

Negative feelings like disappointment and frustration help you because they motivate you to change undesirable

Activating Events. In RET they are called aCs (appropriate
Consequences). Yes, we, too, don't like disappointment
and frustration! However, if you *demand* that they not
exist, when they actually do, you can easily, frantically try
to get rid of them. Then you can make yourself feel hopeless, give up, or get drunk. None of those "solutions" helps
you reach your goals, and that makes those "solutions"
irrational or inappropriate.

The weak link in the ABC chains that bind you is B,
because you create B and can therefore change it. To do so
in the above example, you would identify depression and
drinking as targets (Cs) for change. Between your scheduled self-help sessions you would notice when you felt
depressed and got urges to drink. Then you would ask
yourself right away, "What am I telling myself to *make
myself* depressed and to *give myself* urges to drink?" Then
you would note down those thoughts, such as, "I'm a loser.
I deserve the lousy treatment I get."

Once you identify B, you Dispute it, as we explain in
the next chapter. Ideally, you will train yourself to Dispute
your stinking thinking when it occurs. This takes time and
practice, however. You can begin to build and rehearse
your self-defense during scheduled self-help sessions. Get
in touch with your disturbed feelings and actions (Cs), look
at the stinking thinking (B) that creates them, and write
down what is wrong with it. Then change it to more self-
helpful thinking. You might say, for instance, "Yes, I
screwed up that time and many other times, but that's
what humans are so good at! However, my failings do not
make *me* a failure." Then you *practice* that new, rational
Belief. At the same time you *act* on your rational Beliefs
(rBs) repeatedly until you make them second nature. Thus,
if you are shy, you thoroughly convince yourself, "Being
rejected *won't* make me a loser, but I can *turn myself* into
a person *who* can take refusals and still go after what I

want. By getting rejected I'll learn what to do next time!" In this way you force yourself—yes, *force* yourself—to keep taking social risks.

The next chapter shows you how to study your pattern of self-defeat and begin to change it into a pattern of self-help.

7

What Are Your Self-Help Goals? How Will You Reach Them?

What *is* your goal? A simple question, but of the greatest importance. Stinking thinking and self-defeating behavior lead you away from your goals. Rational thinking directs you toward where you want to go. In developing goals, you can start with your longest-term goals and then work backward to more specific and briefer goals. Most people's main long-term goals are to have more happiness and less pain, and, of course, stay alive. Let's assume that you, too, favor *those* goals. And since you are reading *When AA Doesn't Work for You*, let's assume that you do want to quit drinking. Or learn how to do it so you can help someone *else* do so!

Quit? Entirely? This is where people sometimes say, "Can't I just cut down? What about 'controlled' drinking? Can't you teach me to drink moderately?"

What About Controlled or Moderate Drinking?

What *is* controlled or moderate drinking? It's normal, no-hassle drinking that most people do. The term *con-*

trolled, however, implies that there are two kinds of drinking, controllable and uncontrollable, and two different kinds of people, those who can and those who cannot.

We take, however, another point of view that is well supported by common-sense observation as well as by research. We will explain it more fully in chapter 9: *All drinking is under the control of the drinker.* When you drink, you are pursuing certain goals and are trying to achieve "desirable" effects and feelings with alcohol. Some of your drinking may, of course, be *severely self-defeating.* It could even be fatal! Those who pigheadedly pursue the pleasures and relief of alcohol will *also* get negative results (along with the results they like). So, once you choose to drink too much, you cannot change (or control) some of the bad results you will get. So the *effects* of alcohol are often uncontrollable. But unless you are tied up and have alcohol forcibly poured down your throat, you control whether or not you will drink and how much you drink. Once you decide to seek the good and ignore the bad results of drinking, as fallible humans often do, you still control your decision. What you cannot control is all the effects the alcohol has on your body and your mind.

The real distinction is not between "controlled" and "uncontrolled" drinking. Or between "controlled drinking" and "abstinence." It is between self-defeating and non–self-defeating drinking. To explain the human tendency to defeat oneself, people have made up the idea that their behavior is "out of control." That idea is little better than "the devil made me do it."

Self-defeating drinking springs from irrational Beliefs and stinking thinking. To try to change your drinking behavior *before* you change your Beliefs is to put the cart before the horse. It *might* work, but we wouldn't bet on it.

There are two vital reasons for you to stop drinking completely for a long time *if* you want to change your stinking thinking and irrational Beliefs. The first is that people who have trained themselves to become problem drinkers have almost always given alcohol powers it does not actually have. They falsely believe it bestows virtues like courage and social skills. You rarely will become a moderate or controlled drinker unless you have altered this kind of stinking thinking. That is unlikely to occur if you are a heavy drinker who *sets out* to become a moderate, controlled drinker. Why not?

If you are a dedicated heavy drinker, you have *trained yourself* to *believe* that alcohol has special benefits and that it is *necessary* for various purposes, such as celebration, relaxation, courage, and coping abilities. These are ideas in your head, not facts, but you devoutly believe them. The truth is that alcohol can sedate you and interfere with your thinking and coordination, and that's about it. You have *given* it much more power—placebo power—than it truly has. If you never drink another drop of alcohol, you won't miss much. You can obtain good feelings and develop social skills *without* alcohol (or other chemicals).

In order to highlight the false powers you've attributed to alcohol, you'd better stop drinking for a long time. During that time you will learn a lot about the powers you've given away. Why? Because situations will come up where you think, "I need a drink." For each of those situations, you had better learn *alternative coping skills*.

How long do we advise a heavy drinker to remain abstinent? At least one year *after* you effectively change your stinking thinking *and* learn and practice new coping skills. *Otherwise, you had better remain abstinent for the rest of your life.*

The second reason for you to stop drinking completely for a long time is related to the first one. Most problem drinkers also use alcohol for self-medication of uncomfortable emotions and mood states, such as anxiety and depression. Using the alcohol gets to be a compulsive habit because it reduces uncomfortable or disturbed feelings you erroneously Believe you can't stand. If you keep drinking even moderately, it will be much harder for you to ade-

quately flush out of hiding and highlight the stinking thinking and irrational Beliefs that largely cause your disturbed,
negative emotions in the first place. If you are drinking, it
will be harder for you to *combat* the stinking thinking and
irrational Beliefs and build up alternative, more helpful
Beliefs.

For example, let's say a stinking thought for you is "I
can't stand anxiety," such as the anxiety you feel when you
start social conversations. Your habit has been to drink
abusively to cover up this anxiety. If you are still drinking,
even moderately, you are probably *still* covering it up.
Doing so, you seriously hamper your efforts to catch,
challenge, and effectively change your stinking thinking
and irrational Beliefs. The reason? If you drink, you may
not *feel* anxiety's discomfort sufficiently to *teach* yourself to
stand it. And you may not feel anxious enough in social
situations to push yourself to work forcefully to change the
irrational Beliefs underlying your shyness.

Once you have effectively combatted the stinking
thinking that creates and supports your problem drinking,
and once you have built up alternative coping skills, then
who knows? Who knows what you'll think or what you'll
want at that stage. We don't know, and you don't know.
We are, however, reasonably certain that if you do have a
drinking problem, you are asking for big trouble if your
initial goal is to achieve normal, "controlled" drinking.
Normal drinkers hardly even think about alcohol. If someone said to normal drinkers, "You can never drink again"
(for, let's say, some important medical reason), most of
them would say, "Oh, well." Their whole plan in life would
not be to remain a moderate drinker.

AA is fervently against the mere idea of "controlled"
drinking. It believes that there is a whole category of
people, "true alcoholics," who cannot even in theory learn
to exercise control.[1] AA therefore views any efforts at
teaching controlled drinking as practically criminal. (Many
AA members, also, we suspect, do not realize that "con-

trolled drinking" in experiments involves lengthy, grueling *training*. It is not merely a rehash of the alcohol abuser's promises and vows that have already failed.)

"Controlled" drinking, that is, non–self-defeating drinking, has been taught in a number of experiments. A research team teaches the would-be controlled drinker a detailed procedure. Trainees are required to practice it thoroughly and repeatedly in the lab and in real-life settings. The training is rigorous, well monitored, and quite different from promises to control drinking "this time." For the most part the results of such research have not been greatly impressive, but they have had some success.[2] After all, whole cultures tend to drink non-self-defeatingly, so it's obviously possible. If "controlled drinking" research weren't so controversial, there would be much more of it.

A couple of examples can illustrate the pitfalls, as well as possibilities, of so-called controlled drinking. Ed and Linda came for relationship therapy with me (EV), and the most pressing issue was Ed's drinking. He adamantly said he would not stop drinking, but he was willing to work on controlled drinking. After much negotiation in an individual session, Ed and I agreed to work on that goal for up to two months. If he were still overdoing it at that time, he agreed to go along with Linda's request (and my suggestion) that he stop drinking completely.

While Ed did reduce his overall amount of drinking during that two months, he continued to overdo it. However, Linda wisely refrained from saying, "I told you so." To her surprise, Ed then decided to stop drinking entirely. At last report he had stuck with that decision. Their relationship, however, did not improve. With Ed's drinking and Linda's focus on it out of the way, they saw more clearly that they had fundamental differences. They decided to end their relationship.

I (AE) know a former heavy drinker in the Midwest who directs an addiction-recovery clinic. For years he taught the traditional absolute abstinence model to his patients. He also rigorously abstained himself. Then he read about the experiments that tested controlled drinking and decided to have up to two drinks in a day if he wished. He taught himself controlled drinking by following to a T the steps outlined in the research. Though he does not drink daily, he does drink occasionally. He reports he feels fine, works steadily, continues to relate well with his wife and children. He predicts he'll be able to stick with his moderate drinking pattern. Most of his recovery-oriented friends were horrified over his touching a drop. They explain his results by saying he was not a "real" alcoholic. They also say that he inevitably will find himself back on skid row!

Another possibility is that he had changed his stinking thinking and irrational Beliefs. My observation was that he had learned how to have good feelings, deal with bad feelings, and how to cope—all without alcohol. When he began to drink again (having studied the "controlled" drinking research), he had become a different person from who he was in his heavy drinking days.

While results of "controlled drinking" are meager, follow-ups of problem drinkers who use rigorous abstinence-based treatment are disappointing. The usual abstinence approaches work great *if* the person becomes abstinent and stays that way. The percentages of heavy drinkers, however, who attend AA for ten or more sessions and then remain abstinent is surprisingly low, something like thirty percent, according to AA's own figures. We believe that percentage could be appreciably improved by teaching heavy drinkers to combat their stinking thinking in the many ways described in this book.

If you have a drinking problem and want to achieve and maintain moderate drinking, you'd better try to meet *all* of the following conditions:

1. *Truly* train yourself to give up the irrational Belief (iB) that you *need* alcohol and its effects *at all*. Alcohol use

has a completely different meaning for moderate drinkers than it has had for you. It takes *a good deal of work, which you have yet to do,* to cultivate and practice the attitudes that normal drinkers have.

2. Stop drinking completely for "a long time." At least, we'd say, a year.

3. Teach yourself nonalcohol coping skills (especially social skills) and practice them repeatedly in real-life situations.

4. Prove that you really *can* take alcohol or leave it (rather than just rationalizing that you can do so).

5. Maintain abstinence without having to "white knuckle" it, without staying dry *because of* the fear of probation or parole violation, and without needing Antabuse. You may start out "under the gun," but had better end up feeling self-motivated.

6. Follow your doctor's advice. If he or she says that your liver functioning and other alcohol-related medical problems have returned to the normal range, says that it is okay if you drink moderately, *and* defines "moderately," only then might it be prudent for you to consider any drinking.

Let's consider three possible goals you may have regarding drinking:

Not drink again. The not-drink-again people can be roughly divided into those who are willing to work at it (see below) and those who fondly believe that the decision alone is all it takes. These nonworkers give willpower a bad name. They *will* themselves to change, but they don't put *power* into it. They goof on doing the work and practice necessary to carry through their decision.

Abstinence takes work and practice. It requires you to learn how to combat stinking thinking *and* to reduce or eliminate some tempting situations (A's). Some people say, "Why look at the negative?" and misuse the AA slogan "One day at a time" to mean "I don't need a plan." If this sounds like you, tell yourself forcefully that there is *near zero* chance of your making it with that attitude. To para- phrase George Santayana, people who do not learn from their histories are condemned to repeat them.

Push yourself to face the facts. If you fear the work involved in achieving sobriety, ask yourself where your best *wishful* thinking got you. Educate yourself about the amount of work involved in AA, Rational Recovery, Wom- en For Sobriety, Men For Sobriety, and Secular Organiza- tions for Sobriety. Find out that "One day at a time" means something more like "Make plans, but don't plan the results," or "Easy does it, *but do it.*"

Some drinking. If this is your initial goal, look at why it is. Does it stem from fear of hard work? From hopeless- ness? Ask yourself, "What is my overall goal in life? If I continue to drink or start drinking again, does that help me reach that goal?" Answer honestly. Reread the section above on moderate drinking to see how well qualified for it you seem.

Keep drinking full blast. If this is your goal, see number 2. Are you suffering yet because of alcohol use? If so, why do you have no interest in stopping? Lack of motivation to stop may mean that you have blocked your- self with hopelessness, depression, hostility, shame, and overrebelliousness. Look into those possibilities and work with them. If you simply want to drink and intend to continue doing so, many interventions in this book may prove impractical or useless, but not all of them.

If you do choose self-help, we advise you to make specific appointments with yourself daily and to do self- help in a planned, consistent way. Most people think of self-help as a few meetings, or maybe even ninety meetings in ninety days, with an in-between attitude of hopefulness. You may well want to believe that a hopeful attitude is all you need, but many problems are tougher than that. Turning around a pattern of substance abuse takes work and practice at new ways of thinking, feeling, and behaving. This self-help book can teach you ways to PYA (push your ass) to do that.

How Do You Do It?

If you choose guided self-help, study your drinking history. Look for the patterns you have created. Identify your ways of drinking and relapsing. Two key questions to ask yourself are "How *do* I decide to resume drinking? How *do* I usually justify continued drinking?" Just asking yourself these questions says, "I make choices. I'm going to make better choices." If you go to a therapist or counselor, don't get bogged down in lengthy descriptions of your A's, the situations that *facilitate* your poor choices to drink. Similarly, don't waste much time dwelling on your Cs, your gruesome drinking behavior. Drunkalogs are so boring!

If your therapist or counselor spends much time listening to your gruesome stories and trying to remedy the crises produced by your stinking thinking and poor behavior, watch out! Those activities only "help" you keep getting away with as much as possible and avoiding the real work of changing.

Heavy-duty drinkers *cause themselves* much of their crummy histories, such as jailings, broken relationships, job losses, medical woes, and poor living quarters. Are we blaming the victim? No, we are clearly recognizing what they *do*. Your "poor me" image of yourself as a victim whose early environment and history "made" you what you are today sabotages your recovery process. Further, it denies the reality of the human being, you, who plots and schemes the sacred pursuit of certain *short-range* pleasures. Such as compulsive drinking!

While important, A's and Cs distract from the real bottle lifter—you. A's and Cs affect but do not *create* your self-defeating philosophy that leads to your addiction and that takes away your power. Safely assume that *you* are the most important factor in your lapses and relapses. Even given a perfect environment, if you are relapse-minded, you can easily figure out a way to justify your resuming drinking.

To study your self-defeating decision-making pattern, ask yourself these questions:

"What is my current alcohol abuse pattern?" Look for the amounts, costs, brands, times of day, description of the social and physical environments, and whatever else goes into your plan to justify drinking.

"What is my history of alcohol use and abuse? Have I done better, or worse, at times? If so, what factors were responsible?"

"What are all the treatment attempts I have made? What interfered with them?"

If you at times stopped drinking: "How did I decide to stop? How did I decide to start drinking again?" Develop as complete a description as possible of internal circumstances (thoughts, feelings) and external conditions (arrests, job loss, divorce).

"What influences pushed me to help myself at this time?"

"What are my living circumstances and other factors that may help or hinder my recovery efforts?" These may include medical (health), personal qualities, family relationships, social relationships, work history, legal hassles, and so on.

"Do I have any misconceptions that might interfere with treatment?" For instance, "Do I think treatment has to be easy, free of craving, quick, convenient? Do I think that a slip or a lapse is *awful* and *the end?* Do I think a slip would prove that I'm *a loser who will never make it?*"

Working on Changing the A and Interrupting Drinking

If your self-help project is to work on an alcohol problem, the first step is to stop drinking. This requires an initial decision. You may have heard of Mark Twain's famous remark about quitting smoking: "It's easy to quit smoking. I've done it a thousand times!" Most of us who try to curb our addictions can appreciate his remark. If you ever have quit drinking, but then changed your mind about *staying* stopped, expect that you may quit nondrinking again. "I'll never drink again" sounds good, but may reflect your wishful thinking that a decision alone is all it takes to stay stopped. A whole *range* of changes is usually required. [3]

If you are still drinking, choose a Quit Day. This will be a day, perhaps one with some special significance to you, but not too far distant in the future. You will quit drinking on that day, and stay quit, having planned your strategy well enough in advance that you can see yourself as having ways to cope with whatever hassles quitting brings. In pushing for early abstinence from alcohol, you can use AA sayings, such as, "Take life a day, even a minute, at a time," "Stay away from the first drink," and "Salute the daily progress you make." Or you can study and memorize those "Central Ideas of Alcoholism" from Rational Recovery that seem to hit home for you. [4]

You can often quit drinking by changing your A's (Activating Events, Adversities) in the ABCs of RET. Changes in A's include any modifications you make in your environment, such as reducing your access to alcohol and reducing or eliminating "triggers." Triggers are the stimuli you have decided will "make" you drink—such as a friend-ly bar that you pass on the way home from work. If you see them as tempting, avoid some of these stimuli. Most of us can profit from arranging fewer opportunities to defeat ourselves. (If you could get away from *all* temptations, that might be great, but it would be a miracle!)

The most important thing to remember about your A's is that they do not *make* you decide to drink. They do make it easier for you to *think* about drinking and to *carry out* your decision. Alcohol in your house, for example, does not *make* you pour it down your throat. Many people say that alcohol is so readily available that they might as well keep it at home. Yes, it is easy to obtain, but if it is in your house it is *easier* to obtain. Its immediate presence increases your tendency to think about drinking and to tempt yourself. It also makes your decision to drink easy to carry out. If alcohol is *not* right there with you in your lonely room, you might have to get dressed and go to the store to buy yourself some. But before you got dressed or before you got to the store, you might tell yourself some-thing that would stop you from drinking.

It is important to realize that we ourselves *seek out* and *create* many of our A's (opportunities, stimuli, and temptations). After all, normal drinkers and nondrinkers have the same access to alcohol as you have. An A (Acti-vating Event that "makes" you drink) is an A because you bring *yourself* to it. *You* give meaning to it. Even if you are largely successful in avoiding drinking situations (and re-frain from creating new ones!), you may well not always be successful at doing so. In that case, you have to fall back on your inner resources. If your only resource is avoidance of temptation, you may fall back into drinking when you cannot avoid temptation.

You can change your A's by changing your location or setting. This is the famous geographic cure that applies more to drug abuse than to alcohol abuse because there is no place without alcohol! It's legal; it's everywhere. But certain places are worse than others. If you have practiced heavy drinking in bars, for instance, you can stay away from bars until you feel secure in your sobriety and no longer care about bars. If you *do* still care about bars, then, please, no rationalizations about going to the bar "just to test myself." Life will easily give you plenty of tests. You don't need to set them up (or to set yourself up!). When you reach the point that you no longer "need" alcohol's effects or care about it *at all*, bars will not *mean* the same thing to you they might mean now.

Another "A change" that can help is changing your schedule. Let's say you tie one on with your friends after work each day. If you change your hours so that you work the graveyard shift, then it is unlikely that as many people getting off work at six A.M. will immediately go and tie one on. You could change your schedule by going to the gym right after work, and thereby sidestep your regular drinking habits. Such changes are beneficial, and the more detail you put into plans, the better. If you have only a vague idea about alternatives, like "Oh, I'll have to be sure to do something different today after work," then good luck! Map out your plan as you would a military operation. Leave as little to chance as possible.

If your friends are booze hounds and will not refrain from drinking around you, then you may have to refrain from being around them. Changing your associates is not *necessary*, but it can be damned important. Whether it is a good idea or not depends on your track record. If you have done heavy drinking with certain associates who do *not* stop drinking, and you continue going with them, the forecast for you is dismal.

If you live with, love, or are married to a heavy drinker, you have major problems when you want to stop drinking. The toughest situations are those with family members or mates who are themselves heavy drinkers or who show other major disturbances. If you have tried to change them, invited them to therapy, self-help groups, and so on, and still they refuse to change or "cannot" change, you may choose to separate from them.

In such cases you may do well to sever relationships with heavy drinkers with whom you have socialized and drunk, even if they are family, loved ones, or friends. A parting of the ways can be difficult, but if it were easy for you to get better and change your life, you'd be at a different place already. Again, we do not agree with the idea that your family members *make* you drink, whether they drink or merely act poorly in other ways. While it is true that they don't *make* you drink, they *can* make it difficult—sometimes exceedingly difficult—for you to follow through on your decision to abstain.

Reducing your exposure to drinking situations means getting rid of all remaining booze and all equipment—cocktail shakers, wine glasses and racks, beer kegs—that are part of your pattern. Question yourself closely about this. Are you keeping back an item "for a rainy day" or because of its alleged antique value? Ending exposure can mean making other changes, too, such as getting an unlisted phone number and so reducing chances of contact with old drinking buddies.

Similarly with other addictions. You can make sure that your home is free of alcohol, cigarettes, and fattening foods. You can go to the racetrack or the shopping center with only a limited amount of money and no checks or credit cards. You can see your free-spending friends only in your or their homes, where you and they cannot spend. You can go to restaurants that have only salad bars and health foods. You can go to a picnic or a hike with only diet soft drinks. You can put expensive stores off-limits by cutting up your credit cards.

Sometimes it helps if nondrinkers monitor your behavior and provide support and alternative activities for you during periods of high craving. This is a stopgap measure because your goal is to learn to monitor yourself. It can and does help to have "support." However, it is not your loved ones' responsibility to give you support. You do not *need* them to do so for you to be able to stop drinking and stay stopped. Further, if you decide to resume drinking, it is not their fault, even if they provide the liquor on a silver platter. (If they *do* provide you liquor on a silver platter, you may have a big problem!)

The Achilles Heel of Relying on Changes in the A

We obviously encourage you to change your exposure to alcohol-related situations to help you stop drinking and stay stopped. Such changes can sometimes rapidly help, but they are only part of a self-help program. In fact, if changes in your surroundings work too fast in preventing your drinking, you can easily deceive yourself that *you* have changed, when in fact only your environment has altered. When the environment gets bad again, you will be just as vulnerable as ever.

Suppose, for example, you are a "love addict" and are depressed (C) about the breakup of an intense relationship (A). You think (B), "I *must* not lose this relationship! How *awful!* I *can't stand* living alone! I'll *always* live alone! What a *loser* I am! No wonder no one *will ever* love me!"

But, let's say, *before* you work on your musts, awfuls, I-can't-stand-its, and damnings of yourself, others, and life (and by that achieve a more realistic philosophy), you luck out and find another partner. Lucky you? Complete cure? Maybe—until that relationship also breaks up. Then back to wormhood and trauma you go!

So with substance-abuse problems. You can only go to "recovery" parties at which no alcohol is served. Fine. You can, for instance, avoid drinking with your friends or see them only at places where there is no alcohol. You can carry a couple of nonalcoholic beers with you when you see those friends or ask them to agree not to drink when you get together with them.

However, what about a time when there is no recovery party, but only a party with "normal" drinkers who are having a great time and don't give a plugged nickel about your trying to abstain? At point B you may irrationally tell yourself, "I can't stand having only plain soda when they're having highballs. It's too frustrating! Besides, they'll think I'm a weakling. How awful!" So at point C you foolishly drink with your friends.

Now you could, of course, rationally tell yourself—at point B—"I don't *need* my friend's approval and I *can* stand plain soda!" Then at point C you wouldn't drink.

Norma, who started drinking heavily in college, became abstinent at age thirty-two. She stopped going out with any of her old drinking friends, but she sometimes does see them in her home, where she keeps no liquor. But when one of them, as occasionally happens, brings her or his own liquor to one of Norma's nondrinking gatherings, she copes. She tells herself, "I wish they wouldn't drink in my house, but they don't have to abstain. It *won't kill* me to see them drink. And I certainly *can* stay away from drinking myself, even though a couple of them drink too much in my presence. Their drinking here is boorish, but that doesn't make them horrible, stupid *people*. I'm not completely perfect myself."

Changing the A (or using stimulus control, as it is called in behavior therapy) is not an elegant solution to your compulsive drinking, eating, or spending problems. It does not reveal and Dispute your self-addicting irrational Beliefs. But often it really helps you reduce your destructive compulsions. Don't forget, too: You can change both your irrational Beliefs (iBs) and your A's (Activating Events) simultaneously.

Changing Your A by Staying Busy

"You've got to stay busy!" How many times have you heard this tried but true bit of advice? Chances are, often. This commonsense saying is often true. While boredom does not *make* you drink, still, "Idle hands are the devil's workshop." Your drinking and the crises you cause by indulging in it may almost fill your life. When you stop drinking, your days and nights may be relatively empty. Or when drinking you may make yourself unmotivated and lethargic. "I don't feel like doing anything." If you leave such gaps, it may be easier for you to decide to fill them again with heavy drinking. Sound familiar?

To avoid high-risk situations that go with boredom, schedule "normal" activities that alcohol-related chaos may have displaced. To help you do this, you can adapt the Daily Planned Activity Chart shown in Figure 5.1.

Some people who train themselves to be heavy drinkers have busy lives and take little or no time for leisure activities and other pleasures. A chief attraction of alcohol is that it provides very rapid relief or pleasure and, at first at least, does not require much of your time. Exercise, sleep, hobbies, and so on are much more time-consuming! Alcohol seems to make leisure activities unnecessary. Eventually, however, the drinking itself becomes more and more time-consuming and costly. If so, you had better increase your *non*drinking leisure and relaxation.

Let us say you have little money for "leisure activities." Perhaps you live on a fixed income, are disabled, or unemployed. You may feel bored, at loose ends, trapped, and focused on day-to-day survival. Drinking is as simple as pie, and it may seem to change everything for you, getting your mind off your dreary everyday life. In truth, it keeps you trapped where you are. Instead, use your ingenuity to devise inexpensive activities, such as a trip to the library, taking a walk, stopping and smelling the flowers. You can do it, though of course it would be easier if you were richer.

Put structure into your life to aid your successful recovery plan. Use your Activity and Reward Schedules as part of that structure and make shaping your life an ongoing process. You always can—if you do not combat your stinking thinking—drift back to listless habits. At times, "alcoholism" seems like gravity, always pulling you back down until you've left your old life far behind and new habits are well established.

In the last chapter of this book we will discuss relapse prevention. Meanwhile, don't delude yourself, like many heavy drinkers do, that you have beaten your addiction permanently. Maybe so. But when you are in *true* recovery you will have left substance abuse behind. You will no longer identify yourself as "substance abuser, in recovery." Instead, you will have truly changed by effectively combatting your stinking thinking and acquiring a new way of thinking, feeling, and acting.

Realize, as many "ex-alcoholics" don't, that you can easily fall back to stinking thinking. Don't think you are in the clear and can "lighten up" and "kick back" again. Watch your stinking thinking as it nibbles away at recovery. "It's too much trouble going out and facing rejection." "I'm tired of going to the gym after work. It certainly isn't going to hurt anything if I just watch TV after work. It's been a long time." "I've been sober all these months. I don't think one drink is going to hurt anything. It would loosen me up. I'll be sure and only start up conversations with very sober-looking potential partners at the bar." Beware! Don't gradually drop structure, eliminate leisure time, and forget about relationships. Don't set yourself up for a fall by returning to your original A's—your drink-related situations and temptations.

8

Step by Step

It is not enough just to tell yourself to schedule activities and stay busy. You had better write down your planned and your actual activities in your Daily Journal. Writing helps commit the writer—you—to the scheduled activities and works against your low frustration tolerance cop-out, "I didn't feel like doing it." You will probably benefit from using a Daily Planned Activity Schedule such as Figure 5.1. This form doubles as an Activity Schedule and a Reward Schedule. If you want to use the form as it appears in this guide, photocopy it. Your own creative imagination is the limit. You can have one copy labeled "Daily Planned Activity Schedule" and another copy labeled "Reward Schedule." On still another sheet, you can regularly record your thoughts and feelings. In later portions of this guide we provide forms you can use to challenge and change your disturbing Beliefs. Keep your Daily Planned Activity Schedule at hand. Follow it and review it at the beginning of each self-help session.

When you are in early recovery, you may not feel like doing anything other than sitting around, feeling sorry for yourself and drinking. So you had better forcefully warn yourself, "Don't let my feelings guide me!" Feelings are not sacred. They are products of your way of thinking, body chemistry, and situations. No matter *what* feelings you experience, you do not *have* to "go with" them.

Surprisingly, many problem drinkers don't notably seek pleasure except in their specialty area: alcohol. So when you delete alcohol from your life, you may have a barren and joyless existence. This is because you over-specialized in alcohol! If you put too many eggs in the alcohol basket and then stop drinking, true, you "don't have anything to do." What a sad story! Get going on creating new interests and pleasures.

Changing the A by Being Good to Yourself

Your Daily Activity Schedule can be used as a Reward Schedule. The self-helping part of you can coach and coax the overdrinking part of you to insert various pleasures into your schedule. This works against depression, boredom, and overwork. Pleasures reward you for the trouble you take on to stop drinking. Rewarding activities also help make life seem worth living again. If you think that normal pleasures seem dull compared to alcohol, ask yourself again, "Why *do* I want to stop drinking? What *pains* do I want to eliminate?"

You may not easily plan rewards, even though there are hundreds of possibilities. Some common rewarding activities are walking, reading, going to a movie, calling a friend, having sex (alone or with someone), eating, playing with your dog or cat, gardening, visiting a friend, and so on. Your interests (besides drinking!) are a good place to start as you develop a structure for yourself to replace the structure you may have built around alcohol.

How many such rewarding activities should you work into your new life? It depends on your "baseline." How many nonalcohol pleasures are you used to? If alcohol has dominated your life or if you now feel quite depressed, you had better push yourself to carry out several rewarding activities a day. It is important to be active, whether you feel like it or not. If you predict that what you will do won't be enjoyable, do it and see. Your ideas about lack of enjoyment are only *ideas*—often incorrect, irrational, and unhelpful ideas, not facts. You can Dispute these ideas and replace them with ideas more likely to lead you out of your rut, toward happiness, and into recovery.

If you have always had a happy, activity-filled, pleasurable life (except for the troubles of drinking), then structuring pleasures into your life may not help you much. Direct most of your self-help efforts to curtailing drinking. You may not have to build up a rewarding life to offset the gap once filled with drinking.

Rigorously and vigorously review your Daily Journal, Daily Record, Activity and Reward Schedules, and homework at each self-help session. Remember, you are training yourself to be your own therapist in these sessions. Check your results at the beginning of self-help sessions, just as a Rational-Emotive therapist would do. Doing so reinforces the idea that you get better by work and practice (not talk and insight). It also will interrupt your addiction to *stinking thinking and behaving.*

First You Work, Then You Reap the Rewards

If you fail to do the homework you assigned yourself, focus on its nondoing during your self-help session. Don't just vaguely refer to the importance of doing the homework and then reassign it to yourself. Don't let nondoing slide. Ask yourself, "What did I tell myself to cause me to decide *not* to do what I had agreed to do?" This usually brings out irrational Beliefs like, "I don't need to," "I don't feel like it," "It's too hard," "I already know everything I need to know," and similar excuses. Help yourself combat the stinking thinking that keeps you stuck. Ask yourself, too, "What had I better tell myself next time to get myself *to do* the homework?" A typical *self-helping* statement is "It'll be harder on me if I *don't* do it."

Figure 8.1 is a form you can use to help yourself catch, challenge, and change the stinking thinking that stops your progress. Re-plan exactly when you will do the homework. Be specific. Write the time and place into your Daily Planned Activity Schedule. Brainstorm how you may interfere with your homework and ways to deal with your neglecting it. Work out rewards and penalties that you can use as incentives. For instance, no food or TV until you have done your homework!

Ask someone to help you. Volunteerism is fine and dandy, but volunteer helpers sometimes are not reliable. Plus, they can have odd ideas, such as "Poor little you can't help yourself." This will only encourage you to act like a helpless baby. It works better if you *contract* with a friend. Contract? Yes, you *hire* the friend to help you. Your part of the contract is that you will do, say, two pages of written homework by a certain time. Or you might contract with your friend that you will appear at the gym at a specified hour. Your friend would check the homework or would call at that time. If you do the homework or if you are at the gym, great. If not, you pay the penalty to your friend, say, twenty dollars. Simply for checking, the friend gets, say, two dollars. Expensive? How cheap is your heavy drinking habit? Think of the money you'll save if you go to the trouble of changing your behavior.

How about this for making a more humorous and diabolical contract almost sure to get you off your duff and to work on changing your stinking thinking: You can contract with your friend to turn in two sheets of written homework at a certain place and time. If you have not done so, your friend will send off to a hated organization a hundred dollars of your cash.

Using C Solutions

"Alcoholics" specialize in working directly on their disturbed feelings (Consequences [Cs]), and you may be tempted to do so, too. Typically, these Cs are panic, depression, hostility, hurt, shyness, and other inappropri-

Figure 8.1

How to Get Myself to Do Self-Help Homework

The steps in getting off your duff and getting on with life are:

1. Ask "What did I tell myself to stop myself from doing the homework?" This is your stinking thinking, your irrational Beliefs.
2. Ask "What is unrealistic or illogical about each stinking thought? How does believing it *hurt* me?"
3. Ask "What would be a more helpful, realistic Belief?"

Stinking thinking	*How does it stink? What's nuts about it?*	*It would be more realistic and it would help me more if I believed and told myself:*

ate and self-defeating feelings. You may also, like many problem drinkers, quickly "treat" *appropriate* negative feelings—like concern, disappointment, annoyance, frustration, and sadness. Why? Because you have such low frustration tolerance that you believe that you *can't stand* those uncomfortable feelings, too. You "solve" these "problems" by dissolving them in so much alcohol that you make your "solution" a problem in itself!

Similarly, many heavy drinkers "cure" their problems with tranquilizers such as Valium, Xanax, Klonopin, or Librium. Taking these and other benzos is a bad idea for substance abusers because they have a "cross tolerance" with alcohol and easily substitute for alcohol. If you become physically dependent on benzos, withdrawal can be quite nerve-racking and had better be done under medical supervision.

If you believe you may need medical help or supervision, review the section in chapter 6 regarding inpatient treatment. See your physician and tell her or him that you are a heavy drinker and are kicking alcohol. If there is any likelihood of seizures, your physician will most likely prescribe a sedative like phenobarbital. It will only be necessary for a week or so, if at all. After that, you had better tell yourself, "I *can* stand feeling uncomfortable while I withdraw!" This helps make you more tolerant of frustration. And it helps you stop avoiding pain. You thereby give yourself a chance to learn better coping skills. For perhaps the first time in your life you work on changing your irrational Beliefs (iBs) that greatly increase your feelings of frustration, rather than medicating them away with alcohol, tranquilizers, or other chemicals.

Sometimes you may use medication to change your disturbed Consequences (Cs) when you push for early abstinence. Antidepressants, for instance, help reduce depression, which is a common side effect of alcohol abuse and a common complaint during initial abstinence. You can also simply outwait the depression. You can combat it by using RET on your irrational Beliefs and the stinking thinking that help create it. Thus, you may be making yourself upset by telling yourself, "I *must* not suffer while withdrawing! I *can't stand* withdrawal!" You can change these iBs to: "I *don't like* to suffer while withdrawing, but I'll suffer *more* if I don't withdraw."

Don't forget, however, that you may have made yourself depressed before you drank and may have "treated" your depression with alcohol. Once you stop the alcohol, you may feel depressed again. Depressed people often have a much harder time reaching recovery than do others. And they are much more likely to lapse and relapse. If you are depressed, you may be wise to consider antidepressants. Using medicines appropriately may help you recover—unless you let the drug do all the work and don't also use RET to overcome your depression.

How depressed do you need to be to consider antidepressant medication? There is no firm answer to that question for everyone. However, you can roughly evaluate your degree of depression by asking yourself questions such as these:

1. Do I feel sad and depressed?

2. Do I feel like a failure as a person?

3. Am I discouraged about my future?

4. Am I losing interest in people?

5. Do I feel tired even when I've had rest?

6. Is my appetite as good as it used to be?

7. Have I lost weight recently without meaning to?

8. Do I wake up early and can't go back to sleep?

9. Am I worried about physical problems?

10. Have I lost interest in sex?

11. Am I thinking about suicide?

12. Have I thought of a way to commit suicide?

If you answered yes to even one or two of those questions, it might be a good idea for you to seek professional help to supplement your self-help. If you answered none of them yes, you may not need professional help.

By professional help we mean a psychiatrist, clinical or counseling psychologist, clinical social worker, or other licensed mental health professional. If the person you consult is not a medical doctor, he or she will be able to refer you to a physician for possible use of antidepressants. Don't spend valuable time and money in therapy that does nothing but look back into your past.

You can locate a cognitive-behavioral therapist in your area by contacting the Institute for Rational-Emotive Therapy, or the Association for the Advancement of Behavior Therapy, Rational Recovery Systems (See Appendix A).

If you answered yes to a question about suicide, we strongly recommend you do seek professional help. If you are suicidal, you probably feel hopeless about your situation and your chances for ever improving it. The *feeling* of hopelessness nearly always comes from hopeless *thoughts*. To produce hopeless thoughts, you take negative Activating Events or Adversities (A's) and predict that they will *always* be that way and that you can *never* change them. You are sure that your grim *predictions* about the future are *facts*. They aren't facts. You don't know the future. If you did, you would pick the winning lottery number! We urge you to work on your hopeless thoughts and feelings. Since death comes for us all, why not wait until it comes, give up the "horrors" you predict will occur, and look forward to a nondrinking and undepressed life?

Another key question is number 9, about health problems. Depression is a great copycat. Many of its common symptoms, such as weight loss, aches and pains, low energy, and insomnia or sleeping too much, can result from medical disorders. If you think your depressed feelings may accompany physical symptoms, we recommend that you have a full physical from your doctor. If you don't have a doctor, get one.

You may have irrational objections to taking medicines prescribed by your doctor as part of your recovery efforts. Your desiring not to be on "another drug" may be sincere, but still unrealistic. Weigh your objections, but don't base them on always and never ideas—"You must *never* take a tranquilizer to help you get sober." And don't base them on other people's ideas about what was good for *them*—"I didn't take medication, and you shouldn't, either."

Let your physician know the truth about your use of substances, no matter what they are. Some patients do not disclose substance use for fear their doctor will discriminate against them. If your doctor does that, you had better replace her or him.

You also may obtain Valium or other tranquilizers from your doctor, who has no idea (because you shaded the truth) that you abuse alcohol. You may even hop among several physicians, so that they fail to discover how many tranquilizer prescriptions you get. You understandably want to *feel better* and avoid crummy feelings. However, you have *not* gotten better by addicting yourself to alcohol, and most likely you will not improve by addicting yourself to tranquilizers. Your core Belief that addicts you to alcohol, to illegal drugs, or to prescription tranquilizers may be that you absolutely must, at all costs, avoid bad feelings. Stick with that Belief and see what worse feelings you ultimately get!

Ask yourself, if you think you need tranquilizers, "Has avoidance worked for me?" Usually the answer is "No, I've just dug myself in deeper and deeper by trying to avoid disturbed feelings *and* the work it takes to change them." It might benefit you doubly to tell the truth to your doctor and work at not putting yourself down even if your doctor does chastise you for copping out with pills.

Todd volunteered to make a live therapy demonstration at my (AE's) regular Friday night workshop at the Institute for Rational-Emotive Therapy in New York. He presented a problem of shame when he goes to his AA meeting because he sometimes takes Xanax to calm his anxiety. I worked with him and helped him see that although taking a tranquilizer like Xanax might not be *desirable*, it wasn't awful and shameful. He could therefore accept himself with this poor behavior, as long as his physician was guiding him in using Xanax occasionally. To calm himself more effectively, he could use RET to minimize his anxiety. I recommended he read my book, *How to Stubbornly Refuse to Make Yourself Miserable About Anything—Yes, Anything!*

Later, Todd sent me a note saying he had done so. After reading it, he asked his doctor to prescribe an antidepressant to treat the depression he had felt for many years. Though his AA group had opposed the antidepressant also, Todd felt much less depressed and was able to "take what I want and leave the rest" of the AA teachings.

Many heavy drinkers who have been forced into treatment object violently to taking one medicine. Can you guess which one? Yes, it is Antabuse (disulfiram). If you take Antabuse, and then drink alcohol, you will feel quite ill and sometimes puke your guts out. Quite unpleasant, and quite motivating *not* to take that first drink!

Is Antabuse for Me?

Heavy drinkers who have severely suffered from drinking sometimes can benefit from taking Antabuse. You may object to taking it because you know it will prevent even "occasional" or "recreational" drinking "on special occasions," which may be your secret goal. If your doctor suggests Antabuse, and you "virtuously" spurn it because it is "another drug," honestly ask yourself, "Do I object because it will really stop me from all drinking?" If your secret goal is to magically achieve controlled or moderate drinking, ask again, "Where has that line of reasoning gotten me before?" Answer: "Into great trouble! So, it's stinkin' thinkin'."

Is taking Antabuse advisable for you in your recovery program? It may well be, especially if your drinking pattern includes extreme binges that are dangerous to you and to others. Antabuse requires a prescription, and it has its dangers, so you will have to discuss it with your physician.

You may ask "Shouldn't I be able to stop on my own? Aren't I a weakling if I have to take medication?" There's no shame in seeking help. Rational-Emotive Therapy (RET) teaches you to *accept yourself* even if you have all kinds of weak behaviors or deficits. It also shows you how *not* to accept your failings themselves, but to use any tool to change them. Even a crutch, such as Antabuse, may be a good tool. In truth, if you take Antabuse voluntarily, you *will* be "doing it" on your own.

How about your "I don't want to take medicine forever" objections? First, taking Antabuse or an antidepressant forever probably would not be required. Second, even if it were, how bad would that be compared to the effects of the heavy drinking and binges?

More Self-Medication

As we mentioned above, many "alcoholics" turn to alcohol to "treat" their emotional problems, especially their panic disorders and depressions. If you experience panic, you often think you are having a stroke, a heart attack, are losing control, or will go crazy. Once you panic, you panic about your panic. "What *if* I have an attack? It would be awful and unbearable!" You then may go on to "medicate" yourself with alcohol to *prevent* attacks. You may unknowingly touch off panic attacks by noticing some physical symptom like a racing heart or lightheadedness, which you interpret as a sign of dire danger. Or you may be entering a social situation, like a singles bar, and touch off a panic attack in yourself by *awfulizing* about the prospect of rejection and humiliation.

If you believe you may have a panic disorder or another type of severe anxiety disorder, by all means see a licensed psychotherapist. You can obtain a referral by consulting the organizations listed in Appendix A.

Psychotherapy and medication (and not drinking!) are the proper treatments of choice for major psychiatric disorders. Some of the key symptoms of such disorders are hearing voices that come from outside you, seeing things that are not there, believing that people are plotting against you, noticing personal messages to you on TV or the radio, and believing that people can read your thoughts. If you are experiencing any of these symptoms— whether or not they seem to stem from using alcohol or drugs—quickly seek professional help.

You have probably heard of "manic depression," an inherited tendency to experience mood swings that take weeks or months to go from one end of the swing to the other. If you are happy one minute, then down the next, and back to feeling okay later in the day, that is not the kind of mood swing we mean. "Manic" is the high end of the mood swing and it is quite different from normal high spirits and cheer. It may have nothing to do with your circumstances. When manic, you may have abnormal confidence in yourself, reduced need for sleep, racing thoughts, feel like talking nonstop, and become quite enraged when someone blocks your goals. You may have unrealistic plans and schemes to make money and become famous, and you may think that you have discovered The Truth. Your grand ideas are *not* true, but you believe them and may run up huge bills and act recklessly.

If you believe you have such symptoms, consult a psychiatrist. Lithium is a medication of choice for manic symptoms, and it can be combined with other medications that address the depressed end of the mood swing. Taking cocaine, crack, or speed can cause psychiatric symptoms similar to those of mania. When you discontinue such drugs, you may "crash" into a deeply depressed mood. Symptoms of manic depression differ from those that come from substance abuse. The latter can require medication as well as complete abstinence from the drugs.

Besides medication, there are other interventions possible at point C (Consequences) that can help you overcome a drinking problem. Acupuncture, exercise, improved nutrition, massage, and relaxations may often help. Some people think herbal remedies and megadoses of various vitamins are beneficial. If you are not a medical practitioner, be cautious about prescribing these "cures" for yourself. Talk it over with your doctor.

9

How to Stop
Self-Defeating Bs
(Stinking Thinking)

Thoughts—stinking thinking or irrational Beliefs—lead you to start and continue alcohol use. Once you get into trouble, you may say that you were "out of control," "had no choice," or "couldn't help it." These excuses or cop-outs make you shirk responsibility for your poor choices and take away your power to change. Only by taking responsibility for your self-destructive acts are you likely to correct them.

When you abuse alcohol, you *do not* (versus *cannot*) control your self-sabotaging habits. You *choose* to drink too much because you believe you *must* have the powerful "good" effects you derive from drinking. And you *choose* to ignore the bad results you get from the overdrinking. Eventually, the grim results catch up to you. You may then easily blame external factors that "made" you act foolishly. Nonsense! You were in control of your behavior. But you stubbornly chose to go after only immediate pleasures. The only thing you couldn't control was the fact that *if you persisted* at drinking, then unwanted *bad* results would *also* occur.

If you are a substance abuser hell-bent on obtaining alcohol, you are more than willing to go through lots of trouble to get what you want. *Later*, when you bring on too much trouble, you *see* how crazy you were to stubbornly *persist* at getting momentary good feelings and relief. Then you invent the "fact" that forces outside your control were "responsible" for your self-defeating behavior.

Your Belief that when you compulsively drink you easily get "out of control" is prevalent in our culture. This mistaken Belief, as writers like Stanton Peele have argued, may actually *cause* you to give away your power and behave irresponsibly.[1] How so? Because it tells you that you aren't responsible for what you do. Not only do codependency books and Recovery preachers on TV help you think you are out of control and powerless. Even some researchers devoutly believe in "powerlessness."

I (EV) was at a professional meeting recently where a prominent researcher in eating disorders seriously presented the idea that certain chemicals in the bodies of binge eaters are responsible for their bingeing on the kind of foods they like. The chemicals then "make" them vomit the food up on purpose, binge on more delicious food, throw up on purpose again, and so on. He mentioned that bulimics almost never eat the food in public, much less vomit in public. No one sees them do it. One night, however, at a Chinese restaurant, he saw a young woman eating alone who had a meal, left the table, returned and had another meal. She left the table again, returned, consulted the menu, hailed the food server, ordered, and ate a third meal! She very probably was bingeing and vomiting up the food so she could order, eat, and enjoy some more food.

But out of control? If so, she would hardly throw up only in the women's room. Powerless people are powerless in public as well as in private. And if you are powerless, you do not only choose foods you think taste good. Choosing good-tasting foods means you *are in control*. If you were out of control, you would eat anything. You would grab food from other people's plates and out of the dog's dish. None of that happens, of course, because bulimia is a planned, calculated, voluntary behavior. It is *based on* nutty ideas such as "I *must* be able to eat everything I want and not get fat" and "If I got fat I'd be a terrible, worthless, loveless person."

Therefore we encourage you to admit that you (and other substance abusers) *are in control of yourself most of the time (just like the rest of us)*. You quite consciously measure the amounts of alcohol you believe you need to achieve the effects you want. Research has even shown that "skid row alcoholics" don't drink at every opportunity. They start and stop drinking according to their plans, goals, and resources. They do not drink every drop of alcohol the second it's available, but choose times and places to imbibe.[2] Let us give a real-life example.

Recently I (EV) had some business downtown and ate lunch at a small restaurant in the shambles known as San Francisco's Civic Center. From a window seat, I watched three very dirty, unkempt men seated on cardboard in a nearby doorway. Their faces and noses were puffy and blotched, very wrinkled, and tan. They had a bottle of booze in a paper bag. They passed it among themselves, each taking a drink. The last to take a swig would hand it back to its keeper, who would screw the cap back on and put it away. Meanwhile, they continued to socialize and beg passersby for spare change! Then out would come the bottle and the three men would repeat the ritual. I saw them count and recount their money. After they finished the bottle, one departed with the money, probably to make another alcohol purchase. The other two seemed unconcerned.

Those three men were undoubtedly very heavy drinkers. They did not seem to be strangers to living in doorways. Their coordination was wobbly. But out of control? No. They controlled (but did not moderate!) their intake of alcohol, to make their supply last and to maintain a certain level of inebriation. If they got too drunk, they could not continue to ask for spare change. They were also clearly observing etiquette. Nobody tried to quaff down the whole bottle. As far as I could tell, each in turn would take one good swallow. They had goals and a plan. They had positioned themselves in a corner doorway so that—I suspect—passersby approaching the corner would not see them (and be able to steer clear of their begging!) until it was too late. They cooperated with each other by pooling and counting their earnings. Two of them showed trust for the other by letting him depart with the money.

Many observers would probably *infer* "out of control" and "powerlessness" from the scene just described, *because* the three men were inviting crummy health and surroundings *to obtain the alcohol-related feelings they wanted*. A nonaddict might think, "Since *I* would not hurt myself that way, no one else in their right mind would either, so people who do so *must* be out of control." We think it so unbelievable that anyone would ignore such poor Consequences to get immediate highs and relief that we *dream up* that self-defeating people are out of control. Indeed, you can easily sabotage yourself by drinking, later find it incredible that you would choose to do so, and then make up a "disease" (or the devil) that "made" you do so.

Abusive substances do not just hop into your mouth, nose, or veins. Instead, you *choose* to *think about* the positive feelings or relief you expect to get from them. Brain chemistry does not make us feel and give in to cravings and urges. You, the dedicated abuser, *think* about what you like to think about and *do* what you insist on doing: avoid pain and feel good. These goals are normal human goals. When overdrinking, you merely go too far in *demanding* that you reach them. By doing so, you can't control the fact that you will bring poor results on yourself.

Triggers

Various circumstances that you have trained yourself
to associate with alcohol may trigger thoughts about drinking. For instance, if several times a week you make a
withdrawal from an automatic teller machine and then go
to a bar to have a few drinks, you may associate the
machine, money, and, of course, the bar, with drinking.
After a while, these cues may prompt alcohol-related feelings and thoughts. Like the dogs Pavlov trained to salivate
at the sound of a bell before food was served, we humans
condition ourselves to respond emotionally and physically
to cues. So ask yourself about events and feelings you
associate with your urges and decisions to drink. Keep
notes on this in your Daily Journal.

Some popular alcohol triggers or "cues to drink" are:
when home alone, home not alone, at a friend's house,
before going out, at parties, sporting events, movies, bars,
clubs, concerts, during a drug purchase, driving, at school
or work, when avoiding school or work, before a date,
during a date, sex, first thing in the morning, at lunch,
after payday, carrying money, going past a bar or club, the
smell of your favorite alcohol, approaching a particular
freeway exit, being with particular people, and so on.

You can also train yourself to associate certain negative *or* positive *emotions or feelings* with alcohol and thereby to trigger alcohol-related thoughts and feelings. Some
common feelings you can link to alcohol are: feeling upset,
worried, afraid, anxious, shy, terrified, depressed, discouraged, grief-stricken, hopeless, embarrassed, hostile, hurt,
inadequate, jealous, lonely, and dependent.

As you make yourself into a heavy drinker, you need
fewer triggers before deciding to drink. What are your
triggers? List them. Keep noticing additional triggers.
Then use the list to *rehearse* ways to stop and change your
stinking thinking. You also can list activities or situations in

which you would *not* drink. These situations can be used to schedule nondrinking activities.

Rational-Emotive Imagery

You can use Rational-Emotive Imagery (REI) to *reprogram* your emotional responses and actions so that they help you rather than hurt you. First you list your triggers. Include not just physical situations (A's), but *emotions and feelings* (Cs) associated with your stinking thinking and decisions to drink. In addition, list any thoughts or images you can recall that also are associated with the *beginning* of stinking thinking.

Then take one of your listed items, close your eyes, and visualize a scene that would depict that trigger in action. If, for example, you have toyed with the idea of drinking after a hard day's work, imagine yourself after a hard day's work. Imagine it in as much detail as possible—the sights, sounds, smells, the very *feel* of "after a hard day's work." Then, in your practice session, begin to think and feel your stinking thinking. When you have begun to feel it, *change your thoughts to appropriate ones.* You can, for instance, hear and see and feel yourself say, "To hell with drinking! Once I get home I'll rest or exercise, and that will be a *real* reward for a hard day's work. No matter how much I'd *like* to drink, I never *have* to!"

If one of your triggers is depression, you imagine a scene in which you feel very depressed. Once you are in contact with the depressed feelings, look at the thoughts that create them. For instance, "I *can't stand* feeling so down. I've *got* to have a drink to feel better." Then, emphatically Dispute, challenge, and change that stinking thought. You can think, "Get serious! You think you're depressed *now!* Drinking never really helps you to get over depression, but makes it worse. You'd better *stand* these depressed feelings and get to work to *change them* in a more productive way than drinking."

If one of your triggers is, say, a memory or image of

your ex or of your past drinking cronies—and such images do pop up—you first would get in contact with that image. Then you would hear yourself begin to think stinkingly and to toy with the idea of drinking. Then you would Dispute, challenge, and change the stinking thinking. For example: "So *what* if I never see my ex or my drinking cronies again? Too bad, but I can't change and create a new life for myself if I sit around crying in my beer, pretending that the good old days were only good. Fact is, they were crappy. And look what harm they led to!"

Schedule times to do Rational-Emotive Imagery as you would any homework. Knowing a technique is a start, but *practicing* it leads to improvement. Yes, working on yourself and doing homework *is* a hassle, but *there is no easy, magical way to change your habits. If there were an easy way, you would have found it already*! Perhaps you have thought you found it, and even paid good money for too-good-to-be-true gimmicks, such as subliminal tapes. In that connection, remember what P. T. Barnum, that great nineteenth-century philosopher said, "A sucker is born every minute." You make yourself a sucker when you *demand* an easy way to solve your problems and when you seek out magic and the millions of charlatans eager to sell it to you. In this book we can show you many effective antidrinking techniques, but *all of them take work and practice.*

Another kind of Rational-Emotive Imagery goes like this: Imagine intensely exposing yourself to a most tempting addiction-related image. Stay with this image and stand it until your temptation begins to fade. Do this again and again until your tempting images lose their hold on you. Thus, in imagination (or even in reality), you can dip a cotton ball in your favorite poison—perhaps good rye whisky—and smell it and smell it until you almost drive yourself up the wall. But convince yourself that you can damned well *stand* it. In time, the smell and image of rye whisky will have less and less of a hold on you.

Actively removing your personal triggers is useful.

For example, instead of going to an automatic teller at night that is close to your favorite bar, you can get rid of your ATM card, and can schedule aerobics or a recovery meeting (AA, Secular Organizations for Sobriety, Rational Recovery, or Women For Sobriety). Wherever possible, eliminate the triggers. But not because the triggers *make* you drink. A common trigger may be having a six-pack of beer in the refrigerator on a hot day just after you have felt stressed out. Although beer does not *make* you drink it, it is still good sense to "change the A" by simply not having beer in the refrigerator. Reducing triggers makes it harder for you to choose to drink and aids your self-help program.

Some of your personal triggers, however, *cannot* be eliminated, especially where you have associated almost everything with drinking. Even if you could eliminate all triggers, you can easily create new ones. So teach yourself to live with some triggers and *still* not drink. How? By stopping or changing the stinking thinking that really triggers your triggers.

Techniques for Thought-Stopping

Thought-stopping is hardly a deep or elegant technique, but it can save your life, especially if you use it to stop your pro-drinking thoughts as early as possible after you create them. You'll find it becomes more difficult to stop them if you let them gain momentum. In a self-help session, first close your eyes and imagine, for instance, being at home all alone and lonely. Then think a specific trigger thought, such as, "Passing this bar reminds me of what great times I had when I used to drink there." When you note you are just beginning to "get into" the decision to drink, shout "Stop!" or "No!" loudly, smack the desk or your leg with an open hand, and *force out* your stinking thinking. Then focus on prerehearsed antidrinking thought, such as, "Not going into that bar any longer is one of the most constructive and healthy things I have done in the last ten years!" Repeat the process five or ten times before moving on to stop another thought in another trigger scene. Work from your personal list of triggers.

In time, you can simply *think* loudly "Stop!" or "No!" You can also use a rubber band on your wrist and snap it smartly enough to sting and help interrupt stinking thinking and to penalize yourself if you stubbornly refuse to stop it. You can combine the snapping with the words "Stop!" or "No!"

You can use the thought-stopping techniques when stinking thinking "spontaneously" occurs. However, you had better often use this, Rational-Emotive Imagery, and other RET methods in your scheduled self-help sessions. Practice your coping techniques before you need them. Don't wait till a crisis strikes and you are caught with your pants down and your elbow bent.

Understanding the idea behind a technique like thought-stopping will not make it work for you. Benefits stem from work and practice in your scheduled self-help sessions and at other times. Even well into recovery, you can benefit by reviewing and rehearsing coping techniques. You will probably tend to have recurring alcohol-related thoughts far into recovery. But if you work at interrupting them, you will dwell on them less and less. In time, it simply will not be "you" to dwell on and obsess about them. You will be out of white-knuckle recovery and be getting on with the rest of your life.

Another useful method of thought-stopping is to follow the same procedure as above, but this time to take a whiff of rotten egg or smelling salts (spirits of ammonia) every time you begin to harp again on drink-provoking thoughts. Smelling salts are available over the counter in many drugstores. Before you use them, *clear it with your doctor*.

Other Distraction and Diversion Techniques

Two pieces of good advice that you can use in your self-help sessions are "Don't think about it" (the old way) and "Try to stay busy." Find something different and diverting or distracting when you indulge in drug-related thoughts. Brainstorm about what diversions and distractions might work for you. Then work out and write out a specific plan for how to do them. Rehearse these plans. You can, for instance, imagine the situation in which you dwell on alcohol-related thoughts, then see, hear, and feel yourself *immediately* choosing to engage in some distracting behavior.

Humans have a difficult, if not impossible, time thinking of two things at the same time. Therefore, look at your self-destructive ideas,—such as, "Because I must stop drinking and I still drink, that proves I'm a hopeless weakling from drinking and I'll never be able to stop." Then force yourself to think of something else that will *not* upset you.

You can temporarily change your thoughts in several ways:

1. *Relaxation procedures.* These procedures are diversions that can be helpful in interrupting alcohol-related thoughts and feelings. If you feel empty, nervous, angry, or thirsty for alcohol, you can often relieve these feelings by breathing in deeply through your nose and exhaling very slowly through the mouth. Concentrate on slowing your breathing and on breathing from your lower abdomen rather than from your upper chest.[3]

2. *Meditation.* If you meditate by steadily repeating a mantra, watching your thoughts "objectively," or using other meditative methods, you will usually find it almost impossible to obsess at the same time. Again, this will temporarily dissolve your agitated thinking.

3. *Focusing on pleasures.* If you are upsetting yourself, and you then concentrate on something pleasurable, such

as sex, sports, or entertainment, you will often feel better for a while and may enjoy yourself instead.

4. *Forcefully changing your thoughts.* When you are thinking of something frightening or depressing—such as always getting rejected by those whose approval you want—you can force yourself to keep thinking of more pleasant things, such as romantic daydreams, hobbies, science, literature, inventions, business, current events, or almost anything else.

All these methods of cognitive distraction can drive away your anxious and depressed and raging emotions—temporarily! That's the problem. They then usually slowly come back. Why? Because your disturbance-creating shoulds, oughts, and musts will only be temporarily side-tracked, but hardly changed, by your various kinds of distractions.

Suppose, for an example, you horrify yourself about speaking poorly in social groups and you keep thinking about what an incompetent fool you are for feeling terrified. You use yoga and slow breathing whenever you panic and whenever you damn yourself for your panic, and you are quickly able to relax and to stop your feelings of terror. But you still believe that you *must* speak well in social groups and that it is *awful* when you speak poorly. And you still believe that you *must* never be terrified of speaking and that you are a loser if you do speak poorly or if you show that you are nervous. What do you most probably return to soon after you stop your relaxing, Yoga, and slow breathing? Guess!

So by all means use distraction techniques to calm yourself and waft away your panic and depression when you find it useful to do so. But after you relax, after you meditate, after you breathe yourself out of your panic, go back, if you are wise, to finding your irrational Beliefs. Then actively, forcefully Dispute them until you change them, and subscribe only to your more flexible preferences.

A case in point was Joseph, a lab technician who meditated for two hours every day and did his best to turn all his friends on to doing so, too. He was positive that meditation cured all emotional evils. When he finally met the most attractive partner he had ever found and she refused to meditate too (largely because she had tried it for a few months and found it to be useless and incredibly boring), he became very angry with her. This led to her seeing how immature and self-centered Joseph was. He then depressed himself so severely and drank so heavily when she broke up with him that he barely kept himself from committing suicide. Did his steady meditation help him? Yes, in some ways, to *feel* better, which is good, but not to *get* better, which is far healthier.

In the next few chapters we will describe additional, more lasting ways to change your irrational Beliefs and to *get* better.

10

How to Dispute and Really Change Your Stinking Thinking

As we have been showing in this book, irrational Beliefs (iBs) or stinking thinking are the main (not the only) cause of problem drinking. If you drink compulsively, you usually have irrational Beliefs that help make you anxious, depressed, enraged, or self-pitying. Then, once you upset yourself or act self-defeatingly, you consciously or unconsciously tell yourself more stinking, irrational ideas. For example: "I *must* not be upset!" "I'm not really that upset. Even if I were, I *can't* let others see it." "I *can't stand* feeling upset. I *need* something to get rid of my upsets and feel no pain as quickly as possible." "If I'm an alcoholic, that means that I am less of a person, in fact, a nothing!" "When my drinking bothers others and encourages them to scorn me, I'm a total worm!"

Most of the thoughts that drive you to anxiety and despair, that impel you to drink, and that make you damn yourself for drinking, stem from your irrational, *absolute demands* on yourself, on others, and on the world. Demands? Yes, disturbance stems not from your rational *preferences*, but from *absolute demands* that you succeed, win approval, stop excessive drinking, and avoid discomfort. So the first goal of RET is to help you clearly see that when you disturb yourself about practically anything, you consciously or implicitly change your healthy *wishes* (rational Beliefs) to arrogant *demands* (irrational Beliefs). RET's second goal is to encourage you to uproot these demands and turn them back into sensible preferences. RET's third goal is to help you train yourself to do this so consistently and so well that after a while you rarely return to your grandiose demands.[1]

As you know all too well, thoughts about drinking cannot always be stopped. "Get your mind off it" is often unheeded advice. A much better method of changing your stinking, alcohol-related thinking is to *challenge* and *change* your core irrational Beliefs and their results (automatic disturbed thoughts and rationalizations). You then create new, more realistic and self-helping ways of thinking. If you clearly see how to discover and uproot your core irrational Beliefs (iBs), you will be able to stop your stinking thinking in its tracks.

To find your destructive self-talk, look for the Beliefs you hold with absolute conviction. Listen for Beliefs that distort reality. Take stock of Beliefs that block your goals. Don't pretend, when you feel very upset, that you are merely not getting what you *want*. Look for and honestly face your demandingness and neediness. Do you really only *desire* success, love, or comfort? Or—honest, now!—do you dogmatically insist that you *absolutely must* have it? Are you a sane *wisher* or a crazy *musturbator*? Look at your rigid shoulds, oughts, and musts. Do things really have to be—right now—the way you'd *like* them to be? Or do you Believe they *must* be better than they are? Possibly in the future you can change many of your frustrations. Fine! But where is it written that they *have* to change?

When you musturbate you are light years away from strongly preferring. If you prefer, you feel committed and involved in working for what you want. When you can't get it right now, you feel appropriately disappointed, irritated, frustrated, displeased, and concerned. But when you dream up that you *absolutely must* get what you want and that life *absolutely must not* balk you (as it often does), you usually make yourself feel horrified, depressed, panicked, and ashamed. Musturbation *contributes* to your frustration and failure by sidetracking you and making you inefficient. As some RET slogans put it: "Musturbation leads to self-abuse!" "Stop shoulding on yourself!"

When you powerfully musturbate, you tend to create four other core irrational Beliefs that sabotage your basic goals and purposes. The first derivative of your musts is known as "awfulizing." Instead of seeing an event as "bad" or "unfortunate" (as it well may be) when you don't want it to exist, you exaggeratedly *call* it, *define* it, as being "awful," "horrible," or "terrible." By this kind of labeling, you mean, first, it must not be *as* bad as it really is. Second, that because it *is* that bad, it is *totally*, 100 percent bad. And third, it is *more than* bad, beyond bad, 101 percent bad (or worse!) All three of these labels, if you really think about them, are false (and deadly). But as a devout awfulizer, you invent and rigidly hold on to them.

You often derive from your musts a second Belief known as low frustration tolerance (LFT) or "I-can't-stand-it-itis." With this self-defeating dogma you powerfully convince yourself that because things you don't like must not exist and because (perversely!) they really do exist, "I can't stand it! I can't bear it. Because this awful thing exists, I not only feel less happy, but I can't be happy *at all*." With frustration, you are appropriately sorry and displeased. With low frustration tolerance (LFT) you are inappropriately horrified and utterly miserable.

The third major derivative of musturbation is *rating and blaming*. Rating and blaming represent your human tendency to rate yourself and other people globally as "no-goodniks," "worms," "worthless," "inadequate," "failures," or "idiots." You do this if you or they do something that you believe you or they "must" not do. And you do it if you or they fail to do something that you believe you or they "must" do. You also overgeneralize about conditions and the world and insist that "things are awful!" or "Life is no good!" when you view conditions as being worse than they absolutely *must* be. One of the RET posters illustrates rating and blaming people: "Shouldhood leads to shit-hood!" Another illustrates how to avoid damning life and world conditions: "Shit *should* happen—because it often does."

You can derive a fourth core crazy Belief from mustur-bation by *overgeneralizing, taking things to extremes*, or inventing *always and never* conclusions. Thus, when things go wrong—as, of course, they *must* not!—you over-generalize: "Nothing works out for me," "I never do anything right," "I'll never be happy and overcome my drink-ing problem," "Once a drunk, always a drunk," or "No one ever cared a bit about me, nor ever will." You tend to jump to these silly conclusions because your basic, often un-spoken demand is that things be *exactly* and *always* your way. They aren't (and rarely will be), of course. So then you scream, "Life is *totally* awful, unbearable, damnable!" and "It'll *always* be that way."

The core irrational Beliefs that you are likely to hold—musturbation, awfulizing, low frustration tolerance, rating and blaming, and overgeneralizing (always or never attitude)—can be summarized as follows:

Musturbation (Shoulding, Demandingness)

"*I* have to (should, must, ought to, deserve to) do well and be approved by people I like—or else I am an inade-quate, worthless person!" "*You* have to (should, must, ought to) be considerate, kind, and fair to me—or else you are a rotten, no-good individual!" "*Life* (conditions, things, tasks) has to (must, should, ought to) be the way I need it to be—or else the world is a horrible place and I can't be happy at all!"

Awfulizing

"It's awful, terrible, horrible, catastrophic when I don't perform well (as I must), when you don't give me what I need (as you should), and when conditions frustrate me (as they must not)!"

Low Frustration Tolerance (LFT)

"I can't stand (bear, tolerate) it when I don't get what I need (as I must) or when I do get what I don't want (and must not get)!" "I don't deserve" bad conditions (which must not exist) and I am absolutely entitled to get (and absolutely must have) what I want."

Rating and Blaming

"I am a worthless and damnable person for behaving poorly (as I must not behave)!" "You are a rotten individual for acting badly (as you must not behave)!" "The world is a terrible place for being uncomfortable (as it must not be) and having poor conditions (which it must not have)!"

Overgeneralizing (Always or Never Attitude)

"When I do poorly (as I must not) or things are bad (as they must not be), that proves I'll never be happy, succeed, or get what I want."

Alternatives to Musturbating and Demanding

People are always thinking. Not necessarily sanely, self-helpingly, or logically, but thinking nevertheless. Just try to stop thinking! However, when you interrupt your harmful thoughts, you do not immediately or automatically adopt more constructive ones. You are biologically geared to be a creature of habit. To replace your old self-abusing habits with better ones requires your learning *and practicing* alternatives to musturbation, awfulizing, low frustration tolerance, rating and blaming, and overgeneralizing.

Consider alternatives to your Demanding (stinking thinking, musturbation). Show yourself how to *Desire* instead of *Need*. The Serenity Prayer puts nondemandingness in a nutshell: "Grant me the serenity to accept the things that I cannot change, the courage to change the things that I can, and the wisdom to know the difference."

Stay with preferences and wishes, which are fine and healthy. Refuse to change them into demands, and you will rarely disturb yourself. You *will* experience *appropriate negative feelings*—especially sadness, regret, disappointment, and annoyance—when reality thwarts your desires. These negative emotions are *constructive*. They motivate you to overcome obstacles to reaching your goals. They also help you to accept reality when your desires cannot be met.

Rating your (and others') *acts* as "good" or "bad" is also fine and stops your *awfulizing* about them. If you are deprived or handicapped, tell yourself, "*This* is bad." But if you don't add "I *must* not be deprived," you can accurately view your loss as bad. But not as "awful" or *more than* bad. If you desire money very much, you can legitimately view its lack as *very bad*. But if you irrationally convince yourself that because you want it, you absolutely should have it, you will define its lack as "awful" and "terrible." So, again, go back to merely *desiring*!

Can you plan an alternative to *low frustration tolerance* (LFT) or "I-can't-stand-it-itis"? Yes!—Tolerance. When you are frustrated, you first note and acknowledge that you are not getting what you want. You solidly believe that right now you *should* be deprived—simply because you *are*. Conditions *have a right* to frustrate you. You rate your degree of deprivation from 0 to 99 percent, but not at 100 percent or 101 percent. You actively strive to reduce or eliminate your frustration. If you cannot reduce it, then accept the pain, stop whining about it, and look at other accept the pain, stop whining about it, and look at other pleasures that are available.

Now to the alternative you can use to *rating and blaming* yourself and others: *unconditional acceptance*, or what Carl Rogers called *unconditional positive regard*. To acquire this kind of nondemandingness, work to accept yourself and others as fallible humans who do not have to act other than as they do. But also accept that you would often find it *highly preferable* if they acted better. See people as being too complex and changeable to have a global, one-sided rating. But rate your and others' actions according to how those actions help or hinder you in working toward your goals of happiness and staying alive.

Stop damning and start accepting people and conditions as they now are. Don't think that acceptance implies *resignation*. A rational philosophy of acceptance means that you acknowledge that whatever exists *should* now exist (in the sense that it *does* exist). But acceptance doesn't mean that you are absolutely resigned to its existing forever. Being unresigned, and still disliking crummy reality, you can vigorously push yourself to change it.

As alternatives to *overgeneralizing (always or never attitude)* you can use several constructive sayings you may have heard at AA meetings: "Keep an open mind." "Use your common sense." "Keep it simple." "Practice rigorous honesty." "Live in the now." In other words, "stick with the facts." If you slipped and drank again, for instance, it hardly shows "Nothing I do is right," "I'll always fail," or "Once a drunk, always a drunk." If people are frowning at you, you don't know *as a fact* "They don't like me and they never will" or "I can't *ever* please people." Your overgeneralizing means something about you and your stinking thinking, but nothing factual about the way the world is.

MUSTURBATE No More!

How do you dislodge your demanding, musturbatory, My-will-be-done attitude? Dispute it by asking in many ways, "Where is the evidence that it (what I am screaming for) *has* to be?" Your answer soon becomes almost inevitable: "No matter how much I *prefer* something, I don't *have to* get it" and "No matter how much I *dislike* something, I never *have to* get rid of it." If what you want to exist *had to* exist, it would be that way. And if your dislikes had to be eliminated, they *would* be. Thus, no one demands that gravity has to be or must not be. It simply is. It exists quite independently of human commands. The things that *must* be so (at present) *are* so. Most of the commands we issue about what *has* to be and what has to *not* be mainly upset us. They get us off track from doing what we could do to make reality better.

Dispute your commands that reality *has* to be different. Ask "What are the reasons why this situation is the way it is rather than the way I command it to be?" As you begin to look at an undesirable situation from reality's viewpoint, you'll find that your horror over it lessens. There are always plenty of reasons why unfortunate things exist, whether we like them or not or even know why they are the way they are.

AWFULIZE No More!

Using *awful* as an emotional word means that something you find undesirable should not, must not exist. And therefore when it does exist it is 100 percent bad, or so bad that you can't be happy at all with it, and badder than it *should* be. Calling some situation awful, horrible, or terrible almost always is an exaggeration and leads to disturbed, exaggerated emotions. Is it really *that* bad? Has anyone in recorded history, yourself included, borne up under that type of thing before? If so, what happened? *Make a list of the times you have gotten by in spite of such "awful" stresses.*

Problem drinkers often awfulize about not being able to drink like "normal" people, about the negative results of drinking, about just about everything they can't have or don't like. (Street drug addicts use the word *snivel* to describe the whining that is the hallmark of awfulizing and low frustration tolerance. It is not an attractive word, but then again, it is not an attractive behavior!)

It's easy to see your life as full of chaos and tragedy when "awful" things happen. To antiawfulize, keep asking yourself "Where is the *evidence* that this is *awful?*" Notice that the question is not "Where is the evidence that the situation is *bad and against my interests.*" Lots of things, unfortunately, are against your interests. Ours, too! And we are just as against them as you are. Awfulizing and screaming about them, however, will not improve them. Improvement requires—where it can be done at all—work and practice. It's the same work and practice for you to stop your stinking thinking and problem drinking.

It's a free country, and you can be our guest in calling unpleasant events the end of the world. However, if you don't like making and keeping yourself disturbed, you would do better to ask "Where is the evidence that this unfortunate event is *awful? Absolutely unbearable? Infinitely worse than it should be?*" Answer: "Yes, it is unpleasant, against my interests, inconvenient, and painful, but it's still a part of reality. I *can* cope with and get through it with a minimum of horror and sniveling. That is, *if* I stop *defining* it as 'awful.'"

When you find yourself awfulizing about crummy reality, make a detailed plan about how you could *in fact* deal with it and stand it. Write out your plan. Brainstorm alternatives. Have you coped with similar or worse situations in the past? What if you were awfulizing and whining about some obnoxious event, and we offered you a million dollars in cash, tax free, to come up with a sensible plan to cope with the crummy situation? Could you? *Would* you? Almost certainly, you would. The main reason why you may often *refuse* to cope with lousy realities is that you deeply believe that you *should not have to do so.* Good luck on *this* planet with that attitude!

In combatting awfulizing, don't use positive thinking

and try to convince yourself that unpleasant things are really good. And don't think that bad things necessarily will get better. Some clouds do *not* have silver linings. It is better to look the worst-case scenarios straight in the face, to stubbornly refuse to make yourself miserable about them, and then to figure out ways to cope with even those "horrors."

LOW FRUSTRATION TOLERANCE No More!

Low frustration tolerance (LFT) is an attitude or philosophy *toward* frustration. The LFT attitude states that this particular frustration *must not be*. It doesn't only assert "It's frustrating and unpleasant not getting what I want and getting what I don't want," but also "It's *too* hard! It shouldn't be this hard! I *deserve* it easier and better! How *can* it be this way?" The core of your LFT attitude is the whiny Belief, "Because it's *so* hard, I *can't stand* it!"

Low frustration tolerance is not the same as frustration. Frustration does *not* cause horror, fury, depression, whining, and procrastination. Frustration causes inconvenience, delay, deprivation, and the expenditure of extra effort. But frustration is also life-preserving, in that it stimulates you to work against conditions you find disagreeable. Also, it provides a contrast against which you experience pleasure, harmony, happiness, and other positive feelings. If everything were always pleasurable, serene, and unchallenging, chances are you would get bored and wouldn't like it that much after a while.

When you have notable low frustration tolerance, you decide that you simply cannot bear discomfort. In the short run giving up alcohol or almost any addiction leads to *more* discomfort. LFT is usually the main reason that you fail to stop your addictions. You believe it's *too* much of an effort. You stubbornly refuse to be uncomfortable right now, and thereby give yourself much more discomfort and lack of satisfaction in the future.

When you train yourself diligently into an addiction, such as alcohol abuse, and *persist* at it despite increasingly negative longer-range consequences, you do so because of your severe low frustration tolerance. Addicts "can't"— that is, *won't*—tolerate discomfort. They often view with horror any delay, inconvenience, having to plan, and having to do without pleasure. Everyone has some degree of low frustration tolerance, because it's *adaptive* to be against inconvenience. But substance abusers tend to be at the head of the LFT class.

LFT means *whining about frustration* and includes some of the following self-statements. To check your own low frustration tolerance, take out your notebook and write down what's self-defeating about each of these statements. Then, after reading the next section, "How to Combat Low Frustration Tolerance and Develop Higher Frustration Tolerance," review and revise your answers.

1. "Not only is it hard to do (cutting down quantities of alcohol drunk, the number of cigarettes, calories consumed), but it's *too hard*. It shouldn't be hard, certainly not *so* hard. It shouldn't be *this* hard, but maybe only 50 or 60 percent as hard, then I'd do it."

2. "It *can't* be this hard. There has to be some easier way, and I'll wait till it magically appears!"

3. "I'll do it tomorrow (and tomorrow and tomorrow), when it will be easier."

4. "I don't *feel* like doing it, and I can only do and should only have to do what I *feel* like doing." Or "I will do it when I feel *up* to it and it feels natural and spontaneous. I'll know when the time is right, and, believe me, it isn't now." The reason? "It's too damn hard to do it now."

5. "I deserve it easier, and because the Universe doesn't seem to realize who it's dealing with, I'll hold my breath and refuse to cooperate!"

6. "Because I've always had it easy or always had other things easy, this should be easy too!"

7. "Because I've always had everything hard, that proves that this should be easy, so I'll wait. I deserve this to be easy. It's unfair that this is hard, too!"

8. "I've been addicted too long to be able to change. Maybe I could have stopped earlier, but not now." A variation of this sad song is "I'm too old to change." For the young: "I'll grow out of it."

9. "It would take too long to change, and I can't stand waiting."

10. "Life is unfair" (and it shouldn't be unfair). "Why did I have to get the alcoholic genes?"

11. "I can't stand the idea of having to be deprived and not getting what I want when I want it! I've got to have as much of it as I want!"

12. "Oh, I can cut down on the alcohol, and even stop, but do you mean to tell me that I have to change my life, too! And put out so much effort doing so? No way! Well, perhaps I will, but I will begin my efforts after New Year's."

13. "It's my nature to drink too much. I'm a born alcoholic."

14. "It's too much trouble to use a condom when I have sex with my partner. Besides, screwing doesn't feel as good when I wear a condom."

We think you get the idea. Your LFT philosophy is the demanding, whining, and wailing irrational Belief that reality needs to be easier than it is for you before you can stop drinking or do some other hard task. To say the least, the LFT attitude interferes with problem-solving and helps immensely to keep you addicted the rest of your life.

How to Combat LFT and Develop Higher Frustration Tolerance

Working successfully with your own drinking problems means confronting your low frustration tolerance (LFT) attitude that discomfort is unthinkable. Teach yourself that the easy way out is actually the more difficult way, that avoidance does not work. Teach yourself that the hard way is actually the easy way, that there is *no reason* why things *need* to be easier than they are. Teach yourself that you can divide a job up into pieces. Start now, and give yourself rewards for hard work *after* you do the work.

Often mixed in with LFT is self-downing. You see yourself as too weak and inadequate to stand the frustration. You may use as evidence of your inadequacy the fact that you have not successfully withstood frustrations, at least not for long. To combat this stinking thinking, make a list of instances when you *did* withstand frustration, met challenges, and showed courage. Work out in detail just how you *will* stand the discomfort of giving up alcohol and follow through with the effort it takes to stay sober. Rehearse your plan mentally.

Really look at the idea that you "can't stand" discomfort and "must have" quick relief (alcohol) even though it leads to later pain. List and review the *advantages* of tolerating discomfort and the *disadvantages* of refusing to tolerate it. Teach yourself how to stand specific discomforts, such as feelings of anxiety that you usually drown in alcohol. Teach yourself to wait five, ten, or thirty minutes—and do some rethinking—*before* drinking when you get the impulse to do so. The impulse often lessens.

Develop your action plans that involve taking specific, small steps. Praise your stamina and persistence for completing these steps and point out to yourself that you *can* do and stand these steps. Then take larger steps. Work at adopting the philosophy "First you work, then you play." Take a difficult, boring, anxiety-provoking but constructive step, and then plan a reward for yourself.

Write out the reasons for your cravings. Dispute any excuses about how it's too hard to change. Try relaxation or distraction methods, as noted above. Review the ill effects of your past alcohol abuse. Reward yourself for resisting and escaping temptation. Practice standing discomfort by having your friends play the role of very obnoxious, demanding people while you play the role of Mother Teresa, Albert Schweitzer, Dr. Martin Luther King, Jr., or Gandhi. Really get into the character of the tolerant person.

Having now read the above section, go back and look at your previous rebuttals of LFT statements. How can you strengthen each rebuttal? Sample responses follow that can help you build higher frustration tolerance.

1. "It's not *too* hard. That's a decision. It's just hard. I still want to pursue this goal, so here goes."

2. "Lots of luck! There doesn't *have to be* an easier way."

3. "What makes me think it'll be easier tomorrow?"

4. Where is it written that I must feel like doing it before I can do it? Nowhere! It would be nice if I felt like it, but I'd better get started anyhow. Maybe I'll end up feeling more like doing it."

5. "Maybe *I* think the Universe owes me something, but unfortunately the Universe doesn't agree! I'd better work just the way ordinary mortals do!"

6. "How does that follow? There's no logical connection. No matter how easy things *were* for me, they don't *have to be* easy now."

7. "There's no law of nature that says that because I've had things hard, *this* should be easy."

8. "How does my long history of addiction mean I absolutely *can't* change? It doesn't. At most, it means it's hard. Too bad. I'd better get started and not wait till I grow out of it."

9. "Where is it written that I have to get a difficult task over with rapidly? It would be nice, but it's not absolutely necessary."

10. "Of course, life is unfair. Everybody knows that. But why does it *have to* be fair *for me?*" "So I got tons of alcoholic genes. Too bad. Maybe I find it *easier* to keep drinking than do people without my genes, but I don't have to go along with my inherited tendency."

11. "I can stand anything that happens to me till I die. I don't like being deprived, but I can stand it and still find some happiness."

12. "Where is it written that my project of stopping drinking should require so much effort and no more? Only in my head! I'd better unwrite it, accept the effort of stopping, and get back to work."

13. "Oh? Was I born with booze on my breath? A cigarette in my mouth, a needle in my arm, and junk food in my grocery basket?"

14. "Who said that I absolutely must have exactly as much pleasure wearing a condom as I do not wearing one? And who said that screwing equals sex? There are plenty of erotic things we can do other than intercourse."

Disputing SELF-RATING, SELF-DOWNING and BLAMING (and Phony Pride)

Self-blaming, as we noted above, can sabotage your taking responsibility for your self-defeating actions. Blaming yourself can have an ill effect even when you believe your behavior is good. If you rate yourself as good or have pride in *yourself* when your behavior is "good," you then are okay only as long as you act very well. What happens when human nature strikes again? What happens when you slip and perform imperfectly again? Back to wormhood you go! That is why you'd better not rate yourself at all, and only rate your behavior according to how it helps or hinders you in achieving your goals.

When your actions are faulty, you can Dispute your self-downing with "How does my poor behavior *make* me a loser or a no-goodnik?" Ask yourself this often enough in many ways, and you will discover that your self-worth is a definition you give yourself. If you insist on rating your self, you'd better, to be safe, pick a trait you'll always have. for instance, if you say, "I'm good because I'm human" or "I'm good because I choose to be good," you're fairly safe. Otherwise, if you rate yourself "up" because you have some good trait, you will later rate yourself down when you act less than good. If you stop rating your *self* at all, but only assess what you *do*, then you can focus on changing your behavior.

Always-or-Never Attitude No More! (Well, Most of the Time!)

Combat always-or-never attitudes and other overgeneralizations by catching yourself when you use the words *always* or *never*. These words are so often exaggerations that you had better make them "red flags." Once you catch them, challenge them with the facts. For instance, if you hear yourself moaning "No one loves me, no one ever has loved me, and nobody ever will love me," stop. Ask yourself, "No one? Nobody at all?" If you look, you will find several exceptions. Then, you can say, "Well, X *doesn't* love me, but Y definitely *did*. Now that I see that it's not true that *no one* ever loved me, what can I do to stop flipping out about the fact that X does not love me?"

Automatic Disturbed Thoughts and Excuses and What to Do About Them

Stinking thinking includes automatic disturbing thoughts and excuses (rationalizations). Techniques for catching and nipping them in the bud were emphasized in RET in the 1950s and reemphasized later by Drs. Aaron T. Beck and David Burns.[3] These distortions are unrealistic inferences and false perceptions that easily follow from the three musts:

1. I must succeed and obtain approval.

2. You *have* to behave properly.

3. Life *absolutely should* be fair and easy.

Your core irrational Beliefs (musturbation, awfulizing, low frustration tolerance, rating and blaming, and always or never attitudes) "logically" lead to many automatic conclusions, most of them false. Thus, when your mother catches you with your hand in the cookie jar, you firmly believe "I must not steal and have to avoid my mother's disapproval," and you automatically and "logically" conclude "The cookies fell into my hands" (excuse), "My mother will never forgive me," (always and never overgeneralization), "Everyone will now hate me and boycott me" (catastrophizing), or "I'm a thoroughly rotten kid who deserves no joy in life" (self-blaming and awfulizing). Look behind your disturbed conclusions and you will almost always find the basic *musts*: "I must do well!" "You have to treat me properly!" and "The world has to give me what I want!"

Automatic disturbed thoughts. Let's say you are walking down the street and attempt to catch the eye of someone you consider attractive. To no avail. Then you hear yourself think "All alone forever!" or "There's no use." These are automatic disturbing thoughts that stem from your always or never attitude and from your musturbation. Another example: You make a mistake and hear yourself thinking "Nothing I do is right!" or "Life is useless." You derive these thoughts from self-damning and the always or never attitude.

Automatic negative thoughts that refer to drinking take many forms, and some of them seem so innocent: "I'm thirsty"—meaning "I *must* have a drink of alcohol and *can't stand* not having one right now." Or you dream up automatic mental pictures: For instance, the image of taking a cold beer out of a keg of ice on a hot day may pop into your mind, unbidden. Your real, underlying irrational Belief (iB) is "I've been without a drink so long that I *deserve* one right now!"

Excuses. Excuses, or rationalizations, are usually fairly obvious "reasons" that you make up in order to justify drinking. Excuses also imply that for some reason "this time is different" and there won't be any bad results from the drinking. You may often invent rationalizations to justify bringing yourself to the launch pad for drinking. For instance, "I'll stop by the tavern and just say hi to the guys. No harm in that." "I only drank this time because I was under such pressure at work. When this stress eases up a few weeks from now, I'll easily stop drinking."

You can help yourself stop drinking (and stay stopped) by Disputing your self-sabotaging misperceptions and excuses. Sometimes you can actually change the core irrational musts (iBs) if you challenge and change enough of your automatic disturbed thoughts and excuses that stem from them. However, your core iBs often live on to generate *more* automatic disturbed thoughts and rationalizations (and lapses and relapses), when the next opportunity presents itself (which it will). That is why, as indicated above, it is worth your while to go after the *core* iBs first. If that works, you will find it much easier to combat your habitual automatic unrealistic thoughts and excuses. If Disputing the core iBs doesn't work at first, then you'd better keep challenging your automatic negative inferences and rationalizations.

Automatic destructive thoughts and excuses tend to

fall into categories, which often overlap with each other. If you look for them, you will understand how your stinking thinking falls into predictable patterns. Some common unrealistic conclusions and the rational Beliefs you can substitute for them are as follows:

▶ *All-or-nothing thinking.* You rigidly limit your thinking to two categories. For instance, "I must be totally successful in not drinking one sip, or else I'm a total failure." "Life has to go completely my way, or else it's not worth living." "If I fail at any important task, as I must not, then I'm utterly worthless." "All 'alcoholics' who take a single drink wind up in the gutter."

Rational alternative. Teach yourself to be flexible, to try for *relative* progress, to accept trial and error, to believe in human fallibility. For instance: "I'd *like* to be totally successful in not drinking one sip of alcohol, but I don't *have* to be." "I can, and probably will work and practice better against my stinking thinking. When I fail I can always start again."

▶ *Perfectionism.* This overlaps all-or-nothing thinking. You have to *always* do well or you have a cut-off point below which your performance *must* not fall or else you're a "total failure." "Okay, so I went two years without drinking. Big deal. I shouldn't have slipped, so I haven't really gotten better at all." "Even though I only went out with my drinking friends a few times, that's completely unforgivable!"

Rational alternative. Rate your *actions* in terms of how they help or hinder you from reaching your goals, but don't rate your *self* on the basis of those actions. "To err is human; to forgive is desirable." "It would be nice (I guess!) to do perfectly, but I'm human. Still, I can learn from my mistakes and slips." See that you can accept your actions as reasonably good but still imperfect. Practice accepting your "self" even (or especially!) when you perform poorly.

▶ *Jumping to false conclusions*. You see one event as "proving" a whole pattern. You overgeneralize. Other kinds of jumping to false conclusions include *illogical conclusions* or *non sequiturs*: "Because you must always like me and you frowned when I refused a drink, you dislike me." *Mind reading*: "You didn't enthusiastically agree with me, so I know you think I'm wrong and a fool." *Fortune telling*: "I slipped this time, so I'll soon be back to ten drinks a day." "I'm just a born alcoholic," "You showed me I was wrong this time, so you'll never trust me again." "Because my office mate hates me, she'll turn others against me."

Rational alternative. Question your certainties and change them back to probabilities. Look for evidence against your dogmatic conclusions. See that possible future events *need* not occur. Look for alternative explanations and for more realistic, undramatic, and unexaggerated conclusions. For example: "I'm not *an* alcoholic, but a person who now has a drinking problem." "Is it true that *everything* I do is wrong? Even *I'm* not *that* imperfect!" "True, I may not reach my goal, but I'll just demoralize myself if I think I *always must* reach it." "I *don't* know the future. If I did, I'd pick the winning lottery number!"

▶ *Catastrophizing and focusing on the negative*. When you demand that good things *have to* exist and bad things must *not* exist, you insist that unfortunate events are *awful* and *can't be tolerated*. Your "tunnel vision" helps keep you focused on and exaggerating negative things that do happen. The more you believe that negative happenings absolutely should not occur, the less you see their good side and the less inclined you are to change them. "My husband came home late once last month with beer on his breath. That shows that he soon won't come home at all and there's no hope for our marriage." "The small raise I just got shows that my boss hates me and is looking for a reason to fire me."

Rational alternative. Look at the *whole* picture, see its good and bad points, and figure out what you can do to correct the bad ones rather than simply to horrify yourself over them. "My husband came home late *only* once last month. I'd better make a point of expressing my pleasure at his timeliness. I can also ask him to be sure to let me know when he will be late so we can change our dinner plans." "Perhaps my small raise shows that my boss doesn't like me, but perhaps it mainly shows that my company has financial problems. Let me see what I can do to make my boss like me still more."

▶ *Always and never.* If you have always or never Beliefs, they are overgeneralizations that usually stem from your musturbatory demands that you *should* always have what you want and *must* never have what you do not want. "They never pay attention to me (as they always should!)" "Everything always goes wrong (as it never must!)"

Rational alternative. Look for and *list* instances that go against your always and never claims. Challenge your dramatic exaggerations. Dispute the irrational Belief that you are *entitled* to your way. When you hear yourself use the words *always* and *never*, question and challenge: "*Everything* goes wrong? All that happened was that one traffic light turned red as I approached it! What about the three *green* lights I just made?" "Things often, but hardly *always* go wrong, and they often go okay." "People *sometimes* ignore me and seem uninterested, but *always?* They sometimes *do* pay attention."

▶ *Disqualifying the positive.* When you discount or minimize the positives in your life, you stubbornly down yourself (others, or the world) and say that positives "don't count" or can be attributed to luck or to people feeling sorry for you. If someone does seem to like you (and you've been saying no one does), you may say, "Yeah, but he likes *everybody*," or "If she knew the *real* me, she wouldn't like me." This reinforces your negative thinking even though it is contradicted by many of your own experiences. "Compliments don't count because if they knew the *real* me, they would know I'm a schlemięl, and therefore worthless." "My improvement doesn't count because I shouldn't have *any* bad behavior, and I'll soon fall back anyway." "I only stopped drinking because it got too expensive. As soon as I get out of debt, I bet I'll go back to drinking!"

Rational alternative. Make yourself look at all your acts—positive as well as negative. Work against your perfectionism. "Maybe I do get more compliments than I deserve, but I do well at times and *do* deserve some of them." "Yes, even if I could have done better, I still did okay." "I did wrong in drinking again, but I did stay on the wagon for three months. I *can* get back on the wagon."

▶ *Labeling.* Labels are misleading self-concepts— ratings of *you* and not merely of what you *do*. You start with a *desire* to stop drinking, foolishly make it a *demand*, and then condemn *yourself* for slipping. You label *yourself* a loser, alcoholic, fool, idiot, failure, or hopeless slob on the basis of deficient behaviors. Once you label your *self*, you look for evidence to *confirm* that label and to *predict* that you won't ever be able to change because *you* are a loser. "After all I've been through, I failed again. I'm a complete failure. Why do I bother to pretend? I'd be better off dead." "Let's face it. Now that I got dressed and went out to a bar at one A.M., I might as well admit I'm a hopeless drunk who will *never* change."

Rational alternative. Use RET to give yourself unconditional self-acceptance, whether or not you perform well. Work against self-rating and self-downing. Describe and rate your errors *factually* and *behaviorally.* "I had a drink after having been abstinent for several weeks, and I did so because I started thinking 'Just once won't hurt.' Next time, I will combat that rationalization. I will continue to accept and value myself no matter how many errors I make, but I will continue to work and practice at making fewer such errors." "I lied to my partner, but I am not a *bad person*, only *a person who* acted badly this time."

▶ *Emotional reasoning.* You assume that your disturbed emotions actually describe reality. "I feel like a loser, therefore I am." "I'm so depressed that this obviously *proves* that there's no hope for me." "I feel panicked about taking an airplane trip. Therefore, riding in a plane *is* dangerous."

Rational alternative. See that your disturbed feelings indicate that you have *created* them with irrational Beliefs, and then work at changing these iBs. Emotions only prove that you *feel* something and prove nothing about the outside world. Your thoughts may be quite out of whack with reality. If you thought the bogeyman was outside and was going to get you, you'd feel afraid. But would your fear prove anything about the bogeyman? "I *feel* like a loser. Oh-oh! What am I *telling myself* to make myself feel that way? I'd better figure it out. Let me Dispute it and see that my losing doesn't *make me* a loser." "I feel so ashamed of having slipped that I obviously have no ability to go back to abstaining. Really? My shame only shows that I am damning myself for slipping and not that I must *keep* slipping."

▶ *Personalizing.* You see yourself as the primary cause of some external event when you are not. Or you see some external event as having a special connection to you when it does not. "I shouldn't have failed, and I'm sure they're laughing at me because of it." "Those people are looking at me, so they must be saying nasty things about me." "My lover is drinking again, so I must have done something to make her fall back."

Rational alternative. See yourself as responsible for some events, including your own behavior, but accept that others are responsible for *their* behavior. Work against self-rating and self-downing. "Yes, they laughed, but I don't know as a fact they were laughing at me. Even if they were, I can agree with them or disagree with them about my 'bad' actions." "Those people are looking at me, but I don't know what they're saying about me. Even if they are putting me down, that's too bad, but not *awful*. At worst, they rated what they saw of me, not the whole me." "My lover *decided* to drink and is telling me I'm responsible for her behavior. If only I had such power!"

▶ *Phonyism.* "I may be doing quite well, but I *should* be doing better. Therefore I'm a phony and will soon fall on my face and let them see what a failure I really am." This type of irrational thinking has aspects of overgeneralization, labeling, disqualifying the positive, focusing on the negative, and perfectionism.

Rational alternative. Look at your behavior and only rate *it* as good or bad in the light of your goals. Accept yourself as valuable just because you are alive and human, and don't invent dangerous ideas about worthiness and unworthiness of your "self," "essence," or "totality." "Even if they think I'm doing better than I think I really am, and even if I'm fooling them at times, so what? They have a right to be wrong, and so do I. I'm not *a* phony, but only a person who sometimes *acts* phonily."

Easy Does It (But Do It!): Integrating Rational Ideas Into Your Self-Help Work

As you make notes in your Daily Journal, you will identify thinking patterns that lead you to drink. Identify situations, feelings, and erroneous thoughts that have contributed to past lapses and relapses. Such thoughts usually are not deeply unconscious. For instance, "I want to get a buzz on" shows how you *forget* negatives and *focus* on positives of drinking. It is such an obvious and common thought that you may protest you didn't think anything at all. However, you did! Humans are always thinking. The brain—certainly yours!—never rests completely.

If you have a record of alcohol problems, then for you to decide to drink goes against your long-term interests. Many people say they "didn't think anything" or "have no control" when they see themselves acting repeatedly against their own interests. When they look at their long-range goals it sometimes seems unimaginable that they could have been thinking anything when they began to get themselves back into hot water. Yet they were. And so were you. What typically happened at these choice points is that you *stopped* thinking of the long-term hurts caused by drinking. Then you *refocused* on short-term pleasure and relief. Once you have brought out the thinking, obvious or subtle, involved in your self-defeating decision, you can show yourself how to use the Double Column technique to combat such thinking and avoid self-defeat.

Double Column

Write the date at the top of a blank page in your Daily Journal. Then draw a line down the middle of a page. In the left column list thoughts you've used to justify drinking. These usually are excuses and rationalizations, some more, some less obviously so. Usually they are illogical. In addition they are "incorrect" or irrational, because when you follow them, you tend to bring about *self*-defeat. Label this column "bullshit," "baby wants the bottle," "fiction," "application for admission to the drunk driver program or jail or cemetery," or similar colorful, forceful terms.

Why do normally intelligent people—yourself included—buy into excuses, even momentarily? Because they have an underlying *musturbatory* philosophy of "I *should* be able to have anything I want." This irrational Belief leads to the sorts of distorted thinking we discussed in the previous chapter.

They focus strongly on how they want and *must have* good alcohol feelings and *can't stand* not having them. They focus on how they abhor, *can't stand*, and *must* avoid bad feelings.

They then distort or discount evidence from the past that goes against their demands to drink alcohol. Or they may simply make up evidence to support the idea that they can, too, handle drinking "this time." This kind of wishful thinking is quite characteristic of problem drinkers and other addicts, but it also tends to characterize most people. It is not a disease. It is the normal way people often think. When they do it habitually, we may call it an "emotional disturbance."

Some common rationalizations are "I'll just have *one* drink," "This is a *special* occasion, so it doesn't count if I drink," "I can afford it," "I can't stand being depressed," "I'll just have one for old times," "It's my birthday," "I'm going to just test myself," "What the hell?" and the like. Once you have drawn up a fairly complete list of your excuses, question and challenge each one:

> "Is my thought realistic? What evidence is there *against* its truthfulness or accuracy? How much am I willing to *bet* on the thought?"

> "Does this thought help me reach my goals and feel happier in the long run? Does it cause trouble for me or other people?

Label the right-hand column "the facts of life," "happiness and health," "staying out of the drunk driver program," etc. Write in that column your *rational* Disputes of each self-defeating thought in your left-hand column. Usually you can simply write out the facts, such as "Every time I say it'll just be one drink, it's more. Who am I fooling?"

It also can help if these self-helping statements are catchy slogans you may know. For instance, Narcotics Anonymous's famous warning, "One time is too much, a thousand times is not enough"; Women For Sobriety's "I am responsible for myself and for my actions"; Rational Recovery's "I have considerable voluntary control over my hands and mouth"; and Secular Organizations for Sobriety's "We can not and do not drink, no matter what."

Remember, you invent rationalizations because you think you *have to have* what you want, *should not* have to do without it, and *cannot tolerate* discomfort and deprivation. Poor baby! Strongly tell yourself that if you *really* want pleasure and truly are against suffering as much as you claim you are, then you had better combat the philosophy of short-range pleasure.

To Hell with It!

One of the toughest rationalizations to combat is "To hell with it" and its variations, such as "I don't care" and "What difference does it make?" These rationalizations directly express low frustration tolerance (LFT). They declare that it doesn't make any difference if you do resume drinking and go to hell in a handcart. Challenge this type of rationalization by asking yourself, "Okay, my prediction is that it won't make any difference if I drink again. *Is that true?*" Typically, of course, it is not true or does not stay true for long. You *do* care and do *not* like going to hell in a handcart.

Next, develop a plan for reviewing and rehearsing both columns regularly. Write the plan in your Daily Journal and make appointments with yourself to follow up. People often object to this step because they already "know" the foolishness or falsity of their rationalizations, particularly those that are almost too silly for words, like "I'll just have one drink." They "knew" the same thing, of course, at the time they were getting ready to drink again, *but they weren't actively thinking it.* Insight alone into the foolishness of your self-defeating thoughts has not been enough in the past to prevent your heavy drinking. Your self-help job is to teach yourself strongly to think self-helpingly at the right time, namely, before you defeat yourself.

Rationalizations about not stopping drinking (or resuming it if you have stopped) can be almost ridiculous because they are transparent excuses to justify drinking. For instance, when I (EV) hear my clients use this type of rationalization, I sometimes exaggerate and say, "Oh, that's a *very* good reason to drink! *Another* good one is, 'I have to drink because . . . it's Tuesday!' or 'It's North Dakota statehood day!' or 'It's raining.' " Most people immediately appreciate these exaggerations. They see them as humorously highlighting the crazy thinking they invent to justify getting the short-range pleasures and reliefs that lead to long-term defeat.

At the other end of the spectrum, however, come stressors like the *actual* death of someone you really cared about, loss of a limb, or similar very bad occurrences. Some people who have been through residential treatment programs in particular will use the word *excuse* for these reasons to resume drinking. The word *excuse* implies that you fake your pain to justify getting drunk. Just because you have abused substances does not mean you have no human feelings. Therapists, substance-abuse counselors, and fellow participants at recovery meetings sometimes jump to conclusions. "All alcoholics are alike. Everything they say is an excuse to drink. What a bullshit artist! If you really cared about your family, you should have stopped drinking long ago."

The sad fact is that life does sometimes hurt. Yes, substance abusers often have trained themselves to cover up such feelings with chemicals. The more they do it, the more sensitive to painful feelings they may become and the faster and earlier they may reach for the booze. Often this process does reach the level of pure excuses. To fight the habit of covering up hurt, you can tell yourself "It's better if I do learn to stand emotional pain." "Being human can hurt, but if I accept it, there is sometimes value in the pain, and there are lots of pleasurable parts of life, too."

It still is quite true, however, that very bad occurrences, like the death of a loved one, do not *make* you drink. Drinking is still your choice, although a choice that would strike more people as understandable than choosing to drink because of rainy weather.

Whether your stressors are great or small, whether almost anyone would drink under the same circumstances or almost no one would do so but you, it is important to accept *yourself* with and in spite of your stinking thinking and your self-defeating actions. Then refocus on what you can do differently now and in the future.

An important factor in relapse is that problem drinkers, like many people, tend to forget the negative aspects of their past bouts with alcohol faster than they forget the positive aspects. This tendency helps them talk themselves into relapse. They focus on the positive, magnify it ("euphoric recall"), make it up in their heads that they should be able to drink without problems "this time," and tend to forget the negative. It is a bother and a hassle to remember the negative aspects of reality. Who wouldn't like to escape and avoid such memories? Even if your search for "the happy hour" has ended in unhappiness, depression, and many other problems, your thoughts may still easily center first on alcohol's euphoric and stress-relieving effects and ignore its long-term crummy effects. But it is just such memories that you had better keep alive in your mind to help you avoid bigger bothers and hassles in the future.

This selective memory may heighten your ambivalence about giving up alcohol entirely. To the extent that you continue to view drinking as mainly pleasurable, you increase your potential for relapse. This particularly happens on occasions when you are under stress or emotionally upset.

Phobics and other neurotics appear to show the opposite tendency to that of substance abusers. Phobics focus on and magnify the *negative*. They stubbornly predict negatives again and again and again despite lots of evidence that nothing really bad happened to them. They *discount* positives. They seem to hold the idea that they *must* be guaranteed that *nothing* bad could possibly happen to them.

Euphoric and nostalgic recall and other aspects of the stinking, irrational thinking say "It would be so nice to have a drink. That shows I can get away with it 'this time.'" To counteract it, you had better remind yourself repeatedly of the many alcohol-related *negative* consequences that finally convinced you to *work* at helping yourself achieve sobriety. You had better take every opportunity to help keep alive in your mind the negative results of drinking. A great tool for doing that is the shitlist.

Stinking Thinking and Ye Olde Shitlist

Almost all problem drinkers know the great disadvantages of their destructive behavior. When they are about to take a drink (or overeat or smoke), however, they manage to keep these disadvantages in the rearmost recesses of their minds. They replace grim facts with excuses, rationalizations, and soothing forgetfulness. "Sure," you tell yourself and others, "drinking is deadly and does me great harm. I know that."

But do you *really* know it? You say it, you acknowledge it, you are sure that it is deadly for other people. But for you personally? And for you whenever you are *really* troubled, *really* feel like having a drink?

Hardly! Or perhaps we had better say *lightly*. Insufficiently. Vaguely. For when you are really ready for a drink, what do you *strongly* believe? "Oh, I'll just have one and then stop." "Sure, it's stupid, but who said I'm smart?" "I know that most people can't get away with it, but I'm different!" "I'm so upset about what happened today that I've got to have a drink. I'll go crazy if I don't have at least *one*! And, besides, it's Friday night and everybody else will be having fun." You powerfully, devoutly, believe this drivel. It almost completely swamps your weak, sensible antidrinking Beliefs.

Knowledge about drinking includes a full scale of knowing: its advantages, its disadvantages, and its neutral values. But the knowledge that pushes you to drink mainly emphasizes the first of these categories and notably ignores, or sweeps under the rug, the second.[1] Another remedy for this natural human tendency to forget the bad and focus on the good is "shitlisting."

To use the shitlist technique, make a long *list* of all the *disadvantages* of your drinking problem. Add to it over the days and weeks to make sure that you don't omit any of the important ones. Be sure to include expense, health problems, drunk driving programs, jail, and the like. Go into the *details* of each one. Not just the dollars and cents expense, but what could you have done with that money if you hadn't blown it on booze, accidents, court costs, and so on? What are the *positives* you are missing, have missed, or could miss because of drinking?

Then, as in the double-column technique, develop a plan for frequent review of the list *whether you think you need to or not*. You may say you "know" the material on the shitlist (and of course you do), and therefore do not need to practice. However, *do* you think about and *believe* the truth *before* deciding to resume drinking? Show yourself how you usually forget the suffering you cause yourself with past bouts of drinking and that you had better *train* yourself to think about those past sufferings *before* deciding to drink.

Type or print this list clearly and put it on one, two, or more index cards. (Keep a master list in your Daily Journal). Then, every day, preferably at least five times a day, read over and carefully think about this list. Do so until you sink it indelibly into your head, heart, and habits, and keep it steadily there in the forefront of your attention. Yes, the forefront! Then, whenever you are thirsty for liquor and you start to make up an excuse, pull out the list again and slowly, strongly, and repetitively go over it.

You can make yourself a rule that you will never take a drink until *after* you go over the shitlist. And you can do the same thing for other obsessive-compulsive ideas and actions that harm you. Review their many disadvantages, go over them daily, and don't let them slip from your mind or fade into halfhearted excuses.

Here are some disadvantages of drinking that you can add to your shitlist (if you don't have them already listed). Be sure to be very specific regarding details.

arrest	other injuries to	harm to family
brain damage	health	members
accidents	unsafe sex	increased
depression	lack of energy	emotional
insomnia	poor thinking	problems
high blood	poor job	antisocial
pressure	performance	behavior
cirrhosis of the	hangovers	being a bore
liver	loss of friends	spending money
gastrointestinal	poor relationships	getting into
problems	lies	trouble
		losing jobs

The shitlist is quite useful in combatting resistance, denial, and the tendency to downplay your problem. Often you may harbor the (usually unspoken) desire to return to drinking "occasionally." You may see self-help as a way to build enough self-control to make occasional drinking possible again. And soon. As we suggested earlier, if your first *goal* is to become a moderate drinker, and you have been a heavy drinker in the past, watch out. It is just a little suspicious when your goal *itself* has something to do with continuing to drink. You will have much more likelihood of becoming a moderate drinker some day if your foremost goals have to do with stopping suffering and quitting the stinking thinking that contributes to overdrinking.

Likewise, you also may resist accepting the need to make significant changes in your life, peer group, and social contacts and may not understand how a greater acceptance of the reality of problem drinking can aid your recovery. To counteract this denial, you'd better repeatedly push yourself to focus on the shitlist.

Denial and resistance, no matter how successfully counteracted in self-help efforts, will tend to reappear. This does not necessarily mean that you failed to counteract them earlier. Humans are actively inventive and *creative* in their pursuit of short-range pleasure and relief, and they are devout in their insistence on having it despite the evidence that it causes them long-term pain. So, if (and when) you reinvent your stinking thinking, remember, "To err is human; to forgive is desirable; to change is to work and practice."

Disputing Your Stinking Thinking and Irrational Beliefs

RET, as we will keep showing, provides you with many effective ways to think, feel, and act that will help change your stinking, drinking-oriented thinking. One of its main methods is to have you Dispute—yes, actively, forcefully Dispute (D)—your irrational Beliefs (iBs). Disputing, as RET's leading advocate in India, K. M. Phadke, has pointed out, consists of three other Ds: Detecting, Distinguishing, and Debating.[2]

Detecting your irrational Beliefs (iBs). Whenever you upset yourself emotionally (a C, in the ABC model) about anything—such as failing at an important task or rejection by a respected person—assume that you have, in the front or the back of your mind, some absolutist or unconditional *should, ought, must, need, necessity, imperative, or other demand* (your iB—irrational Belief, in the RET model). Thus, when your Activating Event (A) is performing a task, your iB is, "I absolutely *must* do well at this task!" When your A is trying to win someone's approval, your iB is, "I *have to* have this person's approval!" When your A is drinking too much, your iB is, "People *must* never know I drink too much!"

Maybe you're upsetting yourself without a command. Maybe! So far, we haven't found anyone who does so. Therefore, *cherchez le "should"! Cherchez le "must"!* Look for the should! Look for the must! Don't give up until you find and clearly see the inner (and sometimes, also, outer) demands with which you are arrogantly upsetting yourself. Seek and ye shall find. Be a detective of your self-talk and your disturbed feelings until you accurately find— and get ready to change *forcefully and fully*—your self-defeating musts.[3]

A primary clue that you are musturbating is that you *feel* disturbed—anxious, depressed, enraged, ashamed, or self-hating. Another clue: You *behave* self-defeatingly. Many substance abusers, of course, hardly *let* themselves feel upset and disturbed. They drink to ward off or deaden negative feelings they are afraid to experience. For instance, you may have a shot or two of liquor *before* going to a party, because you know you'll be nervous there, at least at the start. You also believe you "can't stand" feeling nervous.

Distinguishing Your Rational Beliefs (rBs) From Your Stinking Thinking and Irrational Beliefs (iBs)

Whenever you have an irrational, unconditional demand on yourself, on others, or on the world, you can be pretty sure that it is an extension of a reasonable, healthy preference. Thus, to get to "I *absolutely must* do well at this task!" you usually start with "I'd really *like* to do well at this task, but there is no reason I always *have* to." When you arrive at "I *have to have* this person's approval!" you usually also believe and feel "I really *want* this person's approval and would be disappointed if I don't win it. *But* I can survive without it." To reach "I *can't stand* stress," you usually also believe and feel "I don't like stress, but sometimes I have to go through it to get what I want."

Usually, then, whenever you have an irrational, self-defeating (and often socially inappropriate) should or must, you also have a reasonable, self-helping *want, wish,* or *preference*. This preference is flexible and moldable and has a conscious or implied "but" attached to it. "I'd *like* to make a million dollars, *but* I don't have to do so." "I'd *prefer* to have a few more drinks, *but* I can live and be happy without them, because I prefer even more not to have their ill effects."

So whenever you find your irrational Beliefs (iBs) or demands with which you needlessly upset yourself, *also* look for your *rational* Beliefs (rBs) or wishes that accompany them. Detect *both* your demands *and* your wishes and actively *distinguish* between them. It is important to develop your habit of preferring, because this is the way you will think and feel (preferably!) *after* Disputing your musts.

Write down your musts; write down your preferences. Imagine that you believe only the one, then only the other. Do you really feel how and why they are so different? Well, let's say we could pay you $10,000, tax free, each time you practiced making this distinction. Would you then practice it? We can't promise you the money, but we can promise that it will be far more difficult for you in the future if you *don't* practice against stinking thinking. So practice making the distinction between stinking thinking and self-helping thinking. Do so until the differences squarely hit you in your eyes and ears and mind and heart. Don't take our word for it. Do it and do it and do it, and see how much it can help.

Debating Your Self-Defeating, Self-Sabotaging Irrational Beliefs (iBs)

Detecting your upsetting iBs—your stinking thinking—and distinguishing them from your healthy wants and wishes (rBs) are great. That gets you started on the road to emotional sanity. The next, and most important, step is to uproot, minimize, and vigorously contradict these iBs while firmly (not dogmatically) sticking with your preferences. If you only—yes, only—have strong preferences and you never—no, never—change them into arrogant, unrealistic musts, you will rarely (if ever) make yourself miserable over virtually anything. For with wishes and preferences you merely believe that it would be *better* if you achieved this and avoided that—but *better* never means *absolutely necessary*.

So keep your strong wants and hold onto your powerful desires. But stop insisting that you *need* them, completely *must* have them fulfilled. Try like hell to achieve them. Push yourself to get what you desire. But not desperately, not frantically. For then, once again, you fall back into disturbing yourself. And anything that you think you absolutely must have, and that is unavailable, is deadly to your emotional health and happiness. Not the thing itself, of course, but your godlike demand about it.

You would think that almost anyone, yourself included, would realize it does not pay to insist "I absolutely *must* have this!" or "I positively *must not* have that!" If you believe at all times and under all conditions that you must succeed at, say, work, at sports, or at sex, you obviously sometimes won't. Then where are you? Cooked!

Even if you devoutly believe "I must, absolutely must, succeed at my job (or at tennis or at sex) *today!*" you may upset yourself. For how can you be sure that you *will* succeed today? You can't. No matter how well you normally do a task, for many reasons you may easily do poorly today (or tomorrow). Knowing this, you can make yourself anxious—and, being conscious of your anxiety, increase your chances of failing. Even if, today, you perform outstandingly well, you probably will only feel good temporarily, because you quickly start to worry about tomorrow, and the next day, and the day after.

Absolute, unconditional, powerful musts may occasionally motivate and help you. Yes, occasionally. If a rapist or a serial killer attacks you, for instance, it's quite possible that believing "I absolutely must not die and absolutely must survive" will help motivate you to escape or to fight fiercely. Feeling terror or rage in that sort of situation could help. (On the other hand, some people outwit their attackers by keeping cool.) But believing "I must stay alive" is *a bit different* from "I must have a beer!"

For the most part, musts will create needless anxiety and trouble for you. This especially goes for *secondary musts*, that is, your musts about your musts. Thus, you may start with "I must always do very well at my job." But because you often *won't* do that well, your musturbatory demand then makes you anxious, depressed, or self-hating. Then you go to the secondary must: "I must not be anxious! I must not be depressed! I must not have low self-esteem!" Now where are you? Doubly anxious, depressed, and self-hating.

What can you do to interrupt this vicious cycle?

1. Look for and find your rigid shoulds and musts.

2. See that they are different, quite different, from your healthy desires, goals, and preferences.

3. Actively, vigorously, persistently debate and dispute them.

How? By challenging them with scientific thinking.

Science is hardly flawless and does not solve all human problems. It is just a tool, and like any tool has its limitations, particularly when used by fallible human beings! But it is still the best method we have of observing ourselves and the world, trying to figure out what makes us tick and what might make us tick better, and checking out those ideas. After we check, we can modify our ideas so that they fit better with "reality" and are useful for happier living. Science itself is not sacred. Its purpose is not to determine absolute truths or perfect rules but to serve humanity and to help us live longer, happier, and healthier lives.[4]

To this end, science uses three main tools:

1. It develops flexible ideas about reality. It leaves these ideas open to testing, to revision, and even to total abandonment.

2. It continually checks these tentative ideas and laws against observable, empirical "reality."

3. It accepts the fact that there may not be any totally "objective reality," because our environment always includes how we view it and how we interact with it. But science observes, measures, and records what seems to be going on in the world and what we humans do to interact with the universe, with others, and with ourselves. It draws tentative conclusions about these interactions. It checks its fallible observations against its tentative theories. In doing so, science uses empirical findings, logic, predictions, and creative guesswork. It constantly updates its observations and conclusions, applies them to human affairs, and avoids making final, absolutist decisions. It is, when it truly follows its own methods, flexible and alternative-seeking.

In Disputing your irrational Beliefs (iBs) you can use flexible, scientific thinking to question and challenge your rigid, self-upsetting, stinking thinking. Challenge your irrational *musts* and their derivatives, but not your rational, *preferred* goals, and values. The *latter* will hardly ever get you into serious, neurotic trouble. Whatever you *want* is okay; but your dire *need* for it will often unhinge you.

Here are some specific scientific questions you can

use to *falsify* the irrational Beliefs that (*a*) significantly contribute to your anxiety, depression, self-hatred, shame, and rage and (*b*) often encourage you to drink too much and maintain your problem drinking or other addictive behavior.

Must No. 1

A. *Activating Event or Adversity.* You failed in a test or a job interview.

rB. *Rational Beliefs.* "I hate to fail, but it won't kill me and I can try again."

rC. *Realistic, reasonable, or appropriate Consequences.* Feelings of concern and regret; preparation to do better in the future.

iB. *Irrational Belief.* "I *must* not fail and bring on such bad results!"

iC. *Inappropriate, self-defeating Consequences.* Feelings of depression and inadequacy.

D. *Disputing (detecting, distinguishing, debating) and questioning your iBs.* "Where is the evidence that I must not fail and bring on such bad results?"

E. *Effective new philosophy.* "Only in my head! If there were any law of the universe that said I must not fail, then I would have to follow it and succeed. Obviously, it doesn't exist. Because I am fallible, I will often fail. Too bad! But I can live with my failures, learn from them, and still be a happy human. Now let's see what I can do to succeed next time."

Must No. 2

A. *Activating Event or Adversity.* Feelings of anxiety and depression.

rB. *Rational Beliefs.* "I don't like feeling anxious and depressed. I had better get at what I am doing to make myself disturbed and then change it and reduce my upsets."

rC. *Realistic, reasonable, appropriate Consequences.* Feelings of frustration and disappointment. Attempts to remove or minimize disturbances.

iB. *Irrational Beliefs.* "It's *awful* to be so anxious and depressed! Life shouldn't be this way! I *can't stand* this pain another second. I've got to have a drink! I *can't wait* and don't have time to use RET to overcome these feelings!"

iC. *Inappropriate, self-defeating Consequences.* Panic about panic. Low frustration tolerance. "Need" for a drink. Drinking.

D. *Disputing and challenging your iBs.* "Why is it *awful* to be so anxious and depressed? Where is it written that I *must* not be? In what way can't I *stand* these feelings? Prove that I *have* to feel no pain immediately and therefore *must* have a drink. Is it true that I *can't* wait and use RET to overcome my disturbed feelings?"

E. *Effective new philosophy.* "It's not awful or horrible to be so anxious and depressed, but it is highly unpleasant and inconvenient, and I'm determined to change these unfortunate feelings. I must right now be disturbed, because that's the state I've largely put myself in. Of course, I can stand feeling anxious and depressed, but I may not have to keep standing it if I do something constructive to overcome these feelings. There is no proof that I have to immediately feel no pain by drinking. But the sooner I deal with my anxiety and depression adequately, the better off I will be now and later. Certainly I can wait and use RET to overcome my disturbed feelings—and to make sure that I rarely bring them back."

Must No. 3

A. *Activating Event or Adversity.* Drinking steadily and getting into serious trouble at work and at home because of this drinking.

rB. *Rational Beliefs.* "I am stupidly destroying my life

by this drinking and I had damned well better stop this self-defeating and antisocial behavior."

rC. *Realistic, reasonable, or appropriate Consequences.* Feelings of regret and disappointment at your foolish indulgences. Determination to stop drinking. Plans to stop, and action to implement these plans.

iB. *Irrational Beliefs.* "I absolutely should not touch a drop of booze! I have no right to act so stupidly! What a complete loser I am for behaving this way! I'm really hopeless and can't ever stop drinking."

iC. *Inappropriate, self-defeating Consequences.* Feelings of enormous self-hatred and increased depression. More drinking and self-defeating behavior because of drinking.

D. *Disputing irrational Beliefs and distinguishing them from rational Beliefs.* "I am really acting very foolishly when I drink to drown my disturbances, but how does that prove that I *absolutely must* never touch another drop of booze? Where is it written in stone that I have *no right* to act so stupidly? Even if I foolishly keep drinking, how does that make me a complete loser? Is there any reason I'm really hopeless and therefore can't ever stop drinking?"

E. *Effective new philosophy.* "My drinking is bad because it hurts me and my loved ones, but that only proves that it is foolish and that I'd *better* stop it, not that I *absolutely must never* touch another drop. Because drinking greatly sabotages me and people I care for, I am determined and committed to stopping it even though I don't *have* to. Of course, as a human, I have the right and the choice to continue to drink, but it is foolish to exercise that right and that choice. So I shall choose, instead, the right to be sane and healthy. If I foolishly continue to drink and destroy my life, that will never make me a complete failure or a worthless scumball. It would mean I am a person who acted poorly, but who can change. I will be hopeless and unable to stop drinking only if I *think* I am. Hopeless thinking is stinking thinking. If I see that I always can change, and keep working at doing so, I really can quit my stinking thinking and problem drinking!"

As I (AE) have shown in my many writings and cassettes on RET, the main irrational Beliefs with which you needlessly upset yourself consist of, first, your arrogant, absolutist musts, shoulds, oughts, demands on yourself, others, and the world, and, second, several common offshoots of these unconditional musts: especially awfulizing; I-can't-stand-it-itis; hatred (or lack of tolerance) of others, life, or oneself; and an always or never attitude.[5] To Dispute these iBs, actively seek them out and forcefully Dispute and challenge them.

Suppose, for example, your main musturbatory demand is "I absolutely *must* be totally and continually loved by my mate in order to be a lovable, worthwhile, happy person!" Very likely, accompanying this command you will have several major derivatives. Let us now look for these derivatives and actively Dispute them.

Awfulizing and Catastrophizing

Irrational Belief. "If I am not totally loved by my mate, as I absolutely must be, it's awful and catastrophic."

Disputing. "Why is it really awful and catastrophic if I am not loved by my mate?"

Effective New Philosophy. "It isn't. It's only damned unfortunate and inconvenient, and I can still live and be reasonably happy."

I-Can't-Stand-It-Itis (Low Frustration Tolerance)

Irrational Belief. "Since you do not really love me, as you absolutely must, I can't stand it, I can't tolerate it, and I might as well drink myself to death!"

Disputing. "In what way can't I stand your not really loving me? How does your not loving me make my *whole* existence miserable and not worth living?"

Effective New Philosophy. "I'll never like your not really loving me, but I certainly can lump it and stand it. I won't be as happy as I think I would be *with* your loving and appreciating me, but I definitely can and will be an effective, happy person."

Hatred (or Lack of Tolerance and Acceptance) of Others, Life, or Oneself

Irrational Belief. "Because I should be able to gain your love, and I have not gained or kept it as I must, I am an unlovable, inadequate person; you are a louse; and life is not worth living."

Disputing. "Where is it written that my not gaining and keeping your love makes me *anything*, especially an unlovable, inadequate person? How does it make *you* a total worm? How does it make *life* completely worthless?"

Effective New Philosophy. "It's only written in my head. I foolishly *define* my worth as a person in terms of my gaining your love. This is no different from falsely *defining and labeling* myself as 'worthless' or 'contemptible' if I fail at Ping-Pong or bridge. Actually, I am a person who, at this moment, isn't winning your love. That is unfortunate and sad, because I am failing and am deprived. But it never makes me—my whole being—worthless or inadequate."

Overgeneralization (Always or Never Attitude)

Irrational Belief. "Because I don't have your love right now, I'll *never* be able to gain love and will *always* be horribly deprived."

Disputing. "Prove that my present inability to win your love shows that I'll *never* be able to gain any love and will *always* be horribly deprived."

Effective New Philosophy. "I can only prove, at most, that you do not love me as I would prefer you to love me right now. But I may well gain your love—and of course, other people's love—in the future. Even if I am unlucky and unable to win the affection of anyone I truly prefer— and that would be quite unusual if I really keep looking and trying—I can still be a happy person, though perhaps not *as* happy as I would like to be. Now, let me keep trying to establish a good love relationship."

More Ways to Catch Your Stinking Thinking and Turn Affirmations Into Action

As I (AE) showed in my early writings on RET in the 1950s and 1960s, once you command that you *must* do well, have to be approved, need comfort and pleasure, and have to be undisturbed and stop your addictions, you very frequently construct awfulizings; I-can't-stand-its; self-damnings, people-damnings, and life-damning ideas; and always or never attitudes. But that's not all! You also tend to derive a good many other inferences and attributions from your major irrational Beliefs (iBs). These derivatives *seem* valid and logical but are usually exaggerated or distinctly mistaken.

Suppose for example, you would really like a friend to monitor your drinking and stop you from ordering anything but soda or water whenever you dine together. The friend replies, "Oh, no! I'm not going to take responsibility for your not drinking. That's your job! Don't be weak. You'd better monitor your own damned behavior!"

Hearing this, you may easily tell yourself (*a*) "My friend dislikes me;" (*b*) "thinks I'm a weak person," (*c*)

185

"knows I can't stop even with help and realizes that I'm a hopeless drunk." All three of these conclusions are your personal assumptions or inferences about your friend's refusal to monitor your drinking. Quite possibly they are all false. Why so? Because, first, your friend may actually like you but dislike your drinking. Second, your friend may not think you're a weak person but a person who has a weakness for alcohol. Third, rather than judging you as a hopeless drunk, your friend may refuse to monitor you because he or she is confident that you can monitor yourself. He or she may think you would benefit more that way than with supervision, and thus are far from being a hopeless drunk.

Now, why do people very often make false attributions and inferences, even though they are bright and well educated? One answer that sounds flip at first is "That's the way they are." However, experimental psychologists have consistently shown that practically all normal people frequently make errors in judgment. As Seymour Epstein has shown, people may first think in terms of impressions and only later think more critically. That is why they make so many errors of judgment.[1]

Perhaps more to the point is the RET view that once you bring to any situation an underlying, powerful musturbatory core philosophy, this very attitude will prejudice you. It will help you make many misleading attributions and inferences that you would not otherwise make. Thus, once you devoutly believe "I must not keep drinking, and I am an utterly worthless person if I do!" and bring that basic attitude to the situation of asking a friend to help you monitor your drinking, you will probably make judgment errors if she or he refuses to help you with your monitoring.

In any event, RET teaches you to look for and actively dispute your musts; your awfulizings; your I-can't-stand-its; your damnations of yourself, others, and the world; and your always and never overgeneralizations. It also helps you look for and forcefully counterattack the additional misleading attributions and inferences that you often derive from your musts and from your other tendencies to think crookedly. Here are some main additional irrational Beliefs you may employ, with ways of Disputing them.

In chapter 10, we listed the categories into which one's automatic negative, disturbing thoughts may fall. Here, we will list them again, and your task will be to develop Disputes and more rational alternatives for each of them.

1. *All-or-nothing thinking.* "If I fail to stop drinking on a single occasion, as I must not fail, I'll never be able to stop drinking at all!"

   How do you Dispute it?

   _____

   _____

   _____

   _____

   See the end of this section for sample answer.

2. *Perfectionism.* "I Believe I must follow my abstinence program perfectly and be the best abstainer anyone in this group, or any other group, has ever seen. I Believe I must not even be tempted to drink from now on!"

   How do you Dispute it?

   _____

   _____

   _____

   _____

   See the end of this section for sample answer.

3. *Jumping to conclusions.* "Because I think I must not keep drinking and because I have gone back to drinking many times, that proves it's *impossible* for me to stop and stay sober. My friend's refusal to help monitor me means that he recognizes what an incompetent nut I am, that it's useless trying to help me. It means that I'm doomed to fail no matter how much effort he takes to put me on the right track."

How do you Dispute it?

_____

_____

_____

_____

See the end of this section for sample answer.

4. *Focusing on the negative.* "Because I Believe I absolutely must never take another sip of alcohol, that means any slips—like that one yesterday—are awful. I haven't made any progress at all."

How do you Dispute it?

_____

_____

_____

_____

See the end of this section for sample answer.

5. *Always or never attitude.* "Since I Believe I should have made it already, that proves I never do anything right. I always mess up everything I do."

How do you Dispute it?

_____

_____

_____

_____

See the end of this section for sample answer.

6. *Disqualifying the positive.* "When my friends tell me that I am making progress in quitting drinking and in not beating myself up for having been stupidly addicted, they don't realize how little *real* progress I've made. They don't realize how far I still have to go because I should have no faults by this stage of life. If they only knew how rotten I am, they wouldn't support me at all!"

How do you Dispute it?

_____

_____

_____

_____

See the end of this section for sample answer.

7. *Labeling.* "My name is . . . and I am an alcoholic." "Once a drunk, always a drunk."

How do you Dispute it?

_____

_____

_____

_____

See the end of this section for sample answer.

8. *Emotional reasoning.* "If I get the urge to drink after all these years, it proves I'll never make it. I'm just a born alcoholic."

How do you Dispute it?

_____

_____

_____

_____

See the end of this section for sample answer.

9. *Personalizing.* "I notice that they are laughing and I am sure they are laughing at me (as I Believe they must not because I Believe I must have approval) for being such a rotten alcoholic. They know I will never stop drinking and they therefore will keep despising me."

How do you Dispute it?

_____

_____

_____

_____

See the end of this section for sample rational response.

10. *Phonyism.* "Everybody thinks I'm doing so well by stopping drinking but they don't know what a real phony I am. They don't realize that I occasionally feel temptation (as I Believe I should not) to take a sleeping pill or a tranquilizer. If they only knew how inadequate and phony I really am, they'd run me of out of this recovery group!"

How do you Dispute it?

_____

_____

_____

_____

Sample Rational Answers

1. _Sample rational alternative to all or nothing thinking._
   "How can a lapse—or even a few lapses—prove that
   I'll never be able to stop drinking? It doesn't prove
   anything except that I haven't stopped yet. But I have
   many more chances to stop. Even if I occasionally fall
   back to drinking for the rest of my life, that doesn't
   show that I am a hopeless alcoholic."

2. _Sample rational alternative to perfectionism._ "It
   would be great if I followed my abstinence program
   perfectly and never even felt tempted again to drink.
   But why do I have to be so perfect? I don't! I can live
   with my imperfections, and even with occasional slips
   or relapses, and still accept myself as a fallible human.
   Then I'll not only stop drinking but stop my very
   foolish self-downing."

3. _Sample rational alternative to jumping to conclusions._
   "How do I know that my friend just thinks _I_ am
   incompetent and hopeless? Maybe she wouldn't take
   time and trouble to try to help anyone with a problem
   like mine. Maybe she just hasn't the time to devote to
   me and my problems. Her refusing to help may mean
   nothing about her attitude toward me personally.
   Furthermore, lots of people stop and stay stopped
   after many lapses. I more than likely can do it, too,
   especially if I study the factors that contribute to my
   lapses and work against them."

4. *Sample rational response to focusing on the negative.* "My taking an occasional drink can't make me a hopeless alcoholic. A slip is just a slip. I can learn from slips. I've made fairly good progress and it's normal to have ups and downs. Learning is not always a smooth process. Maybe I'd better make a list of the progress I've made, so I can counteract my negative thinking."

5. *Sample rational responses to always or never attitude.* "Wait a minute. Lots of people change their lives, so I can, too, if I work at it. Maybe I mess up many things, but isn't 'always' a bit of an exaggeration?"

6. *Sample rational responses to disqualifying the positive.* "How do I know that my friends are exaggerating my progress? Maybe I have made some good gains. Even if I could do better, that won't ever make me a rotten person who deserves no friendly support."

7. *Sample rational response to labeling.* "Well, it's true that I have trained myself into quite a definite pattern of problem drinking. But I am much more than 'an alcoholic.' I have many, many characteristics—good, bad, and indifferent—and many of them are changing. I harm myself by giving myself a permanent identity based on some of my self-defeating behavior."

8. *Sample rational response to emotional reasoning.* "Get serious. What happened is that I started up some stinking thinking, and I did stop by the tavern for a minute. My thoughts and my surroundings led to my cravings. But cravings are just feelings. I don't have to do what they say. They prove nothing about reality other than the way I'm thinking."

9. *Sample rational response to personalizing.* "What evidence do I have that they are laughing at me? They

could be laughing for several reasons. And even if they were laughing at me right now, that hardly proves that they know I will never stop drinking. It also does not prove that if I keep drinking they will totally despise me."

10. *Sample rational response to phonyism.* "Am I a real phony—or just a person who sometimes isn't always a hundred percent truthful? Is my occasionally taking a sleeping pill or a tranquilizer truly that bad? Will the people in my recovery group actually boycott me if they find out that I sometimes keep things from them? Even if I occasionally hold things back, that hardly makes me a completely rotten and phony person."

Rational Coping Self-Statements

If you actively keep Disputing your self-defeating, irrational Beliefs (iBs) until you really see how invalid they are, you will tend to surrender them. But you also will decrease your tendency to construct new iBs and to gullibly accept others' disturbance-creating ideas. You will become more adept at thinking for yourself and being a personal scientist. You can Dispute your irrational Beliefs (iBs) and thereby arrive at Effective New Philosophies.

But even without Disputing, you can figure out several Effective New Philosophies that will particularly work for you. You can forcefully say them to yourself many times, think about them while you are repeating them, and thereby sink them solidly into your head, heart, and habit. Don't merely parrot or intellectually understand these Effective New Philosophies or rational coping self-statements. But show yourself *why* they are true and *why* they will work to undo your disturbance-creating ideas. Tailor-make them for your own problems, and use them whenever you fall back on anxiety, depression, drinking, or other self-defeating feelings and behaviors.[2]

Turn Your Affirmations Into Actions

What about positive thinking? The modern word for "positive thinking" is *affirmation*. For instance, you might stand in front of the mirror and say, "I am a good person and deserve love." This can help you feel better. A problem with that kind of affirmation is that you may believe it but, underneath, still believe your negative thinking. You may hold the self-defeating thinking more strongly than your positive thinking. Therefore, when the chips are down, you will not be likely to believe and follow your positive affirmations. Negative thinking usually takes priority because it is more basic to survival than is positive thinking. That is why it is so important that you practice the types of Disputes we've suggested above until you succeed at challenging and changing your root stinking thinking.

Another problem with the kind of affirmation in the example above is that it is quite risky to believe you *deserve* love. If your beloved or the world does not give you what you say you deserve, what happens? Yes, "Poor, poor me, treated so unfairly! I think I'll have a drink!"

Therefore, if you use affirmations, make them instructions to yourself. For example, "I will work and practice today at catching, challenging, and changing my stinking thinking. If I do that, more than likely it will benefit me." "I will keep a realistic attitude today and will not make up in my head that I deserve people to love me. I will have a better chance of getting love if I focus on being loving toward others, not on thinking about what I supposedly deserve."

The first kind of coping statements you can use are realistic affirmations of what you can, in reality, do to help yourself. They contradict negative, unrealistic statements with which you frequently tend to sabotage yourself. For example:

"I *can* stop drinking, even though it's hard to do so. It's not too hard, and no matter how much trouble it takes, it's worth it!"

"Yes, I've often failed to do what I promised that I would do, but that doesn't mean that I can't or won't carry out this promise."

"I *am* able to change my stinking thinking no matter who tells me I cannot."

"If I keep ignoring and never giving into my powerful urges to drink, I will make it easier and easier to resist them."

"My strong desires to go back to drinking will not make me lift a bottle to my mouth. Only I can make me—and refuse to make me—do that!"

"I can fully and unconditionally accept myself—yes, even with all my flaws and failings."

"Alcohol seems to quickly cure my problems, but actually makes them worse."

Another kind of rational coping self-statement that you can construct is even more profoundly philosophical because it helps you rip up the musts and the awfulizings, I-can't-stand-its, self-damnations, and always or never attitudes that often accompany these *musturbatory* demands. You can consider self-statements like these:

"At times, I would like very much to drown my troubles in alcohol, but that is never a reason I *have* to do so."

"It's most uncomfortable when I don't get what I really want. But it's not *awful or terrible* unless I choose to *believe* that it is, and I choose to believe something more realistic and helpful."

"I'll never like unfair treatment, but I damned well can stand it and perhaps plot and scheme to stop it."

"No matter *how* many times I fail at an important pursuit, my failure never makes me an incompetent louse. It just makes me *a person who* may have acted incompetently this time."

"I don't absolutely *need* what I want, but I can still be reasonably happy—though not as happy—when I don't get it."

"I strongly *prefer* to be outstanding at my work, but I don't have to be. Too bad if I'm not, but it doesn't make *me* inferior. I can always keep trying to do better without *needing* to do better."

"Many things can help make me sorry and disappointed, but when I demand and command that these things *must* not exist, I then make myself panicked, depressed, and enraged."

"I hate like hell being anxious or depressed, but I don't have to immediately dissolve these feelings in alcohol. When I drink, I temporarily *feel* better about my problems, but I don't *get* better. In the long run, drinking makes them worse."

"People don't enrage me by treating me badly. I pigheadedly *choose* to enrage myself about their bad treatment by demanding and commanding that they act better."

13

Other Cognitive or Thinking Techniques of RET

RET helps you change your stinking thinking, your disturbed feelings, and your self-defeating behavior in many cognitive, emotive, and behavioral ways. For as we have already pointed out, people do not experience beliefs, emotions, and actions in a pure state. These experiences affect each other. Thus, if you strongly think "Mary has to love me!" you feel great when you perceive that she does love you. You horrify yourself when (you think) she doesn't. When she acts lovingly toward you, you move closer. When she acts unlovingly, you either avoid her or compulsively cling to her.

Let's say you feel panicked because you perceive (rightly or wrongly) that Mary no longer loves you. If you want to change your disturbed feelings, you have several options. For example, you can convince yourself that Mary does love you—in her own way. Or she does love you but is unable to show it. Another option is to try to avoid her so you don't find out whether she loves you or not. You might also keep looking for another woman who does love you more than Mary does. If successful, this keeps you from dealing with your dire need for love.

More elegant ways to change your feelings stem from changing your Beliefs. You would better convince yourself, "I wish Mary would love me, but I don't need her to do so. I can still be happy without her love." At the same time, you can work on your feelings about Mary's lack of love for you. You can push yourself to feel appropriately sad and frustrated—but not panicked and horrified. Finally, you probably would try harder (but not frantically) to win Mary's affection. Once you convince yourself that Mary's love is *not* a *necessity*, you would probably solve most of your emotional problem. You will no longer feel horror about losing her affection. (You still would have the practical problem of wanting a lover and not having one). By changing both your feelings and your behavior, you have a better chance of curbing your self-created horror.

In this and the next chapter, we shall present many cognitive methods, besides Disputing irrational Beliefs (iBs), that may help you overcome your addictive drinking problems. These methods also will deal with the emotional upsets that often set you up for addictive drinking. They will also teach you to stop beating up on yourself and making your upsets and drinking problems still worse.

Reframing

Problem drinkers frequently see things in an exceptionally bad light. They make catastrophic and awfulizing predictions about what is going to happen to them. Because they think that losses, failures, and dangers absolutely *must* not occur, they exaggerate their occurrence. They see the proverbial glass as half empty instead of half full. Then they tend to distract themselves and treat their bad feelings by drinking glassfuls of alcohol!

If you often look at life gloomily and ignore many good and neutral events, you can reframe many negative situations. You reframe by deliberately focusing on possible advantages hidden in bad situations, rather than focusing only on their disadvantages. This technique is the opposite of the shitlist technique. In using shitlisting, you *want* to remember negatives and think first about them because doing so *helps* you avoid them.

Suppose, for example, you lose your job and start seeing yourself unemployed forever and on welfare or homeless. You can look at the *advantages* of taking a rest from the work world. For instance, you could live off unemployment insurance, possibly get a better job, have the chance to study for a new career, and so forth. By looking also at the disadvantages of the job you just lost, you may wind up liking the fact that you lost it!

Again, if a potential mate refuses to live with you, you can focus on your good fortune in not having a partner who doesn't care for you. You can feel pleased you did not mate with someone who is so likely to have faults. Even if you have wasted many years drinking, staying at a low level-job, or unassertively staying with the wrong partner, you can reframe realistically. You can show yourself that the "wasted" time was really a good, and sometimes necessary, experience. It prepared you for where you are now: ready to forge ahead and determined to make the rest of your life much better.

RET also shows you how to reframe your inappropriate negative feelings—such as severe anxiety and rage— and to change them into appropriate, self-helping feelings—such as concern or irritation. You can do this by using rational-emotive imagery (REI) (which we explain in the next chapter). Another possibility is to figure out which thoughts would make you feel disappointed instead of enraged. Thus, when you enrage yourself at someone's slighting you, you are probably telling yourself, "He *must* not treat me so unfairly, and is a rotten louse for doing so."

How can you reframe inappropriate feelings of rage to an appropriate feeling of disappointment? You can convince yourself, instead, "I really don't like the way he is treating me and I think that his behavior is unjust and rotten. However, he is a fallible, screwed-up person who is now acting badly but who also has his good points. Too bad that he is treating me unfairly, but I can try to get him to change. Even if I can't get him to change, it won't kill me."

You can particularly use reframing when you attribute negative intentions to people that they may well not have. Let's say John makes a date with you and agrees to go to a vegetarian restaurant, because he knows you are doing your best to stop drinking. However, he takes you to a bar and grill, he drinks a great deal himself, and keeps insisting that you have one. You may feel very angry with him. You may make all kinds of assumptions about his treating you this way, such as "He's deliberately doing this! He *wants* me to go back to drinking! He sees how well I'm getting along with my sobriety and he's jealous of me, because he can't stop drinking himself. How *could* he deliberately do a rotten thing like that to me? That bastard!"

You can reframe your rage-creating ideas by showing yourself that John may just be doing what *he* wants to do. He may have no real intention to harm you. He may merely be forgetful or generally irresponsible. He may have had something to drink before he met you and there-fore be more likely to act insensitively. He may be very upset over something that has recently happened to him—failure to get promoted, for example. This makes him less likely to act considerately toward you—or anyone.

So watch attributing nasty intentions to people. *May-be* they really have them; but it is very possible that they don't. The more you bigotedly *assume* that they absolutely *have* to think mainly about you and act the way *you* want them to, the more likely you will draw false conclusions about them. These inferences will often be false. So when-ever you enrage yourself because you believe other people *intend* to do you in, watch it! Reframe their intentions more realistically.[1]

Check Your Language!

Alfred Korzybski, the founder of general semantics, pioneered in realizing that science and sanity blend into each other and used them in the title of his fine book.[2] He said that when we overgeneralize and thereby think crookedly, we often render ourselves "unsane." He also noted that, being human, we uniquely employ symbols and language, and so our crooked thinking gets into our language. Then our language encourages us to think more irrationally. How right he was!

So one RET technique you can use to reduce your drinking-related difficulties is to *check your language*.[3] Whenever you think, feel, or act self-defeatingly—that is, against your own and society's interests—look at both the content and the form of what you are telling yourself and others. That may help you see how your manner of speech produces needless problems.

Here are some common statements you can analyze and practice changing to more precise and accurate statements. If you use precise language, you can disturb yourself less and undisturb yourself more easily:

Fuzzy language. "You didn't keep your promise, and that upset me."

Clear communication. "All that happened was that we didn't go to the movie as planned because you changed your mind. I like people to keep their promises, but it's hardly horrible that you didn't keep yours. I foolishly chose to upset myself about your changing your mind by demanding that you *absolutely ought* to keep your promise."

Fuzzy language. "You made me so upset that I had to have a couple of drinks to steady my nerves."

Clear communication. "I *told* myself it was awful and unbearable that you broke our date. Then I *decided* to have a couple of drinks to feel better."

Fuzzy language. "I'm an Adult Child of an Alcoholic, and that dooms me to be the mess I am."

Clear communication: "Bullshit! If I believe that crap, then I will doom myself to remain messed up. I have the power to change myself now."

Fuzzy language. "Seeing other people enjoying a good cold beer so much makes me so thirsty! I just can't help giving in."

Clear communication. "Seeing other people drink beer and enjoying it so much helps me *want* it, but does not make me *crave* it. Cravings come from my Believing that I must have what I want and *can't stand* not having it. But cravings are just cravings. Even if I do give myself cravings, they do not *force* me to give in to them and drink. Giving in to them is always a decision."

Fuzzy language. "Because I *need* to get through school, I *absolutely* must get an A on the term paper I am writing! It will be the end of my whole career and my future life if I don't."

Clear communication.. "I very much want to get through school successfully and get an A on the term paper I am writing. If I get a lower mark, or even fail, that may slow down my career but it won't end it completely. I can still try for another career and lead a happy life even if, at the worst, I ruin this present career."

Fuzzy language. "It would be awful if I didn't do a great job on the proposal. If the pressure builds up much more I'm going to have to say, 'To hell with it!' and start drinking again."

Clear communication. "While it would be a pain in the ass if I did a poor job on the proposal, it wouldn't kill me. I'm giving myself most of the stress by musturbating. Then I'm telling myself the stress is so bad that I don't care what happens to me. Phooey on that!"

Fuzzy language. "Because abstinence is my goal, I immediately have to achieve it. Because I have gone back to drinking many times, I *can't* stop and will always be a stupid drunk!"

Clear communication. "Because complete abstinence is my goal, I shall determinedly keep striving for it, but I don't have to achieve it immediately. Because I've gone back to drinking many times, I obviously have trouble staying stopped. Still, there is no reason I can't finally quit my stinking thinking and addictive drinking. I do have voluntary control of my hands and my mouth!"

Cognitive Homework

Rational-Emotive Therapy, as noted above, has many insights, but the three main ones are:

1. You largely choose your Beliefs, consciously or unconsciously, and they mainly upset you—although other people and bad conditions may help you do the job.

2. It doesn't matter how and when you originally began to make yourself disturbed and to form self-defeating habit patterns. If you are still emotionally upset today or acting self-defeatingly, you are now reformulating, and actively recreating, the irrational thoughts, feelings, and behaviors with which you originally plagued yourself. In fact, you often creatively *add* to them!

3. To change your self- and social-sabotaging philosophies and actions, insight into them is not enough. Strong resolution to change is not enough either. Millions of problem drinkers have strongly determined to stop and yet continued to drink till they died. Insight and determination to change are a good start for doing so. But, alas, only work and practice— yes, WORK and PRACTICE—will get you going and keep you going on the path to sobriety. It takes consistent work to overcome the stinking thinking that promotes problem drinking. Unless you repeti-

tively and strongly *practice* new thinking, new feelings, and new habits, you will only temporarily *feel*
better than you previously did. However, your
chances of *getting* better, and particularly of staying
better, are slim.

Cognitively, then, you'd better do your homework,
during and between scheduled self-help or therapy sessions. Steadily practice day after day and look for your
disturbed feelings and the irrational Beliefs that largely
create them. Actively and forcefully Dispute these iBs by
constructing and thinking through rational coping self-
statements, reviewing your shitlist, employing reframing,
and checking your language. In addition, use various other
cognitive-emotive methods that we present in this chapter.

One way is to use DIBS (Disputing Irrational Belief
Systems).[4] Here is a sample DIBS exercise:

Question 1: *What irrational Belief or stinking thought
do I want to Dispute and surrender?*

I can't stand anxiety without drinking.

Question 2: *Can I rationally support this Belief or
stinking thought?*

No.

Question 3: *What evidence exists of the truth of this
Belief or stinking thought?*

*None, really. I stand anxiety all the time, for instance, at work,
where I can't drink.*

Question 4: *What evidence exists of the falseness of
this Belief or stinking thought?*

See above. I stand anxiety, though I hate to do so.

Question 5: *What are the worst things that are actually, factually likely to happen to me if I give up this irrational Belief and act against it?*

I'd just be very anxious, which is a pain in the ass. But eventually the anxiety would fade.

Question 6: *What good things could happen or could I make happen if I give up this irrational Belief?*

Maybe I could make myself stronger. I'm never going to get anywhere if I don't learn to stand anxiety without turning to the bottle.

Below is a blank DIBS form you can use for Disputing your own stinking thinking.

Question 1: *What irrational Belief or stinking thought do I want to Dispute and surrender?*

_____

_____

_____

_____

Question 2: *Can I rationally support this Belief or stinking thought?*

_____

_____

_____

_____

Question 3: *What evidence exists of the truth of this Belief or stinking thought?*

_____

_____

_____

_____

Question 4: *What evidence exists of the falseness of this Belief or stinking thought?*

_____

_____

_____

Question 5: *What is the worst things that are actually, factually likely to happen to me if I give up this irrational Belief and act against it?*

_____

_____

_____

_____

Question 6: *What good things could happen or could I make happen if I give up this irrational Belief?*

_____

_____

_____

_____

Over the years, other Rational-Emotive therapists and I (AE) have devised several RET Self-Help Reports that we have found highly effective with our therapy clients and readers.

A simple, effective way to Dispute your stinking thinking is to fill out an RET Self-Help Form daily[5]. Figure 13.1 shows completed and blank versions of this valuable self-help tool.

Finally, Figure 13.2 is a blank version of another RET self-help tool—A Guide for Solving Your Emotional and Behavioral Problems. You can obtain copies of it and of the RET Self-Help Form from the Institute for Rational-Emotive Therapy (see Appendix A).

If you do fill out these forms whenever you feel or act in a self-defeating way, you will learn the ABCDEs of RET quite well. In time you will have them so solidly in mind that you may then be able to apply them without referring to them.

Dear Inner Child: Grow Up Already!

You also can use these self-help forms about past situations that you made upsetting—including abuse, failure, loss of loved ones, feelings of shame and guilt, and other problems you may have experienced during your childhood, adolescence, or early adulthood. Some therapists and writers tell you that to overcome your emotional problems today you have to get in touch with all the gory details of your past. They tell you to reactivate your "walking wounded inner child" and relive the terrible deprivations that this poor little critter underwent.

Everyone is against genuine child abuse. However, most "inner children" are immature and spoiled and they brattishly claim they were abused whenever they didn't get their own way! It really is time to stop coaxing your "inner child" with teddy bears and to begin acquiring

Figure 13.1

RET SELF-HELP FORM

Institute for Rational-Emotive Therapy
45 East 65th Street, New York, NY 10021
(212) 535-0822

(A) ACTIVATING EVENTS, thoughts, or feelings that happened just before I felt emotionally disturbed or acted self-defeatingly:

I promised myself I would Never drink again but when my friends urged me to drink I started to do so and got stinking drunk.

(C) CONSEQUENCE OR CONDITION—disturbed feeling or self-defeating behavior—that I produced and would like to change:

Anxiety. Depression, Severe self-blaming, Hostile to friends.

(B) BELIEFS—Irrational BELIEFS (IBs) leading to my CONSEQUENCE (emotional disturbance or self-defeating behavior).
 	
Circle all that apply to these ACTIVATING EVENTS (A).
	(D) DISPUTES for each circled Irrational BELIEF (iB).
	  Examples: *"Why MUST I do very well?" "Where is it written* that I am a BAD PERSON?" *"Where is the evidence* that I MUST be approved or accepted?"
		(E) EFFECTIVE RATIONAL BELIEFS (RBs) to replace my Irrational BELIEFS (iBs).
		  Examples: "I'd PREFER to do very well *but I don't* HAVE TO." "I am a PERSON WHO acted badly, *not a* BAD PERSON." *"There is no evidence* that I HAVE TO to approved, though I would LIKE to be."

1. I MUST do well or very well!	*Why MUST I Never have a drink or get drunk?*	*It's most desirable if I Never drink or get drunk but I Never have to act well or stay sober.*
2. I am a BAD OR WORTHLESS PERSON when I act weakly or stupidly.	*How does doing a stupid thing like getting drunk make me a bad or worthless person?*	*It doesn't. It only makes me a person who now acts weakly and badly. I am Not my foolish behavior.*
3. I MUST be approved or accepted by people I find important!	*Why do I have to be approved by my drinking friends?*	*I clearly don't have to be. But it would be Nice if I could give up drinking and still be liked by them.*
4. I NEED to be loved by someone who matters to me a lot!		
5. I am a BAD, UNLOVABLE PERSON if I get rejected.		
6. People MUST treat me fairly and give me what I NEED!	*Do my friends have to treat me fairly and help me stay off alcohol instead of urging me to drink?*	*Of course Not! I wish that they would help me stop drinking but they definitely don't have to help.*

(OVER)

7. People MUST live up to my expectations or it is TERRIBLE!	MUST My friends live up to My expecta-tions!? Is it really terrible if They don't?	Definitely NOT. They can do whatever They do. It's unfortunate, but not Terrible. That They are not helpful.
8. People who act immorally are undeserving, ROTTEN PEOPLE!		
9. I CAN'T STAND really bad things or very difficult people!	Why can't I stand My friends being difficult?	I can! They obvious-ly don't have to be More cooperative Though I wish that They were.
10. My life MUST have few major hassles or troubles.	Why should it not be such a great has-sle for My To stand making	It should be because it is. If I accept Its problem and stop whining about Them I'll be able to stop easier.
11. It's AWFUL or HORRIBLE when major things don't go my way!	what makes it so awful and horrible when I fall back To drinking?	only My Thinking of it as horrible. It's really bad when I fall back but The horror of it is in so is only in My head.
12. I CAN'T STAND IT when life is really unfair!		
13. I NEED a good deal of immediate gratification and HAVE to feel miserable when I don't get it!	Do I really need The immediate gratification of getting drunk and Dowering up My emotional problems?	No, I don't need it. It's Nice To make my self immediately feel No pain by drinking but it's deadly IN The long run.
Additional Irrational Beliefs: My anxiety is awful. I MUST dissolve it immediately IN alcohol.	Awful or inconvenient? Aren't there much bet-Ter ways To reduce it?	It's painful but not awful & more than painful. I can see what I'M Telling myself To create it and use RET To reduce it

(F) FEELINGS and BEHAVIORS I experience after arriving at my **EFFECTIVE RATIONAL BELIEFS:** Disappointment.
Regret. Self-acceptance.

I WILL WORK HARD TO REPEAT MY EFFECTIVE RATIONAL BELIEFS FORCEFULLY TO MYSELF ON MANY OCCASIONS SO THAT I CAN MAKE MYSELF LESS DISTURBED NOW AND ACT LESS SELF-DEFEATINGLY IN THE FUTURE.

Joyce Sichel, Ph.D. and Albert Ellis, Ph.D.
Copyright © 1984 by the Institute for Rational-Emotive Therapy.

100 forms $10.00
1000 forms $80.00

RET SELF-HELP FORM

Institute for Rational-Emotive Therapy
45 East 65th Street, New York, NY 10021
(212) 535-0822

(A) ACTIVATING EVENTS, thoughts, or feelings that happened just before I felt emotionally disturbed or acted self-defeatingly:

_____

(C) CONSEQUENCE OR CONDITION—disturbed feeling or self-defeating behavior—that I produced and would like to change:

_____

(B) BELIEFS—Irrational BELIEFS (IBs) leading to my CONSEQUENCE (emotional disturbance or self-defeating behavior). Circle all that apply to these ACTIVATING EVENTS (A).	**(D) DISPUTES** for each circled Irrational BELIEF (iB). Examples: _"Why MUST I do very well?"_ _"Where is it written that I am a BAD PERSON?"_ _"Where is the evidence that I MUST be approved or accepted?"_	**(E) EFFECTIVE RATIONAL BELIEFS (RBs)** to replace my Irrational BELIEFS (iBs). Examples: _"I'd PREFER to do very well but I don't HAVE TO."_ _"I am a PERSON WHO acted badly, not a BAD PERSON."_ _"There is no evidence that I HAVE TO to approved, though I would LIKE to be."_
1. I MUST do well or very well!		
2. I am a BAD OR WORTHLESS PERSON when I act weakly or stupidly.		
3. I MUST be approved or accepted by people I find important!		
4. I NEED to be loved by someone who matters to me a lot!		
5. I am a BAD, UNLOVABLE PERSON if I get rejected.		
6. People MUST treat me fairly and give me what I NEED!		

(OVER)

7. People MUST live up to my expectations or it is TERRIBLE!

8. People who act immorally are undeserving, ROTTEN PEOPLE!

9. I CAN'T STAND really bad things or very difficult people!

10. My life MUST have few major hassles or troubles.

11. It's AWFUL or HORRIBLE when major things don't go my way!

12. I CAN'T STAND IT when life is really unfair!

13. I NEED a good deal of immediate gratification and HAVE to feel miserable when I don't get it!

Additional Irrational Beliefs:

(F) FEELINGS and BEHAVIORS I experience after arriving at my EFFECTIVE RATIONAL BELIEFS: _____

I WILL WORK HARD TO REPEAT MY EFFECTIVE RATIONAL BELIEFS FORCEFULLY TO MYSELF ON MANY OCCASIONS SO THAT I CAN MAKE MYSELF LESS DISTURBED NOW AND ACT LESS SELF-DEFEATINGLY IN THE FUTURE.

Joyce Sichel, Ph.D. and Albert Ellis, Ph.D.
Copyright © 1984 by the Institute for Rational-Emotive Therapy.

100 forms $10.00
1000 forms $80.00

Figure 13.2
A Guide for Solving Your Emotional
and Behavioral Problems

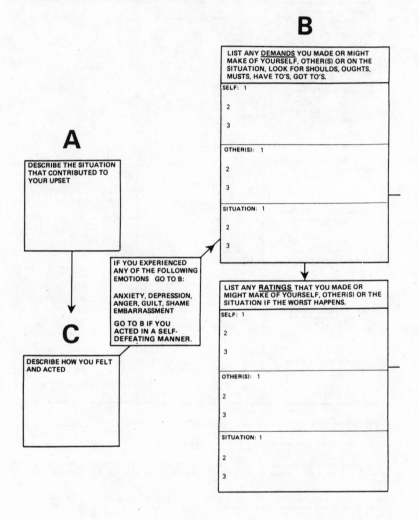

D

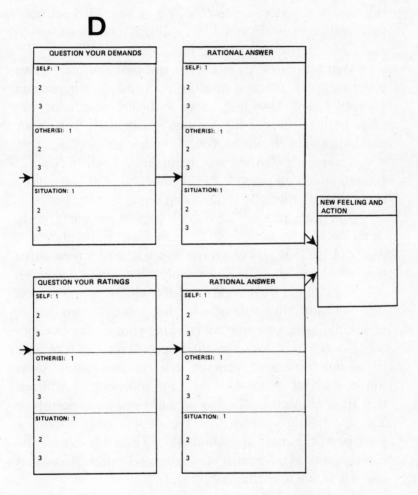

QUESTION YOUR DEMANDS
SELF: 1
2
3
OTHER(S): 1
2
3
SITUATION: 1
2
3

RATIONAL ANSWER
SELF: 1
2
3
OTHER(S): 1
2
3
SITUATION: 1
2
3

NEW FEELING AND ACTION

QUESTION YOUR RATINGS
SELF: 1
2
3
OTHER(S): 1
2
3
SITUATION: 1
2
3

RATIONAL ANSWER
SELF: 1
2
3
OTHER(S): 1
2
3
SITUATION: 1
2
3

feelings and behavior that will serve you well today. Further, you do not need to relive the early traumatic events, such as incidents with your drunken parents, that presumably "made" you a disturbed person and a problem drinker. Ain't it awful? This Freud-inspired detailed reliving of the past and gruesome uncovering of your "primal traumas" will usually do you little good. It may even create obsessions and do you more harm than good.

Why? Because dwelling on the past normally gives you *practice* at empowering the past and disempowering yourself today. Dwelling on your dismal past helps you believe that external happenings, particularly with your parents, originally upset you. It helps you believe that your repression of "traumas" maintains your disturbances. It gives you more practice—as if you needed it!—in feeling miserable. It tilts you toward cop-outs.

You may indeed have had very unfortunate early experiences—as who hasn't? However, remember the ABCs of RET: It was not those happenings *by themselves* that made you neurotic, but mainly what you told yourself *about* childhood frustrations and abuses. Moreover, if you still feel quite upset about what happened to you during your childhood, you *now* are *retelling* yourself how *shameful and horrible* those events were. You are replaying them and convincing yourself that you *can't stand* even thinking about them. You are now repeating to yourself that they *absolutely should not, must not* have occurred. You are telling yourself that the people responsible for your past "traumas" are damnable vermin who should be confronted and who must apologize and suffer. All of that keeps you stuck in the past.

So if you still hang yourself up on what happened in your childhood, you have two choices. You can choose to continue to feel miserable about what occurred and thereby retraumatize yourself about unfortunate events that cannot ever be changed. Or you can effectively use the ABCDEs of RET not only to undo the "hurtful" past but to undo the needless "hurt" and "horror" you *still give your-self about it.*

Let us give a specific, extremely gruesome illustration of a woman who suffered severe abuse as a child. She went on to show many maladjustments as a woman, including alcoholism. Joann, a thirty-three year old problem drinker, had a father who sexually abused her from the age of ten to fourteen. She dearly loved him at first but then grew to feel hatred and terror when he got drunk two or three times a week, left the bed of her stuporously drunken mother, and climbed into Joann's bed. He forced her to masturbate him until, after twenty minutes or so, he had an orgasm and ejaculated on her body. She was sometimes sexually aroused by his hugging her closely while he was having sex with her, felt tremendous guilt about this, and was revolted by his drunkenness, his callousness in only satisfying himself, and his threats to send her away to boarding school if she ever told her mother or anyone else. She felt terribly hurt by both her parents' compulsive drinking and by the fact that they ignored her. They also paid no attention to her obvious psychological problems and poor social relationships.

When Joann was fifteen, she insisted on going away to boarding school even though she was scared that she could never keep up with the sophisticated kids she thought she would find there. However, she did keep up with them by joining the fast crowd, drinking and drugging. While she never enjoyed sex acts and was repelled by them, she was promiscuous. By doing this, she found that at least she would never be alone on weekends. She would always have a boyfriend who was glad to go with the best sexpot on the campus. At sixteen she had a serious gonorrhea infection, got pregnant, and miscarried. She became sterile because of the gonorrhea and the complications of her miscarriage.

I (AE) saw Joann, then a waitress, after she had gone through eight years of therapy—including Gestalt, primal,

and codependency therapy that had not helped her overcome extreme feelings of shame, guilt, and worthlessness
or to relate to any man steadily. She had no close women
friends and described herself as "catty" with other women.
She had also gone to scores of several types of twelve-step
meetings, but they had not helped her to stop drinking.
Partly because of her therapy, she kept having repellent
flashbacks of her father's kissing her passionately with his
disgusting beer breath while panting "Hold it tighter! Rub
me harder!" until he finally came all over her stomach and
then, without another word, went back to her mother's
bed to sleep.

I first helped Joann accept herself fully, in spite of her
continued drinking and drugging. As she did so, she
stopped flogging herself for not finishing school, for not
forming any close relationships, and for not doing anything
with her "wasted life." I also helped her see that when she
was depressed she didn't *have to* "feel no pain" by taking a
pint of gin to bed with her almost every night. By working
on her self-downing and her low frustration tolerance, she
was able to stop drinking. Then she started planning to go
to college to study to be a mental health professional.

Joann's flashbacks and nightmares about her grim
childhood, however, had continued until she did a series of
RET Self-Help Reports on the ABCs of what had happened with her father. Her A's were usually the same:
picturing her panic as she waited for her father to sneak
into her bed, being told that she had to masturbate him,
having him drunkenly and sometimes savagely kiss her
while she was vigorously massaging his sex organs, having
him messily ejaculate all over her, and then having him
suddenly return to her mother's bed, leaving her lonely
and often sexually conflicted.

Joann's Beliefs, as she relived these scenes, were: "He
must not treat me like this! I'm his daughter, not his wife!
How horrible to have him use me as a mere *thing*, and not
give a damn about me or my feelings! And my goddam

mother! She probably gets drunk every night to make sure they can't have sex. She always told me, 'One child is enough of a bother. You can be sure I'll never have another.' So that's her method of birth control—getting dead drunk. I'll bet she even knows what he does to me every night! And she doesn't care. But what am I yelling at her for? Look at me. Yes, I'm letting him do it to me. And for nothing! What a nothing am I! I hate him, I hate him! And I hate myself for letting him get away with it."

When Joann wrote down these ideas on many RET Self-Help Report forms and kept actively Disputing them, she came up with these Effective New Philosophies:

> "My father *should* have acted as badly and un-fatherly as he did, because he was a very sick and irresponsible person, and nutty people will often act badly."

> "It was really unfair and rotten for him to use me as a thing, but it was not horrible, only extremely unfortunate. I can get over it."

> "He never made me into a thing. I did that by foolishly putting myself down and thinking of myself as a thing."

> "He didn't consider my feelings, not because I'm unlovable, but because drunks usually don't consider anyone else's feelings."

> "Sure my mother probably kept getting drunk to avoid having sex, but the poor woman was just too weak to assert herself otherwise. Tragic. But that was her weak nature."

> "Maybe she did know what was going on and willingly looked the other way—giving him my body to save her own. Again, that's what weak, sick people do. She certainly acted badly, but as

RET teaches, she doesn't deserve to be roasted in hell."

"Maybe I acted weakly myself. To some extent, maybe when I was older, I let him get away with what he did by not insisting that he stop. So I did at times want him to love me, caress me, and even give me some sexual satisfaction. What's so wrong about that? And later, when I went with boys my own age and was too afraid of rejection to ask them to satisfy me—how does that make me a 'wimp' or a 'bad person'? It doesn't."

"What went on back then was definitely wrong. My parents were fallible, screwed-up people. Maybe I could have acted differently, too, though I'm not sure how. I'd better leave the past behind, forgive and forget my sick father and mother, and push myself to get on with my life."

Joann repeatedly developed these Effective New Philosophies, mainly by using the RET Self-Help Report. The more she did so, the fewer flashbacks and nightmares she had. In time, she contacted her parents and even felt some small degree of caring for them. However, she decided she did not need or have to be close to them. She solidly concentrated on her relationships, her schooling, and the rest of her life. She never completely forgot her traumatic past, but she made peace with it.

RET Educational Methods

When I (AE) originated RET in 1955, I used it only for one-to-one individual psychotherapy and, a little later, group therapy. (I still have as many as eighty, mostly half-hour, individual sessions and five group therapy sessions every week I am in New York and not traipsing around the country and the world giving many RET talks and work-shops). We both (AE, EV) also "see" many clients by telephone, as RET individual therapy doesn't require face-to-face sessions.

From the start, I recommended reading material to my clients, especially some pamphlets and articles on RET that I had written myself. This material proved so helpful that I realized that RET—or any other effective mode of therapy—is good enough to be given away to the public. So in 1956 I started writing *How to Live With a "Neurot-ic,"* the first popular book on RET and cognitive-behavior therapy. It came out in 1957 and has gone through several hardcover and paperback editions. I'm happy, more than thirty-five years later, to see it still selling well.

So successful was *How to Live With a "Neurotic"* with my clients, and with thousands of self-helpers all over the world who soon started to enthusiastically write me about it, that I have since written more than a score of other RET-oriented self-help books. They have sold millions of copies and have presumably, from the many reports I get, helped great numbers of people to apply rational-emotive principles and methods to their daily life problems. Many other books and articles, with or without giving credit to RET, have also espoused its principles. Some of them, like Wayne Dyer's *Your Erroneous Zones*, and David Burns's *Feeling Good*, have also sold fabulously.

At our large Psychological Clinic at the Institute for Rational-Emotive Therapy in New York, we have found that clients benefit from doing homework consistently. Clients who read the pamphlets on RET that we give each of them and who also read several of our books improve more quickly and deeply than those who do not do so. Several studies of self-help materials have shown that other therapists find suitable readings distinctly helpful to psychotherapy clients as well as to nonclients.[6]

To help yourself learn and apply RET better, we recommend several RET-oriented books. These include my own *New Guide to Rational Living, A Guide to Personal Happiness,* and *How to Stubbornly Refuse to Make Yourself Miserable about Anything—Yes, Anything!,* Paul Hauck's *How to Overcome Depression;* Windy Dryden and Jack Gordon's *Think Your Way to Happiness,* and Howard Young's *Primer of Rational Counseling.*[7]

More specifically to help you overcome your anger and your low frustration tolerance, we recommend my own *Anger—How to Live With It and Without It,* and my and William Knaus's *Overcoming Procrastination,* Paul Hauck's *Overcoming Anger and Frustration,* Windy Dryden's *Dealing With Anger Problems: Rational-Emotive Therapeutic Interventions,* and William Knaus's *How to Get Out of a Rut.*[8]

All these books, and a good many other RET materials, are available at the Institute for Rational-Emotive Therapy in New York. If you write, the Institute will send you a free catalog of RET self-help items. Its address is listed in Appendix A. Materials orders: 1-800-323-IRET.

Specific RET writings showing you how to solve your addiction problems are now beginning to become popular and to prove helpful. These include Jack Trimpey's *Rational Recovery From Alcoholism: The Small Book;* Lois and Jack Trimpey's *Rational Recovery From Fatness: The Small Book; The Journal of Rational Recovery;* Paul J. Woods's *Controlling Your Smoking;* and Albert Ellis and others' *Rational-Emotive Therapy with Alcoholics and Substance Abusers.*[9]

After using RET books and pamphlets to help my clients improve, I (AE) in the early 1970s began to make recordings of some of my talks and workshops. I encouraged clients at the Institute's Psychological Clinic to listen to them repeatedly to supplement their therapy sessions. Again, with great success. Now the Institute distributes thousands of these RET recordings every year. Most of the Institute's clients as well as members of the general public find that if they listen to the RET recordings and think about the messages on them, they get considerable help with their emotional and addiction problems.

Some of the tapes that you can use with profit (and for fun) are my (AE) *I'd Like To Stop, But . . . ; Conquering Low Frustration Tolerance; Rational Living in an Irrational World; Unconditionally Accepting Yourself and Others; Conquering the Dire Need for Love*; William Knaus's *Overcoming Procrastination*; Leonor Lega's *Thinking and Drinking: An RET Approach to Staying Stopped*; and Emmett Velten's *How to Be Unhappy at Work*.[10]

Let us again encourage you: Listen to these tapes, if you will, for instruction, advice, and enjoyment. But take them seriously by thinking about, questioning, and challenging them. This will help you make their messages into thoughtful analyses of your own. Most miracle-promising, positive-thinking tapes will lead you up the garden path to nowhere. RET tapes try to teach you to think for yourself. Napoleon Hill exhorts his readers to think and grow rich. Try to use RET tapes to think and grow.

14

Teaching RET to Others (Twelfth-Stepping, RET Style)

John Dewey pointed out that we often learn a subject best by teaching it to others; and this is what we have found in RET, just as Bill W. and Dr. Bob found in AA. When you learn the fundamentals of Rational-Emotive Therapy, you can teach them to your friends and relatives who have their own addiction and emotional problems. By doing so, you can often help them become less disturbed. Then they can continue to use RET on their own or with the help of a therapist. Some of our own clients, we find, are so rational when they come to see us (after some of our other clients have briefed them on RET) that they require less time in therapy than other clients who were not previously introduced to this new kind of thinking and feeling.

Even if you fail to help your friends and associates to benefit from RET, you will, while making such an effort, often sink it better into your own head, heart, and habits. Thus, when you try to help others, you can considerably help yourself.

Modeling

As Albert Bandura and other psychologists have shown, you can learn good (and bad) behavior by modeling yourself after members of your family, friends, associates, and others.[1] So when you continuously associate with drinkers and drug users, you are likely to do what they do—drink and drug yourself into a stupor.

Obviously, you'd better pick different models! Drop your addicted friends and relatives, or at least see much less of them. Avoid drinking and drugging crowds.

Instead, cultivate sober, healthy friends—people who never had any interest in substance abuse or if they did, have recovered. The best models are people who have graduated not only from alcohol, but from the *identity* of "recovering substance abuser." That is, they no longer think of themselves in that light *at all*. The drawback to modeling yourself after such people's methods of becoming substance free is that they often have little recollection about how they recovered. Plus, they usually aren't interested anymore in that part of the past. It is a closed chapter of their lives.

Second best are people who are currently clean and sober and who attend Rational Recovery, Secular Organizations for Sobriety, Women For Sobriety, Men For Sobriety, or Alcoholics Anonymous meetings. If you attend these groups regularly, especially when you are in the early stages of recovery, you have a chance to expose yourself to and learn from good role models. But keep in mind that you are learning ideas to apply for yourself. You do not *need* a model to copy. Sometimes—often, in fact—that helps. But it is not *necessary*.

One reason for this is that people often do not really understand how they recovered. They may report, for instance, that they recovered because they went to ninety meetings in ninety days and got a sponsor. Going to meetings and getting a sponsor does not *make* you change, but may help you to use ideas *from* meetings to change yourself. Or you may have pushed yourself to change, and part of your change program was to attend ninety meetings in ninety days and to get a sponsor. Then, later, you "see" that the meetings and sponsor stopped you and cured you, but they didn't. You stopped you, *using them as tools.*

Make friends with other group members, particularly those who are doing a good job of nondrinking. Find people who, like yourself, once addicted themselves to alcohol, drugs, smoking, overeating, gambling, or any other harmful compulsion. Discover what they thought and did to give up their addictions. Keep in mind that people often reconstruct the past inaccurately. Sometimes they will miss the main point about how they stopped drinking. Ask them *how* they *decided* not to drink. Ask "*How* did you *change* your attitude toward drinking? What did you *tell yourself* all along the way to *keep* from drinking?"

If you cannot find a sensible self-help group in your community, locate a Rational-Emotive Therapist or a cognitive-behavioral therapist or therapy group. Join it and work with the other members to see what sensible, self-helping Beliefs are and how to actively find and follow them. Model yourself after therapy group members who keep working hard to overcome their emotional and behavioral problems. The Institute for Rational-Emotive Therapy has a referral list of therapists throughout the world who practice RET. You can get a copy by writing the Institute at the address listed in Appendix A.

Rational Recovery Systems now sponsors recovery meetings in many American cities. Its address is Box 800, Lotus, Cal. 95651, and its telephone number is (916) 621–4374. If there is no Rational Recovery group in your area, ask your therapist to consider forming one.

Problem-Solving

As you work and practice at catching, challenging, and changing your irrational Beliefs (iBs) and your self-defeating feelings and behaviors (Cs) that accompany them, go back to your A's—your negative Activating Events or Adversities. Plan and scheme to improve them. If your job, your education, your relationships, or other aspects of your life offer you less of what you want or more of what you don't want, assess them, see what you can do to improve them. Work out specific plans to change them and follow the RET objective of PYA (Push Your Ass!) to make those changes.

Life itself invariably—unless you are unique!—presents you with a long series of problems. Stop whining and screaming about them, stop demanding that they should not, must not exist for a special person such as you, and PYA to examine and solve them. If you don't know them already, read up on methods of time management, overcoming procrastination, and other ways of organizing your life and increasing your efficiency.[2] Construct a specific goal and plan how you want to improve things, and (again) use your head and PYA.

Acquire a Vital Absorbing Interest in Life

Does any kind of cognitive distraction do real good? Yes, probably one. The one that Robert A. Harper and I (AE) advocate in *A New Guide to Rational Living*—a vital, ongoing, absorbing interest. Many years before I became a therapist, I started to write a book entitled, *The Art of Never Making Yourself Desperately Unhappy*. In researching that book, I discovered that a good many people lead happy lives despite their disturbances. They select a vital absorbing interest in life, often at an early age, and enthusiastically pursue this interest for several decades. They work hard at their long-term goal; they devote themselves to it and enjoy it more than their other involvements. As psychologist Anne Roe also showed in a monograph on vocational goals, they often became outstanding achievers in their field.[3] Albert Einstein, for example, was supposed to have remarked after he became famous for his theory of relativity, "I wish most people would stop bothering me and leave me alone so that I can devote more time to my physics."

Why does a long-term vital absorbing interest help you to be content and productive? First, it makes most of your other hassles and problems seem insignificant. If you thoroughly devote yourself to building a business, developing an invention, writing the great American novel, or aiding a political or social cause, you can much more easily put up with minor life difficulties that you might otherwise awfulize and perhaps drive yourself to drink about—such as losing a friend's approval or failing at tennis.

Second, devoting yourself to a vital long-term interest gives you so much to do that you just don't have the time and energy to keep worrying about other trials and tribulations.

Third, and probably most important, choosing to absorb yourself in a major, ongoing project or cause gives you an important purpose or meaning in life. It will help organize and energize your existence for many years to come. Most people seem to lead happier, more exciting lives when they keep pursuing what they view as meaningful projects. If you choose and enthusiastically work for a purpose or big cause, you avoid much apathy and boredom.

Problem drinking itself *becomes* a vitally absorbing interest for millions of compulsive drinkers! What a waste! You can often replace your own destructive compulsions with a well-chosen positive addiction. Thus, you can devote yourself to achieving good physical and mental health; to helping other problem drinkers; to writing, painting, or another art; to some scientific area; to spreading the knowledge of RET self-help methods; or to almost any other goal you enjoy and that will fulfill you for a long time.

"Vital, absorbing interests" can be just about any kind of project. To choose and work at them does not require great financial resources. Take the example of Chris. A crisis unit referred Chris, a "medically indigent adult," to me (EV) after he had become depressed and suicidal because he lived on the street. He once had an adequate job in an X-rated movie theater, but became a dealer in speed and crack, staying one step ahead of the police. He also used speed, crack, and alcohol to the point that he had a very serious psychotic break. After hospitalization in California and later in another state, he was no longer psychotic. He hitchhiked back to San Francisco to reestablish himself, but was getting nowhere.

We focused strongly on practical coping measures Chris could use—step by step—to improve his lot. He took each step as a challenge instead of an awful, intolerable hurdle—and enjoyed the process. He would set goals for himself of figuring out which soup kitchens, for instance, had the most nutritious fare and how to shorten his waiting time in lines. He would figure out how to wake up on time for welfare or job appointments (though he had no alarm clock), take showers, and get his laundry done. After he obtained welfare benefits and temporary housing, he focused on obtaining employment. Chris remained vitally absorbed in making a better life for himself.

Can you turn a positive absorbing interest into a harmful obsession? Yes, you can—if you add a dogmatic must to it. You can, for instance, devoutly convince yourself, "I *must* be the greatest novelist who ever wrote, and *have to* devote all my time to writing!" By devising such a one-sided "positive" addiction, you may fashion a limited, desperate life that allows you few good alternatives.

So, again, be on guard. Any absolutist must—such as "I must under all conditions and at all times be rational!"—tends to make you compulsive and irrational. You can take even your "positive" addictions to self-defeating extremes. Extremism is often the core of disturbance. Beware!

Making a Profound Philosophical Change

Most psychotherapies, as we emphasize in this book, help you *feel better* but not get better. RET features inner growth, not patchwork self-fixing. It says, first, you mainly create your own disturbance, such as compulsive drinking. Second, you carry it on for much of your life and wrongly blame your past and your parents for making you disturbed. Third, you can just about always learn, by consistent work and practice, to undisturb yourself.

Fine. But RET also encourages you to make a *profound philosophic change* and arrive at what it calls the *elegant solution* to your thinking, emotional, and behavioral problems.[4] The elegant solution is an ideal that you may never fully achieve but can at least try to approach. It consists of:

- Reducing or eliminating your disturbed symptoms, such as compulsive drinking.

- Minimizing or eliminating your emotional problems about your symptoms (for example, severe anxiety about failure or disapproval).

- Minimizing your other emotional disturbance, such as rage at people who frustrate you.

- Becoming much less disturbable so that you rarely make yourself severely anxious, depressed, enraged, self-damning, or needlessly self-defeating again.

- Acknowledging, when and if you do upset yourself again, that *you* largely upset yourself and that you can quickly un-upset yourself again.

- Deciding and working to become less disturbable as the years go by.

Impossible? Almost. Utopian? Not entirely. By using RET strongly and consistently, you can approach this kind of profound philosophic change that will keep you largely, but not completely, undisturbable. Some important philosophies that you can teach yourself to do this include:

Acceptance of reality. As Reinhold Niebuhr said in the early part of the twentieth century, give yourself the stamina and courage to change what you can change, to accept what you cannot change, and the wisdom to know the difference. You can also try this Addictability Prayer: "Give me the stupidity to deny my addiction and to ignore its serious problems as I stubbornly demand immediate gratifications!"

Acceptance of human fallibility and imperfection. Accept the fact that all humans—including you—are fallible and imperfect. Too bad—but that's it!

Unconditional acceptance of yourself and others. Always accept yourself and others *whether or not* you and they perform well and whether or not you and they get approval and love. Measure and rate only people's *deeds* and *performances*—and not their *self, essence, or being.*

Acceptance of long-range rather than short-range pleasure-seeking. Try to gratify and enjoy yourself today *and* tomorrow, not merely with short-term gains (like drinking) that sabotage your future.

Acceptance of probability and uncertainty. Accept the likelihood that certainty does not exist, that all things change, and that you can live happily with the laws of probability and chance. The one guarantee that life gives you is that there seem to be no absolute guarantees other than death.

Accept your own and others' importance. Be quite self-interested and absorbed in your own goals, but also have a good deal of social interest.

Almost all humans choose to live in and enjoy the benefits of a social group. Therefore, if you needlessly harm others or your environment, you directly or indirectly sabotage yourself and your loved ones.

Accept the probability that no superhuman or supernatural being is going to stop you from drinking or solve your problems for you. You don't need God to do for you what you can do for yourself. Many phenomenal and strange things exist, but most likely no magic. Yes, zero magic. Not even RET is magical, but requires much hard work and practice.

Accept your own and others' mortality. As far as we know, all living things die. Maybe they some day won't. But don't count on it!

Will acceptance of these kinds of hard-headed, reality-oriented philosophies guarantee you a disturbance-free life? Certainly not. But, it will very likely increase your chances!

How to Get in Touch With Your Feelings . . . and Make Them Better!

Most therapies try to help people get in touch with their feelings. Part of the time this word does mean feelings, that is, emotions. Often, therapists and their clients mean "thoughts" when they say feelings. For instance, people will say, "I felt that it was a bad deal." They really mean, "I *thought* it meant this and then got myself upset over what I thought it meant."

Getting in touch with your feelings can be a good, initial goal if you do not know what your feelings are. Most of the time when you feel miserable, however, you are in plenty of contact with those feelings. When you have a drinking problem, you powerfully and rigidly hold on to your stinking thinking (irrational Beliefs) as well as to the self-defeating feelings and behaviors that they help create. At one and the same time you can easily have *weak* rational Beliefs and *very strong* irrational Beliefs. If so, you had better, says RET, not only actively and persistently Dispute your iBs, but also *forcefully and vigorously* do so. To acquire a rational Belief (rB), to retain it, and to have your feelings and actions eventually follow (or be automatically "conditioned" to) it (after a while), you'd better forcefully

see it, *believe* it, *feel* it, *accept* it, and start pushing yourself
to *act* on it. Strongly! Vigorously!

Remember, you may have practiced your harmful
self-defeating thoughts, feelings, and actions thousands of
times. You can (and do!) do it in your sleep. It's unrealistic
to think that an "insight" into the nature of your habits will
stop you from performing them.

Let's say you drive a car. By magic you are plunked
down in a foreign country where the positions of the gears
are different. To help you learn, you write down a diagram
of the new pattern of gears. After practice you would
become expert (again) at shifting. However, due to some
emergency you have to drive and shift fast before you get
to practice! Would you fall back on your old habit though
you knew that it would be bad for you and that the new
gear pattern would be good for you? Very likely, yes.

Take the example of Dwight. He had tired of AA, had
tried Secular Organizations for Sobriety (SOS), and was
mad at Women For Sobriety because they do not admit
men (there were no Men For Sobriety groups in his area).
He began to attend Rational Recovery meetings looking for
the right insight. As he explained, "When I get a good
grade in school, or get a date with a new woman, or win
some money in the lottery, I figure that I deserve a
reward. So I go to the store and get a couple of six-packs of
beer and drink them. The next morning I feel awful, and
then I absolutely promise myself never ever to do that
again!"

Dwight then went on to ask what RR would say about
why he drank the beer, after vowing not to do so again. He
was looking for an insight, but not just any insight. He
wanted, understandably, an insight that would stop his
self-defeating behavior.

To Dwight's surprise, the RR group focused on *how*
he decided to undo his promise to himself not to drink.
Dwight, of course, replied he didn't decide anything—it
just happened! The group then pointed out that he'd really

already said *how* he changed his decision, by saying something to himself like "I deserve a reward." "That's it?" he asked, disappointed.

When the group advisor (EV), the RR coordinator, and various participants suggested he could label his "I deserve a reward" thinking as "The Beast" (an RR term that dramatizes stinking thinking), and that he had better energetically practice Disputing the Beast, Dwight did not understand. He immediately went back to asking those present what they thought made him keep returning to drink although he knew it was self-defeating. He wanted an *idea* to stop him rather than to have to stop himself. He expected there to be a deep, dark, dramatic insight that would stop him. No such luck!

The whole history of Freudian therapy—from when Freud rode supreme in Vienna to when Bradshaw rides supreme on the Public Broadcasting System—shows this: *Insights* do not change you. *You* have to change you.

Take heed! You can lightly parrot rational material, such as "I know that drinking is very bad for me, and I am going to stop it." At the same time (or later) you can strongly and vigorously tell yourself, "I *need* a few drinks to calm down. I *can't stand* not having them. It would be *awful* if I didn't drink." Which one of these thoughts will usually win out?

RET provides you with a number of powerful emotive methods that will help you vigorously Dispute your stinking thinking and act against it.[1] Here are some of these methods:

Rational-Emotive Imagery

Maxie C. Maultsby, Jr., M.D., created rational-emotive imagery (REI) in 1971, and I (AE) modified it to make it more dramatic and powerful.[2] You can use REI as follows:

Close your eyes and imagine one of the worst—yes, worst—things you think might happen to you. For instance, maybe letting some "friends" talk you into having some drinks, getting intoxicated, acting outlandishly, and having everyone in the restaurant or bar laugh at you. Let yourself feel as bad as you can about this image. For example, feel self-downing, depressed, and ashamed. Get in touch with these disturbed feelings, really feel them, and make them as strong as possible.

After feeling your self-defeating pain for a minute, *work on yourself* and change your feelings. Make yourself feel, instead, *only* sorry, disappointed, and sad about your foolish behavior, but no longer self-downing, depressed, and ashamed. You can do this. Because you largely create your inappropriate feelings, you can almost invariably change them into appropriate ones. How? By changing your ideas.

Thus, when you are making yourself feel down, you may be *strongly* telling yourself something like "I did a stupid thing by allowing myself to get talked into drinking. How idiotic! What a weak and stupid person I am for doing this and acting so ridiculously. How shameful! I'll never be able to face these people again. Fool!"

Obviously, such stinking Beliefs will not help you lick your liquor problem and become a happier person. If anything, they will cripple you more. Of course, you'd better not feel indifferent about your crummy behavior. Feeling bad or sorry about it helps, because feeling bad can motivate you to change. But when you then say "my behavior equals me," you will feel bad about *you*. You may then conclude "*I'm* a nothing," "I never do anything right," "There's no use trying." All these are self-defeating, shame-creating Beliefs. This line of thinking will hardly encourage you to *study* and *target* your habits or to change those that hurt you.

To make yourself feel better about your *self*, but appropriately bad about your crummy *behaviors*, you can make yourself think "Yes, I did a stupid thing by drinking like that, but weak behavior never makes *me* a weak, stupid person. Yes, I behaved ridiculously, but I, a *total human*, am not ridiculous. People are laughing at my silly actions but may not be putting *me* down. Even if they are, I don't have to agree with them and put myself down. If they really think I'm a fool, instead of, as I choose to see it, a person who acted foolishly this time, that is their view. I refuse to see it that way. I fully intend to face them again, look them in the eye, admit to them that I acted foolishly, but not bow my head in shame. Too bad I did so poorly, but I can learn from my mistake and give myself a much better chance of not repeating it."

I (EV) worked with Rebecca, a thirty-eight-year-old architect, who had lived in California several years after having had a severe problem with alcohol and cocaine back east. After her father died and she was to come into a good deal of money, she was to go back east to deal with details of her father's estate. At A, the Activating Event or Adversity, she was to be back where she'd been a severe substance abuser, she would see her brother, with whom she had steadily been drunk, and she was to inherit a lot of money. Quite a high-risk situation.

Rebecca's instinctive approach, like most people's, was to "hope" she wouldn't see her brother and to ask her mother not to let any of her old cronies know she'd be there. Her fear was, of course, that temptation at A would lead to drinking and drugging (and blowing her money) at C.

In therapy Rebecca and I used REI this way: She imagined each of six or seven likely high-risk situations, such as having had a six-pack of beer and then having cocaine dealers directly approach her. In imagery, she would first see and feel herself being strongly tempted. Then she accepted herself with her temptation ("It's too bad I'm still weak, but that doesn't make me a bad person"). Then she imagined herself leaving the tempting situation after having firmly declined to drink and use drugs. We also did role-playing in which I played the cronies and she played her (new) part—someone who knew enough to pass up such bountiful opportunities to screw herself.

If you imagine one of the worst things happening, tell yourself rational coping statements after your images make you upset. Continue to make yourself feel appropriately sorry and frustrated instead of inappropriately panicked, depressed, and enraged. By doing so, Rational-Emotive Imagery (REI) will probably help you. If you do it about a "horrible" or "terrible" image, and repeat this for twenty or thirty days, you will soon train yourself to automatically feel *only* appropriately sorry, disappointed, and sad when you imagine yourself acting foolishly—or when you actually do foolish things. You can do the same thing with rage, low frustration tolerance, or other self-defeating emotions.

If, for example, you often enrage yourself at people who treat you badly or inconsiderately, you can vividly imagine them doing so. Let yourself feel enormously enraged for several seconds, but *then* make yourself only feel appropriately frustrated and displeased with what they are *doing*, but not infuriated at *them*. How can you change your feelings? By working on them and by telling yourself rational Beliefs, such as "I think they are acting very unfairly (though they may see it otherwise). Even if I am right and they are being quite unfair and unjust, that is their nature, to act that way right now. They have a right, as fallible human beings, to be wrong. So, though I dislike their behavior and will oppose it, I am not going to condemn *them* for doing it. It's too bad they are acting wrongly, but I shall try, without rage, to get them to change. If I succeed, great! But if I don't, maybe I can avoid them. Even if that is impossible, I can still *refuse* to enrage myself. I can still lead a reasonably happy life in spite of their unfair doings."

If you hate and condemn others for their crummy behavior, chances are you will eventually go back to hating yourself for *your* fallible, crummy behavior. So use

Rational-Emotive Imagery to overcome your enraged feelings.

Shame-Attacking Exercises

Shame, as such writers as John Bradshaw see so well, is a main contributor to overdrinking and other substance-abuse problems. We differ with Bradshaw, however, about where the shame comes from and how to rid yourself of it. He believes, as do a host of codependency and Adult Child therapists and Freudians, that your parents treated you crummily as a child and *that made you* the ashamed and disturbed person you are today. If you can just get the right insight about the past happenings and "get your feelings out" by emoting to high heaven about them, then, magic! All better. It sounds great, but in practice your whining and crying Inner Child voice gets louder, not softer, as you "champion" and coax the little bugger with teddy bears.

Soon after I (AE) first used the term Rational Therapy in January 1955 for the therapy I was developing, I realized what I had not seen before when I was a psychoanalyst for six years. Shame, humiliation, and embarrassment are the essence of much neurosis. For when you make yourself ashamed of doing something, and especially of others' knowing you do it, you usually tell yourself two things. The first may be very accurate and sane, but the second is quite nutty and self-sabotaging.

Thus:

1. *Rational Belief (rB)*. "I did something stupid or wrong and the people who know that I did it may put me down and think I'm no good for doing it. If so, that is sad and deplorable and I'd better stop doing this silly thing, make amends, and see that I don't repeat it. It's frustrating when I behave foolishly and others disapprove of me. However, it's not terrible, and I can get

by and probably do better next time with work and practice."

2. *Irrational Belief (iB)*. "Because I did something stupid or wrong and others may put me down for doing it, I'm a stupid, incompetent person. They're right in seeing me that way, as I'm sure they all do! I *must never* behave so poorly and get people's disapproval! I *can't stand* their thinking badly of me! It's *horrible* if they laugh at me! Then I'll be a nothing."

To use RET to overcome shame, embarrassment, and humiliation, first realize that you're acting badly *plus* defaming yourself *as a person* for acting that way and for possibly being looked down upon by others. If we assume that you would like to reach your goals, then to feel bad about your self-defeating *actions* is good. When you feel ashamed or humiliated, however, you usually overgeneralize and believe that *you* are no good, that everyone agrees that *you* are worthless, and that they are right about this. Shame or embarrassment, as Bradshaw sees, is usually *self*-downing. It is not merely the blaming of your *behavior*.

Delia made herself ashamed to eat with her friends because they spent a good deal of money on lunch and dinner and she could not afford to do so. Her "solutions": (*a*) Avoid eating with them even when she wanted to do so; (*b*) eat with them and spend money she could ill afford; (*c*) eat with them, pretend she had little appetite, and order very little.

Each of these "solutions" was foolish and anxiety-provoking for Delia. Each increased her feelings of shame instead of minimizing or eliminating them. Using RET, Delia was able to change her feelings of shame to appropriate feelings of sorrow and disappointment that she wasn't as well off as her friends were. She was then able to let them know that she rarely ate out because of the expense, that she would confine herself to having coffee and dessert, and that they should not feel unduly restricted when she ate with them.

To show people how to overcome their feelings of shame and replace them with feelings of sorrow and regret, I (AE) created my famous shame-attacking exercises in the 1960s.[3] If you repeatedly do some of these "shameful" behaviors, and refuse to down yourself when you do them, you reduce your tendency to feel ashamed of yourself when you make errors and show flaws. While you perform shame-attacking exercises, you convince yourself that you are never really a shameful person. At worst, you are *a person who* acted foolishly or ridiculously that time. Also, convince yourself that even when people criticize you for your "shameful" actions, you don't have to take them too seriously and you never have to put yourself down.

Doing shame-attacking exercises may help you immensely. To do one, you first select an act that you personally consider "shameful" or "embarrassing." Then you do it in public and risk the disapproval of those who see you do it. Don't pick anything that could harm anyone else—like denting someone's car in traffic. Don't do anything that would harm you, like getting arrested for going nude or telling off your boss and risking getting yourself fired. But do something harmless that you definitely consider stupid and "shameful." Then, while you do it, *work* at not feeling embarrassed or humiliated *even if* the people who observe you are sure you are a fool, an idiot, a nerd, or mentally ill.

The most famous and funniest shame-attacking exercises include:

Calling out stops on the bus, subway, or elevator (and not getting off).

Walking a banana.

Wearing odd, mismatched clothes.

Asking strangers for spare change "so I can buy some cheap wine."

Singing badly on the street.

Talking to yourself in public in a made-up foreign language.

Picking your nose in public.

Getting on a bus without proper change and asking some of the passengers to change a ten dollar bill.

Going into a hardware store and asking for a left-handed monkey wrench.

Reading a book or magazine upside down in public.

Standing on Broadway and asking people where Broadway is.

Going up to someone on the street and announcing that you were just released from the looney bin and asking what town you're in.

Asking in a pharmacy if they have any small condoms because the regular size ones are much too big for you (or your boyfriend).

We think you get the idea!

Do some of these "shameful" behaviors repeatedly, until you convince yourself that you are not a shameful person and until you no longer feel embarrassed for doing these "humiliating" things. Remember, shame-attacks are two-part exercises: One, you do the nutty behavior in public. But, two, you work on *refusing to rate yourself* because of your dumb behavior and people's likely putting you down when they see you do it.

In addition, you can do something practical that you would really like to do but feel ashamed to do, such as wearing an outfit you have in the closet for three years but that you find too garish to wear. Or refusing to tip a waiter who gives you bad service. Or returning an article you bought and then find is not suitable. Or asking an exceptionally good-looking or successful person for a date.

Sensitizing Techniques

The thought-stopping techniques described in chapter 9 rely on a mild form of aversive conditioning: the use of a mild punisher to terminate a response (your alcohol-related thoughts). But the punishers in this method are artificial because they are not images of real-life negative results stemming from alcohol abuse. You can, however, use images of real-life consequences in a variation on thought-stopping that we call sensitizing. It is far better to suffer poor results in your imagination than to suffer them for real!

Desensitizing is a technique that reduces anxieties by disconnecting them from your thoughts and images. Sensitizing, instead, *better* connects your anxiety and discomfort to thoughts and images that help drive you to seek and drink alcohol. You sensitize yourself by thinking of drinking and something unpleasant at the same time.

Therapists sometimes object that sensitizing consists of using "scare" tactics. It is really a way to teach yourself to think ahead easily and see bad consequences that you will likely bring about. You had better *sanely* be afraid of the poor results of some of your actions. Your *not* connecting drinking with its destructive outcome is often a hallmark of alcohol abuse. *Nonabusive* drinkers automatically think ahead to "What if I got drunk? Had an accident? Turned people off?" They *then* decide *not* to imbibe heavily. As an "alcoholic-in-training," however, you focus on *good* feelings and *relief* from bad feelings that drinking brings. You do *not* think about negatives, you brush off their possible occurrence or tell yourself "I don't care."

To use a sensitizing image to teach yourself appropriate fear, first imagine quite bad consequences of your stinking thinking that you might bring about in some real-life situation. For example, shut your eyes and see yourself at home, bored, and thinking "Maybe I'll go down to the bar and have just one. It's been several days. I think I can handle it." Then see yourself in jail with the door clanging shut behind you. Or see your mate leaving you because you got drunk again. Do this several times until you really feel appropriately fearful and motivated *not* to indulge your stinking thinking.

Gruesome? Yes. Torture? Well, maybe. But wouldn't it be nice *only* to go through it *in your mind* and not do so in real life? Think about it.

Also, forcefully show yourself the link between your thoughts about drinking and what later happens to you. For instance, "If I go to that party, I'll see people who are drinking heavily and I may drink. I may tie one on, easily get into a brawl, drive while intoxicated, and maybe kill myself and others."

Then vividly imagine some good things that will happen when you refuse to drink. Describe to yourself, aloud or silently, what you could actually do to cope with or avoid the drinking situation. For instance, imagine: "When John said there'd be a party, I knew there'd be tons of booze there, so I said, 'Thanks, but no thanks. I'm clean and sober and staying that way.' Then I called up my sober friend, Bob, and we went and shot some pool together and after that I went to a Rational Recovery meeting." You then visualize possible good results.

For instance, you can envision money saved, reestablishment of visitation rights with your children, getting your driver's license reinstated, or doing well at work. Let yourself feel happy at those possibilities. Forcefully tell yourself *out loud* the link between "no" and positive consequences. "If I say no, my anxiety will go down and I will save money." Or "If I stop drinking, I can have a much better social life."

Forceful Coping Self-Statements

You have probably practiced your irrational Beliefs and stinking thinking thousands of times. So don't be surprised if you use regular coping self-statements (chapter 12) and they don't seem to be convincing. Try doing them more forcefully. If you do them with power and energy, you give them a chance to catch up with your irrational, stinking thinking. Practically pound them into your head and heart and habits.[4] You can, for instance, very vigorously tell yourself, either aloud or in your head, some of the following sayings and slogans from Rational-Emotive Therapy (RET):

"I do *not* need a drink to be able to face people at a party! If I die of anxiety, I die!"

"I do *not* deserve a six-pack as a reward! It would be a *punishment*, not a reward!"

"I *never, never* need what I want. I *only, only, only* prefer it! And I *can* take the frustration of not getting what I want."

"People often *will* treat me quite badly and un-fairly. So they will! I usually cannot change this, but I *can and will* gracefully lump it."

"There is no shithood without *shouldhood*."

"I'd like *very much* to be loved by the person I love the most. But there is no reason he has to love me. I can definitely be happy even if that *never* happens."

"No one *makes* me angry but myself, and I *can* stop angering myself even though I have a hard time doing so!"

"Yes, my life is hard and may become even harder. *Tough!* I *can* stand these hassles, and I *will* cope better with them without alcohol!"

"Musturbation leads to self-abuse!"

You also can use some slogans and mottos of Women For Sobriety, Secular Organizations for Sobriety, Rational Recovery, AA, and Narcotics Anonymous. For example:

"Make plans, but don't plan the results!"

"One day at a time."

"Live and let live."

"Easy does it."

"I have complete voluntary control over my mouth and hands."

"I have a problem that once had me."

Again, tell yourself these coping self-statements many times, and forcefully, until you really believe them. Do not rely on insight. People are perpetually surprised that insights don't work to make them better. This encourages them to think they need *deeper and better* insights. What they need is *work and practice* in carrying out the insights.

Sometimes say your forceful coping statements in front of a mirror and do them with strong accompanying gestures. Think about them while strongly saying them, and prove to yourself that they are really correct and helpful. Sometimes you can put them on a cassette tape and listen to them repeatedly. If you have a therapist or friend who knows RET, let her or him listen to your coping self-statements to make sure that they are realistic and strong.

Tom was a forty-five-year-old restaurant worker who kept berating himself for being angry at work and ruining most of his jobs. I (AE) and his therapy group found that he kept resisting our RET view that he was not a bad person even when he did bad things. As a homework assignment that we suggested to him, he stood in front of a mirror several times a day and practically shouted at himself, "Look, I don't give a damn how badly I screwed up and fought with my boss last week. I'm not a shit! I can't *be* a shit. No matter what I do, I can fully accept myself, yes, *with* my stupid hostility. I am okay just because I decide to be okay. Damn it, I really am all right, no matter what crap I still believe and stupidly act on!"

For possibly the first time in his forty-five years, Tom began thoroughly accepting himself despite his distinct failings. He made a dramatic change during the next few weeks. At last report, three years after stopping therapy, he is still unusually self-accepting and rarely makes himself depressed and angry. In addition, he reports a much better relationship with his boyfriend.

Forceful Self-Dialogues

Take a cassette recorder and tape one of your main irrational Beliefs (iBs), such as "If the people who are important disapprove of me and criticize me, I am worthless. They make me angry with them for being so critical." Listen to this iB that you have recorded and then, on the same tape, powerfully Dispute it. For example, "*Why must* I have their approval? Is it *awful, horrible, and terrible* if I don't? Do I *have* to feel worthless if important people disapprove of me and criticize me? Do they really *make* me angry with them for being so critical?"

Effective New Philosophy: "No, they may criticize what I do, but they may well not be putting *me* down or damning *me* for doing it. Even *if* they are wrongly putting me down, and not merely my behavior, I never have to go along with them and damn myself. They may be criticizing me unfairly, but they can't get into my gut and make me angry. Only *I* can do that. So I had better stop taking them too seriously and stop foolishly angering myself about what they seem to be doing. I dislike their *criticism*, but I don't have to hate *them*! Besides, I'm not exactly perfect. Maybe I can learn something from their feedback."

When you do this kind of forceful self-dialogue on tape and listen to it to see how accurate, powerful, and convincing it is, let your friends or your therapist listen to it, too. In that way they can judge how strong and convincing it seems. If you find that your recorded Disputation is too weak or unconvincing, do it over until you (and others who listen to it) find it sufficiently powerful. The real proof is in your results. Did you change your thinking and feeling habits? You had better practice your Disputing and Effective New Philosophies until you truly believe them and start to act on them. If you lightly believe them you have so-called intellectual insight. Only when you strongly believe them will you begin to show "emotional insight."[5]

How do you know you show emotional insight? Simple. You behave differently in the face of the same old A (Activating Event, Adversity). So Dispute strongly—and convincingly. Do it and do it and do it, until you really believe and feel your Effective New Philosophies. And *act* on them!

Role-Playing

You can often use role-playing to overcome your tendencies toward problem drinking and the stinking thinking (irrational Beliefs) that usually promote problem drinking. Thus, if you are afraid that you will succumb to drinking when people at a party offer you a drink, you can practice your responses ahead of time. You can have someone play the role of the persuader and you play the role of the resister. You can then tape this role-playing, or have friends observe it, to see how well you resist the persuader. If you do a poor job of resisting, you can repeat the role-playing until you start doing much better at refusing to drink. Thus, you can practice being straightforward and saying, "No, thank you," or "No, thank you, I don't drink."

If you become anxious, angry, or otherwise upset during the role-playing, you can use RET to discover exactly what you are telling yourself to make yourself disturbed. Then you can practice effective Disputes of the irrational Beliefs with which you are upsetting yourself. It is useful to play the "worst-case scenarios" rather than to hope they don't occur. For instance, your persuader in a role play says, "Can't you handle even one drink? Look, let's face it. You're just a weakling who can't even take a single drink and stop right there." If you feel anxious and worthless when he says this, you can stop the role play, and look at what you are thinking to feel anxious and worthless.[6] Show yourself that you are not "a weakling," that refusing a drink is a strong act, and that even if you sometimes behave weakly, you are never a worthless person.

Using Figures of Speech

Using dramatic metaphors, analogies, and other figures of speech can help sink rational Beliefs into your head, heart, and habit system. Thus, when you rationally tell yourself "Drinking is just not for me, no matter how much other people may harmlessly enjoy it," you can picture yourself as a stalwart oak that bends only slightly in the wind while the thinner trees around it move easily in the same wind but eventually bend and crack and are often uprooted. Or, when you *irrationally* tell yourself "I can drink just as much as anyone can and not do myself any harm," you can picture yourself as a lamb who is pretending to be a lion, and who, while frolicking around with the lions, gets eaten alive.

Use any dramatic metaphors, analogies, fables, and stories that you can to encourage your rational thinking and appropriate feelings. Doing so will tend to discourage your irrational philosophies and inappropriate emotions and may help you give up your problem drinking and maintain your sobriety.[7]

Using Humor

When you disturb yourself before, during, and after drinking, you usually lose your sense of humor and take things to ridiculous extremes. But at that time you don't see it that way. Thus, you tell yourself "If I even *smell* beer, I'd *have to* have one, and if I have a single drop, I'll end up on skid row. My only hope is to stay as far from beer as possible!" If you really think about this extreme Belief, you can easily see that it is ridiculous. But you don't bother to analyze and review it, so you unhumorously believe it.

Stinking thinking and irrational Beliefs thrive on your taking them with deadly seriousness. Poking fun at them will often remove much of their power to influence you. To Dispute and dismantle your irrational Beliefs (iBs), you can often effectively use humor. You can take your iBs to ridiculous extremes, reduce them to absurdity, make jokes about them, refer to them wittily, highlight their contradictions, and in many other ways emphasize their humorous side.[8]

Thus, Sharon, a school nurse, told herself "If I even *look* at a bottle of whisky, the mere sight of it will make me think of drinking. If I have a single thought about drinking, I'm doomed to become a drunk for the rest of my life! My resistance to alcohol is so low that even if I were putting rubbing alcohol on a child's cut, I would shove the child away and pour the rest of the bottle down my gullet until I die gagging on it!" This wildly exaggerated image amused Sharon and helped her see she did have voluntary control of her hands and her mouth.

You could, for instance, imagine that someone was following you around with a gun, forced you to take one drink out of a full whiskey bottle, and then told you he would shoot one of your toes off each time thereafter that you took another drink from the bottle. Would you or would you not be able to control yourself? Or let's say you were drinking out of an open container while driving and the highway patrol happened to pull into view. You, of course, would immediately put the container out of sight. Let's say that for the next several hours the patrol car was next to you, in front of you, or behind you in traffic. Would you or would you *not* control yourself? Would you or would you not pull out the beer and take a swig with the highway patrol in plain view? The answer is obvious. Which means: Your "I can't help myself" whinings are pretty funny. You'd better laugh them out of your life.

I (EV) saw a very bright, well-educated clergyman in therapy for a severe drinking problem. He reported he had stopped drinking after several emergency room trips for alcohol-related problems. After that, he went to Alcoholics Anonymous and was told he could never *ever* have any mood-altering chemicals (cigarettes and coffee were exceptions!). He found the idea depressing that his identity in life forevermore would be "alcoholic." He obsessed about this issue. While discussing another problem at a later session, he mentioned that he regularly partook of communion wine in performing daily services! It did not "disinhibit" him. However, in mentioning the communion wine, he made no connection with his worry about being "an" alcoholic who would instantly lose control. When I pointed it out, he laughed, and after that essentially dropped his worry about "being" an "alcoholic." Nor did he begin to drink again. He really had little interest in it.

Rational Humorous Songs

RET uses rational humorous songs to help people see how they foolishly and needlessly upset themselves. You can sing some of these songs to yourself or with other people to help overcome your drinking related problems.

These songs work very well at public gatherings, such as workshops. They could spice up Rational Recovery, Secular Organizations for Sobriety, Women For Sobriety, Men For Sobriety, or even extremely sober Alcoholics Anonymous meetings! Many of them, set to popular tunes, are available from the Institute for Rational-Emotive Therapy on cassette and in a book of sheet music. Here, for example, are some that you can try alone or at meetings.

Drinking, I'm Always Thinking of You
(Tune: "Margie"
by Con Conrad and J. Russell Robinson)

Drinking, I'm always thinking of you!
Drinking, I'll tell the world I love you!
Don't forget your promise to me—
I can drink and never sink beyond the brink!
Oh, drinking, with you to sweetly guide me,
  I am never blue!
After all is said and done,
There is really only one—
Oh, stinking drinking, it's you!

Beautiful Drinking
(Tune: "Beautiful Dreamer" by Stephen Foster)

Beautiful drinking, why should we part,
When we have shared our whole lives from the start?
We are so used to going in hock,
Oh, what a crime it would be to detox!
Beautiful drinking, don't go away!
Who will befriend me, if you don't stay?
Though you still make me look like a jerk,
Living without you would take too much work!
Living without you would take too much work!

Whine, Whine, Whine!
(Also known as, Wine, Wine, Wine!)
(Tune: "Yale Whiffenpoof Song"
by Guy Scull [a Harvard man])

I cannot have all of my wishes filled,
Whine, whine, wine!
I cannot have every frustration stilled,
Whine, wine, wine!
Life really owes me the things that I miss,
Fate has to grant me eternal bliss,
And since I must settle for less than this,
Wine, wine, wine!

Stink, Think, Drink
(Tune: "The Band Played On"
by Charles B. Ward)

When anything slightly goes wrong with my life,
I just stink, think, drink!
Whenever I'm stricken with chickenshit strife,
I fall off the brink!
When life isn't fated to be consecrated
I can't tolerate it at all!
When anything slightly goes wrong I just sink
Into drink, drink, drink!

Drinking Is the Thing for Me!
(Tune: "Yankee Doodle")

Drinking is the thing for me!
With its stinking thinking,
I can feel alive and free
When I'm really drinking!
Drinking, drinking, keep it up!
With the booze be handy!
Keep pretending, yup, yup, yup,
That I'm fine and dandy!

When I'm acting like a fool
And my ways are shitty,
Drinking makes me feel real cool
And immensely witty!
Drinking, drinking, keep it up!
With the booze be handy!
Keep pretending, yup, yup, yup,
That I'm fine and dandy!

You for Me and Me for Beer
(Tune: "Tea for Two"
by Vincent Youmans)

Picture you upon my knee,
Just you for me, and me for beer!
And then you'll see
How happy I will be, dear!
Though you beseech me
You never will reach me—
For I am autistic
As any real mystic!
And only relate to
Myself with a full six-pack, dear!
If you dare to try to care
You'll see my caring will soon wear,
For I can't pair and make our sharing fair!
If you want a family,
We'll both agree you'll enable me—
Then you'll see how happy I will be!

I Wish I Were Recovered!
(Tune: "Dixie" by Dan Emmet)

Oh, I wish I were not codependent!
Not at meetings without ending!
Oh, how great to be rated innately sedate!
But as an Adult Child I'm fated

To be rather aberrated—
Oh, how sad to be mad as my mom and my dad!

Oh, I wish I were not crazy! Hooray, hooray!
I wish my mind were less inclined
To be the kind that's hazy!
I could agree to really be less crazy.
But I, alas, am just too goddamned lazy!

Maybe I'll Move My Ass
(Tune: "After the Ball"
by Charles K. Harris)

After you make things easy,
And you provide the grass.
After you squeeze and please me,
Maybe I'll move my ass!
Make my life nice and breezy,
And serve me glass by glass!
And, possibly, if things are easy,
I'll move my ass!

Perfect Rationality
(Tune: "Funiculi Funicula" by Luigi Denza)

Some think the world must have a right direction,
And so do I! And so do I!
Some think that with the slightest imperfection,
They can't get by— and so do I!
For I, I have to prove I'm superhuman,
And better far, than people are!
To show I have miraculous acumen—
And always rate, among the Great!

Perfect, perfect rationality!!
Is, of course, the only thing for me!
How can I ever think of being if I must live fallibly?
Rationality must be a perfect thing for me!

(Song lyrics by Albert Ellis, copyright 1977 to 1992 by the Institute for Rational-Emotive Therapy)

Role Reversal Disputing

If you hold on vigorously to your nutty, self-sabotaging ideas and have trouble giving them up, you can try the RET method of role reversal disputing. To do this, you get a friend, relative, or therapist to play your role and to hold firmly to one of your irrational Beliefs (iBs), such as "I *can't stand* bad feelings. I can't function *at all* if I'm anxious. Whenever I am *in any way* anxious, I *have to* have a drink to calm me down. Any bit of anxiety throws me into a dither, and I *have to* quickly drown it in alcohol!"

Let your friend, relative, or therapist strongly uphold this self-defeating view while you keep trying to talk him or her out of it. No matter how you argue against it, the person playing you refuses to budge and acknowledge the error of his or her ways. This kind of reverse role-playing gives you a good opportunity to vigorously try to talk the other person—yourself—out of the self-defeating hogwash that you yourself often rigidly hold.[9]

Tina, for example, once had a major drinking problem, and she was terrified of going back to drinking and ruining her relationship with her lover, Dan, who had left her when she was drinking and only took her back when she quit and solemnly promised never to take another drop. She knew if she felt any kind of upset—anxiety, depression, or rage—she would think she *had* to have a drink. So she got her best friend to role-play herself and *insist* that she absolutely *couldn't stand* any stress and would *have to* drink if she got "stressed out."

"Let's face it," said her friend in the role-play, "I can't possibly stay away from boozing it up if Dan doesn't love me and I feel anxious about his leaving me. Yes, I know that that's Catch 22. Because, if I feel anxious about losing his love and I *do* drink to calm myself down, he will see that I'm drinking and will leave me. So, if I drink I'll lose him, and I can't stand that. But if I *don't* drink, I'll be so anxious about his still not loving me that I'll show him how needy I am. Then he won't love me because of my neediness and insecurity. So, drinking or sober, I can't win!"

Tina had to keep vigorously trying to talk her friend (and thereby herself) out of the bind and was able to show her several important things: (*a*) Even if she were anxious and depressed, she didn't have to dissolve temporarily her upsetness in alcohol. (*b*) Instead, she could tolerate her disturbed feelings and for the moment live with them. (*c*) She could then undo her upsetness by seeing what she was believing—her iBs—to create it. (*d*) She could then tackle these iBs and give them up. In particular she could tackle the ideas that she had to have Dan love her and that she became an unworthy person who could never be happy if Dan failed to love her.

How to Use RET's
Behavioral Methods

When I (AE) started practicing Rational-Emotive Therapy (RET) in January 1955, it was the pioneering cognitive-behavioral therapy. I derived much of its theory from philosophers—especially from Buddha, Epictetus, Marcus Aurelius, Baruch Spinoza, John Dewey, and Bertrand Russell. However, I derived a good deal of its practice from John B. Watson, Knight Dunlap, B. F. Skinner, and other early behaviorists. From the start, RET has always encouraged people to make a basic philosophic change and to engage in habit-breaking homework assignments.

This is certainly the case with overdrinkers, who have not only "emotional" but also distinct behavioral problems. Thus, if you compulsively drink, eat, or smoke or have addicted yourself to some other substance or activity, you engage in stinking thinking and *act* self-defeatingly. You can therefore change your thinking from "I *must* have a drink when I feel anxious or depressed" to "I'd *like* to drink when I feel anxious or depressed. But I don't have to *have* a drink, and it would be much better if I didn't." However, if you change your thinking, you may still have a strong, almost automatic *habit* of drinking heavily when you feel miserable.

What can you do to tackle this? As several philosophers and early behaviorists saw, and as RET reaffirms, you had better *forcefully* Dispute your pro-drinking irrational Beliefs (iBs) and self-defeating behaviors. Then, you had better act consistently against them. First, you repetitively and vigorously change your stinking thinking. At the same time, you had better also make yourself stop drinking and start breaking habits that often precede your decisions to drink.

The proof, obviously, is in your results. Nobody really gets over the neurotic fear of, say, riding in elevators unless they keep—keep—pushing themselves and their asses into many elevators. No one. Similarly, no one stops drinking until he or she stops and keeps steadily stopping. Are we exaggerating? Can you recall anyone you ever met who didn't have to refuse alcohol many times before remaining truly abstinent?

Back to RET Insight No. 3: There is no way but work and practice—work and practice—to recover from problem drinking. Certain insights can be helpful. Thinking against stinking thoughts is great. Feeling against it is marvelous. *Acting* against it is still necessary.[1] So let us, in this chapter, show you how to use some of the best behavioral methods in RET. These methods teach you how to overcome your self-defeating drinking and the serious emotional problems that usually, though not always, lead to and accompany it.

Toughening Yourself Up

People often do themselves in by training themselves to be too sensitive to stresses and then to always avoid these stresses. Avoidance works at first, but soon it does more harm than good. Thus, if you are nervous talking to strangers, you may feel better at first by avoiding them or by having a few drinks when you can't avoid them. If, however, you keep shunning them or drowning your anxiety in booze, you may well create an overwhelming phobia or a drinking problem. If you continue to pander to your fears by avoiding strangers, you may even go beyond this. You may make yourself phobic of everyone, including relatives and friends.

Behaviorists and behavior therapists, like John B. Watson, Ivan Pavlov, B. F. Skinner, H. J. Eysenck, and Joseph Wolpe, developed methods of deconditioning people's fears.[2] RET, which always includes behavioral, emotive, and cognitive techniques, specializes in exposure methods. To use these methods, you forcefully act against your irrational fears.

Suppose, for example, you are afraid to talk to people at a social gathering because you might say something stupid or show them how anxious you are. You therefore avoid such gatherings. Or when you do go, you immediately bolt down a few drinks to make yourself relax and cover up your anxiety. You can first use Wolpe's technique of slow exposure (slowly toughening yourself up) by imagining yourself talking to critical people at a party a month from now. You let yourself feel panicked as you visualize walking over to speak to someone. You then use a relaxation method (such as Edmund Jacobson's progressive relaxation technique), to calm yourself down. You keep imagining yourself getting closer and closer to the date of the party, and each time you feel anxious about this, you again relax.

If you keep making yourself anxious and relaxed, anxious and relaxed, over and over again, you will be able to desensitize yourself to anxiety-provoking images. This procedure often carries over quite well to the real-life situation. You find, for instance, that you are no longer so sensitive and panicky when at social gatherings.

Instead of Wolpe's slow-exposure method, you can use a specific RET version. First, you imagine a "horrifying" situation, such as handing in an important report to the director of your organization and being severely criticized for its inadequacy. This leads to your having a strong urge to drink to steady your nerves. Second, let yourself feel very anxious and depressed. Third, strongly tell yourself some rational coping statements, such as "Maybe it really was an inadequate report but that doesn't make me an incompetent person. If I can learn by mistakes and do better next time, great! Even if the director hates me and fires me, that's really unfortunate, but I can still accept myself and lead a decent life." Fourth, you continue to imagine the worst and make yourself feel only sorry and disappointed, not anxious or depressed. You repeat this procedure until you finally lose your panic and your urge to drink.

Some ancient philosophers—Gautama Buddha, Demosthenes, Epictetus—discovered that if you force yourself, however uncomfortably, to counteract your phobias and do what you are terrified of doing, you will often overcome your irrational fears. You will become comfortable and finally may even enjoy the actions you agonizingly avoided.[3]

I (AE), for example, panicked myself during all of my childhood and adolescence about the thought and act of public speaking. When I deliberately forced myself, at the age of nineteen, to speak and speak and speak in front of groups, I completely overcame my fear of doing so. To my surprise, I also started to enjoy public speaking and now look forward eagerly to giving talks and workshops. Where I once felt horror about appearing before ten or twenty people, I now feel disappointed if only a few hundred show up!

You can use the RET method of imagined exposure, but as several studies have shown, real-life exposure is even better and is therefore often used in RET. You may succeed in imagining yourself calmly facing a feared audience or an authority figure and desensitize yourself in your head to such "terror." However, only when you can face and undergo the "terrible" situation in real life and get yourself used to it can you be reasonably sure that you have conquered your panic. So we often recommend toughening yourself up in the real-life situation.

If you fear social gatherings, as described above, you can unlearn your fear as follows:

Actually force yourself, yes, force yourself, to go to social gatherings that you dread attending.

Acknowledge, before attending such an affair, that yes, you may speak badly to others and may show them how anxious you are.

Then strongly, very strongly, keep convincing yourself that if this happens, you can handle it. You can refuse to severely upset yourself about it.

Rehearse what you can do to cope if the worst thing happens at the affair. For example, you can plod on although you are speaking badly. You can tell yourself "It's only anxiety. It won't kill me, and if it does, then I won't be anxious any longer. At first my anxiety may be high, but if I face it and just focus on being interested in other people rather than thinking of me, me, me, me, the anxiety will lessen."

Rehearse in advance some Effective New Philosophies to believe in case you do fail at the affair. Such as "Too bad I was anxious and didn't socialize well. But if I keep trying, I can definitely overcome my anxiety and do better. Even if I am never great at socializing, I can still enjoy social gatherings, refuse to put myself down, and lead a good life."

Keep going to a good many social gatherings, toughening yourself up, and working on your

rational coping self-statements until you really
see and feel that such events are not terrifying
and can even be enjoyable.

Plunge Into It

RET attempts to be efficient as well as effective. It
favors techniques that, if successful, will uproot disturbances as soon as possible. When many decades ago I (AE)
overcame my enormous fears of public speaking and of
talking to women in whom I was interested, I made a vital
discovery. I found that if I forced myself *repeatedly* to do
the things I was afraid of, I much more rapidly, easily, and
completely overcame my fears than if I gradually and
slowly acted against them.

I have also found the same thing with my individual
and group therapy clients at the Psychological Clinic of the
Institute for Rational-Emotive Therapy in New York. The
more often and the more vigorously they plunge into doing
their panic-attacking real-life homework, the quicker and
better they overcome their neurotic fears.

So if you want to get over your horror of socializing, of
craving, of criticism, of public speaking, or almost any
other activity, try to arrange to do the thing you fear
vigorously and many times in a row. Simultaneously convince yourself that doing it is not really dangerous, won't
destroy you, is merely uncomfortable, and won't show that
you are an RP (Rotten Person). Stay with the uncomfortable feelings until you feel distinctly better. If you often
keep forcing yourself to face "terrible" activities, while
strongly convincing yourself that it is only uncomfortable
and not "awful" to do so, you will be surprised how many
"horrendous" irrational fears you can conquer.

Tolerating Discomfort While Anti-Awfulizing

Millions of people, including large numbers of "alcoholics," run away from uncomfortable situations by drink-

ing their cares away rather than by coping. You may leave a good job because you are nervous around your customers or angry with your boss. You may resort to three-martini lunches to stop your panic about the project you have to tackle that afternoon. Or you may be depressed about a class you are taking, angry that you have to study when "everybody else" is playing, and say, "To hell with it." Then you may drink a couple of glasses of wine to "relax" and "reward" yourself for your "horrendous" labors. Then you may quit school rather than work on your depression and get through the course and finish your degree. Or you may feel so anxious about a relationship that is going badly that to quell your terror you take to drinking and push your partner into leaving the relationship. In cases like these, RET encourages you to stay in the difficult situation, not to cop out, to work on your emotional problems, and only *later* decide whether you had better leave the problem situation.[4]

Tony enraged himself about the behavior of his boss and his roommate. As he saw it, they were both treating him "most unfairly" regarding his duties at work and household duties at home. He made himself so angry that he decided that he couldn't stand it any longer and was going to move to another city and rid himself completely of both these "bastards." Tony agreed with his therapy group that he would put off moving for at least three months. During this time he would work on his problem of enraging himself against people like his boss and his roommate. His group thought that if he left town he would merely take his tendency to infuriate himself to a new boss and new roommate. Tony admitted that he well might do so.

So we worked on Tony's rage for several weeks, until he convinced himself that his boss *should* treat him badly because he usually did act unfairly. Further, he convinced himself that his roommate *should* unjustly give him all the responsibility for cleaning and fixing up their apartment because this man felt very depressed and was unable to deal fairly with their living situation. Once Tony accepted—without at all liking—these two grim realities, he rid himself of his rage and saw that his job and his living arrangements had more advantages than disadvantages. He then had no trouble staying with the job and asserting himself with his roommate.

Can you think of a situation that you are avoiding? If so, whenever you are in that "awful" situation and are upsetting yourself greatly about it, stay with it, at least temporarily. Stay with it until you make yourself appropriately sorry and displeased, but not horrified and incensed, about it. When you have removed your needless horror and your undue anguish, decide whether it is wise for you to leave. Then, possibly, leave the situation. This is especially important, naturally, when you are about to drink and cop out on facing difficult conditions. Stay with the situation, vigorously use RET to un-upset yourself about it, work on the low frustration tolerance that can drive you to drink, refuse to have a single drop, and *then* decide what to do about the problem.

Using Reinforcements

People obviously use alcohol because they find drinking pleasurable and reinforcing. A few drinks—or more!—may make you feel good, give you a buzz, increase your confidence, make you more convivial, sedate your anxiety, and cause other "great" results. Quickly and magically! No sweat!

Such chemical reinforcement, even when it creates later grim results, is very hard to forgo. Humans pretty obviously are geared, through evolution, to like to avoid negative or dangerous situations. Therefore, substance abuse—and other addictions—can easily become habitual. Unless, that is, as millions of people have found, you use other powerful reinforcers to help break your overdrinking habits. Thus, there are many, naturally occurring instances when addicts gave up alcohol—or cigarettes, overeating, or gambling— mainly because their employer, family, or potential spouse said they had to, "or else."

People change their behavior to get less pain and more enjoyment. This is the natural way. You can use this fact to design some self-help interventions. Specifically, allow yourself some valued pleasures or reinforcements only *after* you have significantly cut down or entirely stopped your drinking. And, often, get your relatives, friends, partners, and others to help with this by monitoring you to see that you really stick with it. For it's fine to *say* you will do something enjoyable only after you stop drinking. Unless you reinforce that resolve, your marvelous resolution will often get you nowhere. Nowhere but where you already are.[5]

Sandy had one hell of a time stopping drinking even though she kept losing one good job after another by getting soused and by not showing up for the next few days. Her doctor's warnings about her sadly deteriorated liver also didn't help keep her off her daily diet of four or five bloody Marys. Sandy and I (AE) were hard put to find reinforcers that would help her become abstinent, but we finally worked one out. Sandy was attached to and practically lived with her eighty-year-old grandfather. He had almost singlehandedly raised her when her father deserted the family. Her mother, who had lived with her and her grandfather, worked during the day and drank herself into oblivion almost every night.

Sandy's grandfather was now in a nursing home, had lung cancer, and was given only six months to a year to live. Her greatest pleasure was to visit him every Sunday. She would take him some of the comforts that made his life easier and talk with him about the wonderful times they had had together during her childhood and teens. Sandy and I agreed that she would only allow herself these visits if she had no drinks from Monday to Saturday, and, at most, one glass of wine with her grandfather when she visited

him on Sunday. For eight months, until her grandfather
died, Sandy was able to keep up this program; she got used
to it and saw such good results that after his death she still
drank nothing during the week and occasionally, on a
Sunday, she would have a glass of wine.

Sandy's plan worked so well that I have recommended a similar one to several other heavy drinkers. By
depriving themselves of alcohol and other chemicals, they
have then, and only then, allowed themselves to have
love, friendship, or sexual relations with partners for whom
they very much care. This kind of reinforcement program
is no panacea for all drinking problems. But it often helps.

Other self-rewards for not drinking or for doing your
RET homework are also often effective. Letting yourself,
for instance—after you work at your goals—watch TV,
read, listen to music, take a shower, or take vacations.

Using Penalties

It is great when reinforcements work to help people
overcome their substance abuse problems, but don't count
on it. Many heavy drinkers and other addicts are quite
unreinforceable—*except* with the alcohol or other drugs
they want. Fine whiskey or cocaine is so exciting and
satisfying to them that no other pleasures can replace it. If
that sounds like you, consider using stiff penalties instead
of—or besides—reinforcements.

Suppose, for instance, you knew that every time you
took a drink you would hit your thumb hard with a ham-
mer? Or that you would have sex with someone you hated?
Or that you would burn your paycheck? Or that you would
sleep all night in a bedbug-infested bed?

If you really knew that you would experience these
kinds of penalties every time you had a drink, would you
still indulge? And for how long?

So give this matter some serious thought. If you want
to give up practically any addiction, set yourself a stiff—a

very stiff—penalty every time you slip and indulge in it and see what happens. Providing of course, that you really steadily enact this penalty.

In case you shirk on your agreement with yourself and do not enforce the penalty after you've set it and then "earned" it, enlist the aid of a confederate. The confederate will be a friend or someone else who can monitor you and help you enforce the penalty. For instance, let's say that you give a hundred dollars in cash to the friend. Your friend would then mail it to an organization you hate as a penalty when he or she found you not doing what you had agreed to do. This is easier to do in situations, such as weight loss, where there is a clear measure of progress (or lack of progress). Be creative and you can figure out a way. The guidelines are: Clearly define what your assignment is, and give yourself a stiff penalty as soon as possible after you fail to carry it out.[6]

Let us say that you have been "trying" to work on your taxes. You have an extension from the IRS, but still are goofing off. You could arrange with your confederate to send in, say, a $100 *donation* to the IRS if you do not show her or him, by a certain date, that you have done and mailed in your taxes. What does this have to do with alcohol? Well, many people, while avoiding something stressful such as doing their taxes, drink. They then "reason" that having had a couple of drinks, they can't work on the taxes. The alcohol supports the goofing off and reduces anxiety about getting poor results. Such drinkers cleverly blame the drink for their delays and for other problems they experience. The real culprit is their stinking thinking.

Suppose you keep drinking up all your money. You arrange to show a friend a deposit slip showing that you put an agreed-upon amount of money in the bank each month. If you cannot do so because of your drinking sprees, your friend burns a sum of money you have left with him or her or sends it to a group you oppose, such as the KKK or American Nazi party. In our therapy with substance abusers, we have had pacifist clients whose self-imposed penalty was to send money to the National Rifle Association! And gay and lesbian clients whose self-imposed penalty was to send money to the Senator Jesse Helms reelection campaign! And right-wing clients whose penalty was to donate to liberal causes.

If you really want to change your behavior and you have been what we call in RET a Difficult Customer—a DC—dream up a real lulu of a penalty! You may not give up drinking by looking at the later penalties—such as ill health and job loss—you will probably suffer from your abusing alcohol, but you can still give yourself present, immediate, stiff penalties every time you drink.

In RET, giving yourself penalties does not mean punishing or damning yourself. As we noted previously, you can criticize what you *do* but had better not castigate your *self* for your foolish behavior. So penalize your *acts* at times, but without damning your personhood. And you can reward yourself, too, for improvements without falsely thinking "I'm a great person because I've improved." Remember, you can use both methods—penalties and rewards—and derive double benefits.

Using Willpower

You might think we would put the use of willpower under the heading of thinking or emotive techniques of RET. However, we see it more properly as a behavioral method even though it includes powerful cognitive and emotive elements. Willpower, as the history of addiction and "alcoholism" clearly shows, frequently doesn't work. Millions of substance abusers vow that they will stop drinking and drugging, do stop for a short while, and then return to their ruinous behavior. Because they don't realize (or want to realize) that they have *many* decisions to make before they succeed at their willing. The "will" in willpower is like signing a contract. It says what you will do. It doesn't make you do it. That takes effort and power.

RET-oriented willpower is different from, and works better than, the usual ineffective kind of willing yourself to stop drinking. RET defines willpower as consisting of several important steps:

You firmly decide to do something or to stop doing something—for example, you decide to stop drinking.

You work at making yourself strongly determined to carry out—that is, to *act* on—your decision. Thus, you strongly decide to *push yourself* to stop drinking.

You fully realize that you will most probably have a difficult time following out your decision and your determination. So you accept this difficulty and push on in spite of it.

You look for your irrational Beliefs (iBs) that lie behind your resistance to changing. Typical iBs that block change are "I must change beautifully and perfectly or else I am an inadequate, weak person!" and "I must easily and effortlessly change!" Forcefully Dispute and act against these iBs.

You keep working and practicing to act, act, act on your decision to change. For you fully realize that the power in your "willpower" is not merely your decision and determination to change. It is your steady, persistent *action* to implement your decision. Willpower equals your clear-cut decision and determination to change *plus* your acceptance of the pain of changing *plus* your action to implement change. Without discomfort and action, you may have strong *will*, but no real *power*.

You steadily persist in your decision, your determination, and your action to change your addicted behavior and to keep it changed. You therefore keep working at stopping, stopping, stopping, and staying stopped.

You finally—perhaps!—become a habitual stable, easy nondrinker. You rarely plague yourself about your drinking problem even though you may never completely lose some desire to drink. When, occasionally, your urge to drink again returns, you're able to ward it off without too much trouble. If you indulge again, you deplore your misbehavior, but you accept *yourself* with this indulgence and then return to abstinence and noncompulsion again.

From the above outline, you can see that RET-oriented "willpower" entails a set of procedures that go far beyond your mere will or decision to change and that involve several RET methods. We have taught it to our addicted clients for many years. Though it is hardly a panacea for all self-defeating compulsions, it can lead to willpowerful results.

17

Relapse Prevention: Getting to Recovery, Staying There, and Moving On

Mark Twain's famous remark, "It's easy to quit smoking—I've done it a thousand times," hits home with most would-be ex-addicts. Quitting *is* easy—compared to staying quit. Twain could have been talking about drinking and drug problems, obesity and weight loss, gambling, you name it. For every hundred people who progress in self-help or therapy, many fall back and do so repeatedly. But you don't have to be among that number!

Sometimes, when you work at erasing your emotional misery, you take two steps forward—and one back. Sometimes you completely free yourself of addiction. Then you fall right back. At times, you never experience an old problem, such as a fear of public speaking. But then you bring on an entirely new one, such as a fear of job hunting.

You can use many of the powerful techniques we have described in this book to reduce your chances of slipping back into drinking. You also can use the same techniques to reduce your chances of giving yourself new kinds of problems. But before reviewing this material as it applies to preventing relapses, let's look at how to think about the whole issue of relapses. And how to think about *yourself* if you relapse.

AA and RET both teach that recovery is a lifelong process. Their reasons differ, however, as do their definitions of recovery. The twelve-step theory says you have a Disease and if you drink one drop, you're a goner. Therefore, you can never recover. RET, on the other hand, says you *can* recover from substance abuse—after all, millions of people have done so. *But you can never recover from being human!*

And human equals fallible. Human equals being prone to think "I *must* have what I want." Human equals being prone to think "I *deserve* what I want." Human equals easily convincing oneself (against the evidence) "Yes, I *can* have harmful things I want and not suffer this time." This is no Disease. It's *human nature*.

Very few if any people completely and forever free themselves of human nature, and their leanings toward "messing up." Including you! Rather than upset yourself and catastrophize about your human failings, you can work constructively on them.

The tendency towards addictions stems from the natural human inclination to want to feel good and to reduce discomfort. This tendency is life-preserving. If food and drink didn't taste good, sex didn't feel good, and getting bitten by a saber-toothed tiger didn't feel bad, the human race would have died out ages ago! However, once you escalate your wants and desires into demands and musts, you get into trouble. In addiction, you demand good feelings and insist that the consequences be damned! You demand immediate relief and don't think about or care about the long-term ill effects of alcohol and other noxious substances.

RET holds that humans are born with these leanings towards irrational, self-defeating thinking, feelings, and actions. But humans also are born with leanings toward rational, self-creating thinking, feelings, and actions. Thus, you have a talent for creating problems for yourself and for returning to old problems after you have worked to overcome them.

But you also have a talent for learning to rise above your limitations—your surroundings, parents, family, and past history. You have a talent for changing and transforming yourself. Your ability to grow and transform yourself and your life is easily hampered by adopting *any* rigid ideas about yourself. This includes the label "I'm in recovery." RET agrees with AA that it is far better to call "alcoholism" a Disease than to call it a moral wrong.

However, "I am an alcoholic" identifies your behavior, not a Disease. If you believe you "have" the Disease, it makes the "Disease" into a lifelong deadly opponent that can only be beaten by holding on with white knuckles "one day at a time" and "one meeting a day" for the rest of the one life you'll have. This way of looking at your drinking problems hampers your natural growth and graduation from them.

We think it's more useful to say:

1. You have the ability and power to change your thinking, behavior, and feelings.

2. You may have inborn tendencies toward many, if not most, of the emotional problems you actively, if unthinkingly, work hard to develop.

3. Substance-abuse problems are just one category of difficulties you may give yourself. They are not special. And you are not special and different because you have given yourself such problems. You are just human.

4. No matter where your leanings toward substance abuse came from and what contributed to them, you

yourself are now responsible for your feelings and actions.

5. Endless search for the early examples and roots of your self-destructive behavior gives away your power and can become a cop-out. Because it implies that externals, not you, are responsible for your stinking thinking and problem drinking.

6. Your past, current, and future self-sabotaging is largely your doing. It's a product of your way of looking at yourself, others, and life.

7. You can accept responsibility for your past, present, and future poor behavior *without* putting yourself down and blaming yourself.

8. When you *do* defeat yourself, the root of it usually is your devout Belief in a *must*.

9. Your musts are about yourself, others, and life conditions.

10. When you Believe that you *must, should, ought*, and *have to* succeed at anything, including abstinence, rationality, or rational self-help, you set yourself up. When you Believe you *must, should, ought*, and *have to* gain approval from anyone, including your parents, your peers, your recovery group, your therapist, you set yourself up. Why? Because—being human—you *will* often fail and very often get rejected.

11. *Then* you will put yourself down and feel guilty, depressed, and ashamed. You will deny your responsibility for your behavior. You will defensively blame others and external conditions for your feelings and actions. You will fail to work on and solve your problems. And you will avoid trying new activities that you predict you won't be great at.

12. Worse yet, when you keep musturbating, you continue to drink or drug. Or you easily resume drinking and drugging after having quit. The alcohol and the drugs do deaden pain, give positive feelings, and create many distractions to keep your mind off your feelings of worthlessness. But they lead to huge problems.

You may for a while find it easy to change your feelings. But you'd better keep working to maintain your gains. What can you do to maintain and enhance the self-help gains you have made?

You first can make yourself aware of—and laugh at—some of the myths about maintaining your progress and preventing relapse.

Perhaps the most common myth is that being "normal," that is, not addicted, will result in—at the very least—ecstasy! Even if you know being normal is not ecstasy, it is easy to demand that normal not be the crummy way you may often feel without alcohol. For if you are like most of us, you easily—and sometimes rapidly—forget how bad the "alcoholism" itself caused you to feel.

What you may easily recall is the genuinely pleasurable feelings the alcohol or drugs gave you. You may magnify these feelings and convince yourself that your good feelings were in the majority, when the truth is that they became a very small minority. You may also tell yourself that feeling normal is completely boring and intolerable. You may convince yourself that the hassles and negatives of everyday life are *awful*. You may convince yourself that normal negative feelings are far worse than the "minor" problems you might have suffered from your addiction. With myths like these, you convince yourself that pure, cold logic compels you to resume drinking and drugging!

What is the antidote to this all-too-human way of thinking? One effective antidote is to review your shitlist we discussed in chapter 11. Go over it in gruesome detail. Imagine in depth and detail exactly what some of the items *felt* like. Do this kind of review regularly.

Another antidote is to make a pie chart representing "drinking" or "using drugs." Yes, one segment is the pleasure and relief they give you. The other slices are the many gruesome, miserable, painful results and lost opportunities due to "drinking" and "drug use." As you look at the crummy slices of the pie, remember what they *felt* like.

Yet another antidote—after you review the shitlist and make a pie chart—is to look at the practical problems you face. What are you telling yourself to musturbate and awfulize about those problems? What are you telling yourself that stops you from working toward solutions? What could you *do* to work constructively toward solutions?

Another myth is that *drinking and drug use* lead to relapse. The truth is that the drinking and drug use themselves are mere icing on the cake. By the time you raise the bottle to your lips or stick the needle in your arm, you have gone through a whole process of goofing off in your efforts toward sobriety and gone back to indulging your stinking thinking.

A related myth is that slips and relapses "just happen." It may seem like they "just happen," but it will only seem that way if you have been steadily ignoring the danger signals and refusing to take preventive action. The truth is that slips and relapses are quite predictable.

How do you predict them? Simple. You watch for the same old stinking thinking and actions that was "you" back in the bad old, good old days. You look for the addictive attitudes you exercised the many times you went right back to drinking and the many times you fought off those who tried to stop you.

Yet another common myth about slips and relapses is that they prove you are not motivated and "don't care."

The idea is that *if* you cared, you obviously wouldn't drink or drug again. We disagree. You can care, but you can still fail to let go of the hope that "this time" you can drink or use drugs and not suffer ill effects. Relapses may only prove that you let up in your efforts before you were firmly set in a new orbit and a new way of life. Like a rocket bound for a new planet, you blast yourself away from the Planet Alcohol. However, you may cut your engines before you are beyond the pull of gravity. You begin to coast. And where do you coast? Downward. Back to where you've already been and don't want to go again.

What can you do, then, to maintain your improvement and to deal with backsliding? Try these ideas and methods:

1. Review your Daily Journal and summarize what you have learned about yourself. Especially look at the very earliest entries in your journal. Force yourself to remember and recognize the stinking thinking, the settings, and the feelings that went with addiction. What are the situations— times, places, people—in which you are prone to decide to drink? What are the feelings and moods that prompt you to drink? And, most important, what are the thoughts and decisions you use to get yourself to drink?

2. Summarize what you have learned about all those factors. Remind yourself of stinking thinking, feelings, and behaviors that you have changed and that you have helped yourself by changing.

3. Keep up a schedule of rational self-help. Continue to schedule appointments with yourself. Reduce their frequency, but don't phase them out until you have been in recovery for a long time.

4. Review your Daily Journal, RET Self-Help Reports, Activity and Reward Schedules, and other forms and homework sheets. Work on them systematically.

5. Review your shitlist. Again.

6. Do a double-column every day. Look back at all your old rationalizations and stinking thinking. Then forcefully Dispute it and talk back to it.

7. Continue to work on making yourself less sensitive to triggers by developing coping skills and alternative actions, by toughening yourself up, and by focusing on the poor results you'll get if you "go with" impulses prompted by triggers.

8. Go to Rational Recovery, Women For Sobriety, Men For Sobriety, Secular Organizations for Sobriety, or Alcoholics Anonymous meetings for one year after you have achieved Sobriety As You Understand It.

9. Limit yourself to one or two meetings a week. Assuming you some day want to leave behind the world of "alcoholism" and addiction *and* the world of recovery meetings, it is important not to addict yourself to meetings. Meetings are just a tool. When you have built what you need with the tool, you lay it down and do other things.

10. Identify and work on catching, challenging, and changing your stinking thinking and irrational Beliefs. One of the all-time stinking thoughts is that a slip or a single lapse *leads to* and *equals* a full relapse: "One drink, one drunk." If you believe so, you can make it a self-fulfilling prophecy. The same thing happens if you believe you are a hopeless loser when you violate your vows of abstinence. How do losers act? Do they try to learn from their mistakes? Usually not. Do they study and combat the stinking thinking that led to the lapse? No. They give up.

11. When you fall back to alcohol-promoting feelings of anxiety, depression, or self-downing, zero in on the exact thoughts, feelings, and behaviors you use to

create these disturbances and that you once changed to make yourself improve. If you again feel depressed, think back to how you previously used RET to make yourself undepressed. For example, you may remember that: (*a*) You stopped telling yourself that you were worthless and that you couldn't ever succeed in getting what you wanted; (*b*) You did well in a job and proved to yourself that you did have some ability to succeed. (*c*) You forced yourself to go to job interviews instead of avoiding them and thereby overcame your anxiety about them.

12. Keep thinking, thinking, and thinking rational Beliefs (rBs) or coping statements, such as "It's great to succeed, but I can fully accept myself as a person and enjoy life considerably even when I fail!" "It would be great to feel no pain, but the best way to have the least pain in life is for me to be willing to forgo short-term pleasures, like drinking alcohol."

    Don't merely parrot these statements but carefully think them through many times. Yes, strongly think them through until you really begin to believe and feel that they are true.

13. Keep looking for, discovering, and Disputing the stinking thinking and irrational Beliefs (iBs) with which you are once again upsetting yourself. Take each important irrational Belief, such as "I *have to* succeed in order to be a worthwhile person!" Keep asking yourself. "Why is this Belief false?" "Where is the evidence that my worth as a person depends on my succeeding?" "In what way would I be a *complete loser* if I failed at an important task?"

    Keep forcefully Disputing your irrational Beliefs whenever you see that you are letting them creep back again. And even when you are not bothering yourself, realize that you *may* bring them back. So ask yourself in advance what you think they are, make yourself fully conscious of them, and vigorously Dispute them.

14. Keep taking risks and doing things that you irrationally fear. Some of these risks include foregoing short-range pleasures, asking for dates, starting conversations, job hunting, socializing, or trying new activities. As you are overcoming one of your irrational fears, keep thinking and acting against it on a regular basis. Do what you are afraid to do, and do it very often!

    If you feel uncomfortable when you force yourself to do things you irrationally fear, to hell with the discomfort! Don't allow yourself to cop out and thereby preserve your fears forever! Often, make yourself as uncomfortable as you can be, in order to erase your fears and to become unanxious and comfortable later.

15. When you get deprived, learn to clearly see the difference between *appropriate* bad feelings, such as those of sorrow, regret, and frustration, and *inappropriate* bad feelings, such as those of depression, anxiety, self-hatred, and self-pity. Whenever you feel overconcerned (panicked) or *needlessly* miserable (depressed), admit that you are having a very common but an unhealthy feeling and that you are bringing it on yourself with some dogmatic *shoulds, oughts*, or *musts*. See Appendix B for information about the twelve negative emotions—six helpful and six unhelpful ones.

    Realize that you are quite capable of changing your inappropriate (or musturbatory) feelings back into appropriate (or preferred) ones. Get in touch with your depressed feelings and work on them until you only feel sorry and regretful. Get in touch with your anxious feelings and work on them until you only feel concerned and vigilant.

16. Use Rational-Emotive Imagery to vividly imagine unpleasant Activating Events even before they happen. Let yourself feel *inappropriately* upset (anxious, depressed, enraged, or self-downing) as you imagine them. Then work on your feelings to change them to *appropriate* negative emotions (concern, sorrow, annoyance, or regret) as you keep imagining some of the worst things happening. Don't give up until you actually do change your feelings.

17. Avoid procrastination. Do unpleasant tasks *today!* Do them *before* pleasant tasks. If you still procrastinate, reward yourself with certain things that you enjoy—for example, eating, vacationing, reading, and socializing—*after* you have performed the tasks that you easily avoid. If this won't work, give yourself a severe penalty—such as talking to a boring person for two hours or burning a hundred dollar bill—every time you procrastinate.

18. Make an absorbing challenge and an adventure out of maintaining your emotional health and keeping yourself reasonably happy even if misfortunes assail you. Make the removal of your misery one of the most important things in your life—something you are utterly determined to achieve. Fully admit that you always have some choice about how to think, feel, and behave. Throw yourself actively into making that choice for yourself.

19. Remember—and use—the three main insights of RET that were first outlined in AE's *Reason and Emotion in Psychotherapy* in 1962:

Insight No. 1: You largely *choose* to disturb yourself about the "upsetting" events of your life. You mainly feel the way you think. When obnoxious and frustrating things happen to you at point A (Activating Events), you consciously or unconsciously select rational Beliefs (rBs) that lead you to feel sad, regretful, annoyed, or frustrated. But you also *select* irrational Beliefs (iBs) that lead you to feel anxious, depressed, hostile, and self-hating.

Insight No. 2: No matter how or when you acquired your irrational Beliefs and habits, you now, in the present, *choose* to maintain them. That is why you are now disturbed. Poor conditions (in the past and present) *affect* you. They do *help* you carry out decisions to drink. But they don't disturb you. Your present philosophy creates your present disturbance.

Insight No. 3: There is no magical way for you to change your personality and your strong tendencies to upset yourself, drink too much, and indulge your addictions. You truly change with WORK AND PRACTICE. *Your* work and *your* practice.

20. Keep looking steadily but unfrantically for personal pleasures and enjoyments, such as reading, entertainment, sports, hobbies, art, science, and other vital absorbing interests. Make your major life goal the achievement of emotional health and also that of long-term enjoyment, not the short-term "enjoyment" afforded by alcohol.

    Involve yourself in a long-term purpose, goal, meaning, or interest in which you can remain truly absorbed. Make yourself a good, happy life by giving yourself something to live for. In that way you will distract yourself from serious woes and help preserve your mental health.

21. Keep in touch with several other people who know something about RET and who can help review it with you. Tell them about your problems and let them know how you are using RET to overcome

them. See if they agree with your solutions and can suggest additional RET methods to work against your irrational Beliefs. Visit a Rational Recovery group periodically. Better, set one up and rotate with others as the RR group Coordinator. This will help you keep rational thinking in the forefront of your mind.

22. Practice using RET with some of your friends and associates who will let you try to help them with it. The more often you use it with others, and try to talk them out of their self-defeating ideas, the more you will understand the main principles of RET and be able to use them with yourself. When you see other people irrational and upset, try to figure out—with or without talking to them about it—their main irrational Beliefs and how these can be actively and vigorously Disputed. This, again, gives you practice in working on your own stinking thinking.

23. Keep reading RET writings and listening to RET audio and video cassettes. Read and listen to several of these—particularly my (AE's) books: *How to Stubbornly Refuse to Make Yourself Miserable About Anything—Yes, Anything!*; *Why Am I Always Broke? (How to Be Sane About Money)* (with Patricia A. Hunter); *A Guide to Personal Happiness* (with Irving Becker); *A New Guide to Rational Living* (with Robert A. Harper); and *Overcoming Procrastination* (with William Knaus); as well as Paul Hauck's *Overcoming Depression*; and Howard Young's *Rational Counseling Primer.*[1]

In addition, listen and relisten to rational tapes, including my (AE's) *I'd Like to Stop, But . . . Overcoming Addiction*; *Conquering Low Frustration Tolerance*; *Overcoming the Dire Need for Love*; *How to Refuse to Be Angry, Vindictive, and Unforgiving*; and Emmett Velten's *How to Be Unhappy at Work.*[2]

Keep going back to this RET material, to remind yourself of some of the main Rational-Emotive ideas.

24. Keep observing and acknowledging your backsliding at RET or at anything else. Keep noticing how often and how nicely you let yourself strive for some kind of immediate gratification rather than for long-range gain and happiness. Stubbornly refuse to put yourself down for your low frustration tolerance. Then keep working to eliminate it. With actual addictive, compulsive, and indulgent behaviors, force yourself many times to stop them. And when you later fall back—as you often may—to indulging in them again, force yourself, no matter how hard it is, to give them up again.

25. Because most harmful habits give you some kind of quick pleasure or payoff, use the principles of reward and reinforcement to help you give them up. When you reinforce yourself for having chosen not to drink, you can pick some action or behavior that is very pleasurable, and preferably even more pleasurable than the habit you are trying to give up. Then you may allow yourself this pleasure only *after* you have refused to indulge in the habit you are trying to break.

    Stiff penalties work even better, if you use them properly. As you obviously feel real pain or discomfort when you are trying to break a bad habit, pick something even *more* uncomfortable. Make yourself do that thing whenever you refuse to give up your harmful habit or whenever you temporarily give it up and then fall back to it again.

    Use the principles of immediate reinforcement and quick (and inevitable!) penalties on every occasion when you indulge in bad habits or fail to engage in good habits (like exercising or doing at least an hour's work on a paper you are writing). This won't absolutely make you give up your low frustration tolerance and your tendency to indulge yourself in pernicious behavior. But it will definitely help!

If You Backslide, Try, Try Again!

When you improve your *emotional disturbances, it will be a miracle if you never backslide.* When you *do, back to the RET drawing board.* Try, try again!

1. Accept your backsliding as normal—as something that happens to almost everyone who is learning to act and feel better. See backsliding as part of your being a fallible human being.

   Don't damn yourself when some of your old problems return. You don't have to handle them entirely by yourself. It isn't wrong or weak if you seek help from others.

2. When you backslide, look at your self-defeating behavior as unfortunate. Work very hard at refusing to put yourself down for engaging in this behavior. Gather your thoughts. Then use the highly important RET philosophy of refusing to rate *you, yourself,* or your *being* and measure only your *acts, deeds, and traits.*

   Remember to think of yourself as a *person who* may act well or badly—but never as a *good person* or a *bad person.* No matter how badly you may fall back and upset yourself again, you can always accept yourself with or without this self-defeating behavior. Then keep right on working to change this behavior.

3. Go back to the ABCs of RET and see what you did to fall back into your old anxiety or depression. At A (Activating Event) you probably experienced some failure or rejection once again. At rB (rational Belief) you probably told yourself that you didn't like failing and didn't want to be rejected. If you only stayed with these rational Beliefs, you would merely feel sorry, regretful, disappointed, or frustrated.

But when you felt depressed again, you probably then went on to irrational Beliefs (iBs), such as "I must not fail! It's *horrible* when I do!" "I *have to* be accepted, because if I'm not accepted, that makes me an *unlovable, worthless person!*" Then, after convincing yourself of these iBs, you felt, at C (emotional Consequence), once again depressed and self-downing.

4. When you find irrational Beliefs with which you are once again disturbing yourself, immediately and *persistently* use Disputing (D). Thus, you can ask yourself, "Why *must* I not fail? Is it really *horrible* if I do?"

   And you can answer: "There is no reason why I must not fail, though I can think of several reasons why it would be highly undesirable. It's not horrible if I do fail—only quite inconvenient."

   You can also Dispute your other irrational Beliefs by asking yourself, "Where is it written that I *have* to gain acceptance? How do I become an *unlovable, worthless person* if I am rejected?" And you can answer: "I never *have to* be accepted, though I would very much prefer to be. If I am rejected, that makes me, alas, a *person who* is rejected this time. But it hardly makes me an *unlovable, worthless person* who will always be rejected by anyone for whom I really care."

5. Keep looking for and vigorously Disputing your irrational Beliefs. Keep doing this, over and over, until you build emotional muscle. Yes, you exercise your mind to build *emotional* muscle just the way you would build *physical* muscle by exercising your body.

6. Don't fool yourself into believing that by merely changing your language you will always change your thinking. You may neurotically tell yourself "I must succeed and be approved," and then you may sanely change this to "I *prefer* to succeed and be approved."

However, you may still believe "But I really *have to* do well and truly *must* be loved."

Before you stop your Disputing and before you are satisfied with your rational answers, keep on working until you are really *convinced* of these rational answers and until your anxiety, depression, and rage truly decline. Then do the same thing many times, strongly and vigorously—until your Effective New Philosophy becomes firm. It almost always will, if you keep reworking and repeating it.

Thus, you can powerfully convince yourself, until you really feel it: "I do not need what I want! I never *have* to succeed, no matter how greatly I *wish to* do so!" "I *can* stand being rejected by someone I care for. It won't kill me—and I *still* can lead a happy life!" "No person is damnable and worthless—including and especially me!"

Graduation Day

We believe that most people who reach genuine recovery drop the whole idea of "alcoholism," drug abuse, addiction, *and* recovery. They move into a different identity. They no longer say, "I'm in recovery." If they say anything about it, they say, "I'm *recovered*." They have left that whole identity behind. They have better things to do than talk about the past and go to meetings.

Yes, they have not recovered from being human. We wouldn't want them to. They have not recovered from being fallible. They couldn't no matter how long they tried. They *could* (if they chose) reinvent their past substance abuse, but that is not their interest any more. They have no interest in Diseases, controlled drinking, or in any of the other ideas that would show they are stuck in the past. They are busy living, growing, enjoying, and giving meaning to their lives.

Notes

Chapter 1: How Do You Know When Alcohol Is a Problem?

1. Centers for Disease Control, 1988. The last year for which complete figures are available is 1988. Alcohol caused 125,000 deaths in the U.S. that year. In combination with other drugs, it caused 4,000 additional deaths. Tobacco, however, killed 471,175 Americans in 1988. Heroin and other opiates caused 4,000 deaths. (This figure does not include AIDS-related deaths). And cocaine—at the height of the crack epidemic in 1988—caused only 2,000 deaths.

2. Bernard, 1986, 1991; Dryden & DiGiuseppe, 1990; Dryden & Gordon, 1991; Ellis, 1957, 1962, 1971a, 1973, 1988a, 1991; Ellis & Becker, 1982; Ellis & Bernard, 1985; Ellis & Dryden, 1987, 1990, 1991; Ellis & Harper, 1961, 1975; Ellis, McInerney, DiGiuseppe, & Yeager, 1988; Grieger & Boyd, 1980; Walen, DiGiuseppe, & Wessler, 1980; Wessler & Wessler, 1980.

Chapter 2: How Do I Know When My Drinking Is a Problem?

1. Critchlow, 1984.

2. Peele & Brodsky, with Arnold, 1991; Critchlow, 1984.

3. Critchlow, 1984; Dobash & Dobash, 1979; Gelles, 1972; Wilson, 1957, 1985; (No author listed) Pass it on: Bill Wilson and the A.A. message, 1984.

4. Peele & Brodsky, with Arnold, 1991.

5. Fillmore, 1975; Fingarette, 1988; Peele, 1987, 1989; Temple & Fillmore, 1986.

6. Korzybski, 1933.

7. WFS: Women For Sobriety, Box 618, Quakertown, PA 18915; 215-536-8026; 1-800-333-1606. This is a non-twelve-step, woman-positive recovery organization.

8. Marlatt & Gordon, 1985.

9. Ellis, 1962, 1963 (reprinted and revised, 1985), 1972, 1976; Miller, T., 1986.

10. Peele & Brodsky, with Arnold, 1991; Trimpey, J., 1989; Trimpey, J., Velten, & Dain, 1992.

Chapter 3: Denial

1. Bufe, 1991; Wilson, 1957, 1985; (No author listed), *Pass it on: Bill Wilson and the AA message*, 1984.

2. Bufe, 1991; Wilson, 1957, 1985; (No author listed), *Pass it on: Bill Wilson and the AA message*, 1984.

3. Peele & Brodsky, with Arnold, 1991; Trimpey, J., 1989.

4. Beattie, 1987; Bradshaw, 1990.

5. Ellis, 1957, 1977a, 1977b, 1979, 1980, 1986, 1988a, 1988b, 1990, 1991d, 1991f, 1992; Ellis & Dryden, 1987; Ellis & Dryden, 1990; Ellis & Harper, 1961; Ellis & Harper, 1975; Ellis & Hunter, 1991; Ellis, Sichel, Yeager, DiMattia, & DiGiuseppe, 1989; Hauck, 1972; Huber & Baruth, 1989.

6. Lester, 1988.

7. Nagoshi & Wilson, 1987; Peele, 1989.

8. Ellis, 1975.

9. Nagoshi & Wilson, 1987.

Chapter 4: Alcohol and Drugs Addicted Me

1. Korzybski, 1933.

2. Hauck, 1991.

Chapter 5: Why Do People Drink Too Much and Addict Themselves? & What Does It Take to Change?

1. Siegel, 1989.

2. RR: *Rational Recovery Systems*, Box 800, Lotus, CA 95651; 916-621-4374; SOS: *Secular Organizations for Sobriety* (also known as Save Our Selves), Box 5, Buffalo, NY 14215-0005; 716-834-2922. WFS: *Women For Sobriety*, Box 618, Quakertown, PA 18915; 215-536-8026; 1-800-333-1606. MFS: *Men For Sobriety*, same address and telephone number as WFS.

Chapter 6: But Therapy Doesn't Work!

1. Kurtz, 1988; Pittman, 1988; Robertson, 1988.

2. WFS: *Women For Sobriety*, Box 618, Quakertown, PA

18915; 215-536-8026; 1-800-333-1606; Christopher, 1988, 1989; Trimpey, J., 1989; Trimpey, L. & Trimpey, J., 1990.

3. Ellis, 1989b.

4. Ellis, 1971b (revised and reprinted, 1974).

5. De Angelis, 1991; Marlatt, Demming, & Reid, 1973; Marlatt & Rohsenow, 1980; Merry, 1966; Langenbucher & Nathan, 1983.

Chapter 7: What Are Your Self-Help Goals? How Will You Reach Them?

1. Wilson, 1957, 1985.

2. Miller & Munoz, 1982; Pace, with Cross, 1984; Peele, 1984; Vogler & Bartz, 1982.

3. Ellis, McInerney, DiGiuseppe, & Yeager, 1988; Trimpey, 1989; Woods, 1990.

4. Trimpey, 1989; Trimpey, L. & Trimpey, J., 1990.

Chapter 8: (no notes)

Chapter 9: How To Stop Self-Defeating Bs (Stinking Thinking)

1. Ellis & Schoenfeld, 1990; Peele & Brodsky, with Arnold, 1991; Trimpey, J., Velten, & Dain, 1992.

2. Cohen, Liebson, Fallace, & Speers, 1971; Cohen, Liebson, Fallace, & Allen, 1971; Heather & Robertson, 1981; Mello & Mendelson, 1972; Mendelson, 1964; Gottheil, Alterman, Skoloda, & Murphy, 1973; Miller, P. 1976.

3. Barlow & Craske, 1989; Warren & Zgourides, 1991; Wolpe, 1982.

Chapter 10: How To Dispute and Really Change Your Stinking Thinking

1. Bernard, 1991; Ellis, 1957, 1962, 1971b, 1983b, 1988a, 1990f, 1991g; Ellis & Dryden, 1987, 1990, 1991; Ellis & Whiteley, 1979.

2. Bernard, 1986; 1991; Dryden, 1990b; Dryden & Gordon, 1991; Ellis, 1962, 1978, 1979a, 1979c, 1980a, 1985b, 1988a; Ellis & Dryden, 1987, 1990; Ellis & Knaus, 1977; Ellis, McInerney, DiGiuseppe, & Yeager, 1988; Ellis & Whiteley, 1979.

3. Beck, 1976; Burns, 1980; Velten, 1986.

Chapter 11: Easy Does It (But Do It!): Integrating Rational Ideas Into Your Self-Help Work

1. Danysh, 1974; Ellis, 1988a; Ellis & Becker, 1982; Ellis & Harper, 1975; Ellis & Whiteley, 1979; Velten, 1986.
2. Phadke, 1982.
3. Ellis, 1973b, 1985b, 1987a, 1987b, 1988a, 1991c, 1991f, 1992.
4. Bartley, 1984; Bateson, 1979; Ellis, 1962, 1965, 1973b, 1988a, 1990b, 1991c, 1991e, 1991g, D. Miller, 1985; Popper, 1962, 1985b; Russell, 1965.
5. Ellis, 1971, 1972a, 1972c, 1972e, 1973a, 1973b, 1973c, 1974a, 1974b, 1976b, 1977a, 1977b, 1978, 1985b, 1988a; Ellis & Harper, 1975; Ellis & Whiteley, 1979.

Chapter 12: More Ways to Catch Your Stinking Thinking and Turn Affirmations Into Actions

1. Epstein, 1990.
2. Ellis, 1957, 1962, 1973b, 1985b, 1988a.

Chapter 13: Other Cognitive or Thinking Techniques of RET

1. Ellis, 1985b, 1988a; Ellis, McInerney, DiGiuseppe, & Yeager, 1988.
2. Korzybski, 1933.
3. Danysh, 1974.
4. Ellis, 1974b, 1992.
5. Sichel & Ellis, 1984.
6. Ellis, 1990g, 1991g; Burns, Adams, & Anastopoulos, 1985; Persons, Burns, & Perloff, 1989.
7. Ellis & Harper, 1975; Ellis & Becker, 1982; Ellis, 1988a; Hauck, 1973; Dryden & Gordon, 1991; Young, 1974.
8. Ellis, 1977a; Knaus, 1976; Hauck, 1974; Dryden, 1990a; Ellis & Knaus, 1977; Knaus, 1982.
9. Trimpey, J., 1989; Trimpey, L. & Trimpey, J., 1990; Woods, 1990; Ellis, McInerney, DiGiuseppe, & Yeager, 1988.
10. Ellis, 1974a, 1976b, 1977b, 1978, 1988b; Knaus, 1976; Lega et al., 1985; Velten, 1989.

Chapter 14: Teaching RET to Others (Twelfth Stepping, RET Style)

1. Bandura, 1986.
2. Bayer, 1990; Eisenberg, with Kelly, 1986; Lakein, 1973.

3. Roe, 1953.

4. Ellis, 1962, 1972a, 1973b, 1980b, 1983a, 1983b, 1985a, 1985b, 1988a; Ellis & Dryden, 1987, 1990, 1991.

Chapter 15: How to Get in Touch With Your Feelings ... and Make Them Better!

1. Bernard, 1986, 1991; Ellis, 1969, 1972a, 1972c, 1973a, 1974b, 1977a, 1977c, 1977d, 1979c, 1980b, 1981, 1985b, 1987c, 1988a, 1990f, 1991g, 1992; Ellis & Dryden, 1987, 1991.

2. Maultsby, 1971; Maultsby & Ellis, 1974.

3. Ellis, 1969, 1971, 1972e, 1973a, 1985b, 1988a.

4. Ellis, 1969, 1973a, 1985b, 1988a; Ellis & Dryden, 1987, 1991.

5. Ellis, 1972c, 1973a, 1985b, 1988a, 1990a, 1990c, 1990f, 1991g.

6. Ellis, 1985b, 1988a, 1990a.

7. Ellis, 1979c, 1985b, 1986b, 1988a, 1990b, 1990f, 1991a.

8. Ellis, 1977b, 1977c, 1977d, 1978, 1980c, 1981a, 1987c, 1990a; Velten, 1989.

9. Ellis, 1990a.

Chapter 16: How to Use RET's Behavioral Methods

1. Ellis, 1957; 1962; 1969, 1971, 1972e, 1973a, 1973b, 1974a, 1975, 1976b, 1976d, 1977a, 1985b, 1988a, 1990a, 1990c, 1990f, 1990d, 1991f, 1991g; Ellis & Dryden, 1987, 1991.

2. Wolpe, 1982.

3. Epictetus, 1890; Low, 1950; Marcus Aurelius, 1890.

4. Ellis, 1962, 1969, 1971, 1973a, 1973b, 1976b, 1985b, 1988a.

5. Ellis, 1973a, 1973b, 1976b, 1985b, 1988a, 1990b.

6. Ellis, 1973a, 1973b, 1976b, 1985b, 1988a, 1990b; Ellis & Abrahms, 1978.

Chapter 17: Relapse Prevention: Getting to Recovery, Staying There, and Moving On

1. Ellis, 1988a; Ellis & Hunter, 191; Ellis & Becker, 1982; Ellis & Knaus, 1977; Hauck, 1973; Young, 1974.

2. Ellis, 1978, 1976b; Ellis, 1991h; Velten, 1989.

APPENDIX

A

Sources of Help

To profit from therapy for psychological, family, relationship, or substance abuse and addiction problems, by all means see a licensed cognitive-behavioral psychotherapist. You can obtain a referral by consulting the organizations listed here.

Institute for Rational-Emotive Therapy
45 East Sixth-fifth Street
New York, N.Y. 10021
(212) 535–0822; fax: (212) 249–3582
Materials orders: 1-800-323-IRET

Association for the Advancement of Behavior Therapy
15 West Thirty-sixth Street
New York, N.Y. 10018
(212) 279–7970.

Anxiety Disorders Association of America
6000 Executive Blvd., Suite 200
Rockville, Md. 20852
(301) 231–9350.

Another good referral source is Rational Recovery Systems at Box 800, Lotus, CA 95651; (916) 621–4374.

The Twelve Negative Emotions: Accept the Appropriate Ones, and Work to Change the Inappropriate Ones

We have mentioned above that one of the ways that you can dig yourself deeper into addictions is to make yourself allergic to negative emotions. Yes, negative emotions feel bad. However, certain negative emotions can add to the richness of life. They can prompt us to work our tails off and help us to improve our situations. Some are inappropriate—they interfere with our problem-solving. They don't help us to improve our situations. In the list that follows, the first negative emotion in each pair is appropriate. The second negative emotion in each pair is inappropriate.

1. Concern vs. anxiety. Concern is an emotion that is associated with your Belief "I hope that this threat does not happen, but if it does, it would be unfortu-

nate. I can deal with it and still have a happy life."
Anxiety occurs when you believe, "This threat *must*
not happen, and it would be *awful* if it does. I can't
cope with it!"

2. Sadness vs. depression. Sadness occurs when you
   believe "It is very unfortunate that I have experienced
   this loss, but there is no reason why it should not have
   happened." Depression, on the other hand, stems
   from your Belief "This loss should not have occurred,
   and it is terrible that it did." With depression you may
   feel responsible for the loss. You may tend to damn
   yourself: "I am no good." If, however, the loss is
   outside your control, you may tend to damn the
   world/life conditions: "It is terrible. I can't stand it!"

   As shown earlier, RET theory holds that it is the
   philosophy of musturbation implicit in such evaluations that leads you to conclude that you will never
   get what you want. This leads to your feeling hopeless. Example, "Because I must always get the things
   I really want and did not get it this time, I'll never get
   it at all. It's hopeless."

3. Regret vs. guilt. Feelings of regret or remorse occur
   when you admit that you have done something bad,
   but accept yourself as a fallible human being for doing
   so. You feel bad about the act or deed but not about
   yourself because you hold the Belief, "I prefer not to
   act badly, but if I do, too bad! I'll try to do better next
   time." Guilt occurs when you damn yourself as bad,
   wicked, or rotten for acting badly. Here you feel bad
   both about the act and your "self" because you hold
   the Belief" I must not act badly, and if I do it's awful
   and I am a rotten person!"

4. Disappointment vs. shame or embarrassment. Feelings of disappointment occur when you act "stupidly"
   in public, acknowledge the stupid act, but accept

yourself in the process. You feel disappointed about your actions but not with yourself because you prefer but do not demand that you act well. Shame and embarrassment occur when you again recognize that you have acted "stupidly" in public and then condemn yourself for acting in a way that you *absolutely should not* have done. When you experience shame and embarrassment, you expect the watching audience to think badly of you, and you tend to agree with these perceived judgments. Thus, you believe that you absolutely *need* the approval of these others.

5. Annoyance vs. anger. Annoyance occurs when another person disregards your rules of living. When annoyed, you do not like what the other has done but do not damn him or her for doing it. You tend to believe "I wish the other person did not do that and I don't like what he or she did, but it does not follow that he or she must not break my rule." In anger, however, you believe the other person absolutely must not break your rule and thus you damn the other for doing so.

6. Frustration vs. horror. Frustration at not getting what you want feels bad. It stems from thinking, "I don't like this! It's annoying! What can I do to get past this obstacle and get what I want?" Frustration motivates you to keep working for what you want. It also, ironically, increases enjoyment because you can contrast the frustrated feelings with the pleasurable feelings. Horror, on the other hand, stems from the Belief, "This obstacle is horrible! It must not be this way! How can life give me such an awful obstacle!? I *can't stand* it!"

APPENDIX

The Twelve Criteria
of Psychological Health

What are people in true recovery like? They often show:

Self-interest and social interest. Sensible and emotionally healthy people tend to be interested in themselves and to put their own interests at least a little above the interests of others. They sacrifice themselves to some degree for those for whom they care, but not overwhelmingly or completely.

Social interest is usually rational and self-helping because most people choose to live and enjoy themselves in a social group or community; if they do not act morally, protect the rights of others, and aid social survival, it is unlikely they will create the kind of world in which they themselves can live comfortably and happily.

Self-direction. Healthy people tend to mainly assume responsibility for their own lives while simultaneously preferring to cooperate with others. They do not need or demand considerable support or succoring from others.

High frustration tolerance. Rational individuals give both themselves and others the right to be wrong. Even when they intensely dislike their own and others' behavior, they refrain from damning themselves or others, as persons, for unacceptable or obnoxious behavior. They change frustrations that they can change, accept (but still dislike) what they can't change, and have the wisdom to seek and achieve a reasonably happy life. They often give up immediate gratification (such as boozing and drugging) for long-range goals (such as good health and effective living.)

Flexibility. Healthy and mature people tend to be flexible in their thinking, open to change, and unbigoted in their view of other people. They do not make rigid rules for themselves and others.

Acceptance of uncertainty. Healthy people tend to acknowledge and accept the idea that we seem to live in a world of probability and chance where absolute certainties do not, and probably never will, exist. They realize that it is often fascinating and exciting, but not awful, to live in such a world. They enjoy a good degree of order, but they do not demand to know exactly what the future will bring or what will happen to them.

Commitment to creative pursuits. Most people tend to be healthier and happier when they are vitally absorbed in something outside themselves and preferably have a least one strong creative interest, as well as some major human involvement, that they consider so important that they structure a good part of their daily existence around it.

Scientific thinking. Nondisturbed people tend to be more realistic, rational, and scientific than more disturbed people. They are able to feel deeply and act concertedly, but they tend to regulate their emotions and actions by reflecting on them and evaluating their consequences in terms of the extent to which they lead to the attainment of short-term *and* long-term goals.

Self-acceptance. Healthy people are usually glad to be alive and accept themselves just because they are alive and have some capacity to enjoy themselves. They refuse to measure their intrinsic worth by their extrinsic achievements or by what others think of them. They frankly choose to accept themselves unconditionally, and they try to completely avoid rating themselves—their totality or their being. They attempt to enjoy rather than to prove themselves.

Risk-taking. Emotionally healthy people tend to take a fair amount of risk and try to do what they want to do, even when there is a good chance that they may fail. They tend to be adventurous, but not foolhardy.

Long-range pleasure-seeking. Well-adjusted people tend to seek both the pleasures of the moment and those of the future and do not often court future pain for present gain. They seek happiness and avoid pain, but they assume they will probably live for quite a few years and that they had therefore better think of both today and tomorrow and not be obsessed with immediate gratification.

No heaven on earth. Healthy people accept the fact that heaven on earth is probably not achiev-

able and that they are never likely to get everything they want or to avoid everything they don't
want. They refuse to unrealistically demand total
joy, complete happiness, or perfection, or for
total lack of anxiety, depression, self-downing,
and hostility.

*Self-responsibility for own emotional distur-
bance.* Healthy people tend to accept a great
deal of responsibility for their own disturbance
rather than defensively blaming others or social
conditions for their self-defeating thoughts, feelings, and actions.

References

Note: The items preceded by an asterisk (*) in the following list of references are recommended for readers of this book who want to obtain more details of rational-emotive therapy (RET) and cognitive-behavior therapy (CBT). Most of these materials are obtainable from the Institute for Rational-Emotive Therapy, 45 East 65th Street, New York, NY 10021-6593, (212) 535-0822. The Institute's free catalogue and the materials it distributes may be ordered by phone (800-323-IRET) or by fax (212) 249-3582. The Institute will continue to make available these and other materials, as well as to present talks, workshops, training practica, and other presentations in the area of human growth and rational living and to list these in its regular catalogues.

Abelson, R. P. (1963). Computer simulation of "hot" cognition. In S. S. Tompkins & S. Messick (Eds.), *Computer simulation of personality.* New York: Wiley.

*Adler, A. (1958). *What life should mean to you.* New York: Capricorn.

Adler, A. (1964). *Superiority and social interest.* Ed. by H. L. Ansbacher and R. R. Ansbacher. Evanston, IL: Northwestern University Press.

*Alberti, R. F., & Emmons, M. L. (1990). *Your perfect right* (6th ed.). San Luis Obispo, CA: Impact.

Bandura, A. (1986). *Social foundations of thought and action: A social cognitive theory.* Englewood Cliffs, NJ: Prentice-Hall.

*Bard, J. (1987). *I don't like asparagus.* Cleveland, OH: Psychology Department, Cleveland State University.

Barlow, D. H., & Craske, M. G. (1989). *Mastery of your anxiety and panic.* Albany, NY: Center for Stress and Anxiety Disorders.

Bartley, W. W., III. (1984). *The retreat to commitment* (rev. ed.). Peru, IL: Open Court.

Bateson, G. (1979). *Mind and nature: A necessary unit.* New York: Dutton.

Beck, A. T. (1976). *Cognitive therapy and the emotional disorders.* New York: International Universities Press.

Beck, A. T. (1991). Cognitive therapy: A 30-year retrospective. *American Psychologist, 46,* 382–389.

*Bernard, M. E. (1986). *Staying rational in an irrational world: Albert Ellis and rational-emotive therapy.* Carlton, Victoria, Australia: McCulloch Publishing (in association with The Macmillan Company of Australia). Secaucus, NJ: Carol Publishing Group.

*Bernard, M. E. (Ed.). (1991). *Using rational-emotive therapy effectively: A practitioner's guide.* New York: Plenum.

*Bufe, C. (1991). *Alcoholics anonymous: Cult or cure?* San Francisco: See Sharp Press, Box 6118, San Francisco, CA 94101. Available from Upper Access, Inc., Box 457, Hinesburg, VT 05461.

*Burns, D. D. (1980). *Feeling good: The new mood therapy.* New York: Morrow.

*Burns, D. D. (1989). *Feeling good handbook.* New York: Morrow.

Burns, D. D., Adams, R. L., & Anastopoulos, A. D. (1985). The role of self-help assignments in the treatment of depression. In E. E. Beckham & W. R. Leber (Eds.), *Handbook for the diagnosis, treatment, and research of depression.* Homewood, IL: Dorsey Press.

Christopher, J. (1988). *How to stay sober: Recovery without religion.* Buffalo, NY: Prometheus Books.

Christopher, J. (1989). *Unhooked: Staying sober and drug-free.* Buffalo, NY: Prometheus Books.

Cohen, M., Liebson, I., Fallace, L., & Speers, W. (1971). Alcoholism: Controlled drinking and incentives for abstinence. *Psychological Reports, 28,* 575–580.

Cohen, M., Liebson, I., Fallace, L., & Allen, R. (1971). Moderate drinking by chronic alcoholics: A schedule-dependent phenomenon. *Journal of Nerous and Mental Disease, 153,* 434–444.

Crawford, T., & Ellis, A. (1989). A dictionary of rational-emotive feelings and behaviors. *Journal of Rational-Emotive and Cognitive-Behavior Therapy, 7*(1), 3–27.

Critchlow, B. (1984). The powers of John Barleycorn: Beliefs about the effects of alcohol on social behavior. *American Psychologist, 41,* 751–764.

Danysh, J. (1974). *Stop without quitting.* San Francisco: International Society for General Semantics.

DeAngelis, T. (1991, May). Drunkenness caused by placebos. *APA Monitor, 22*(5), 17.

Dobash, R. E., & Dobash, R. (1979). *Violence against wives: A case against the patriarchy.* New York: Free Press.

*Dryden, W. (1990). *Rational-emotive counseling in action.* London: Sage.

*Dryden, W., & DiGiuseppe, R. (1990). *A primer on rational-emotive therapy.* Champaign, IL: Research Press.

*Dryden, W., & Gordon, J. (1991). *Think your way to happiness.* London: Sheldon Press.

Eisenberg, R., with Kelly, K. (1986). *Organize yourself!* New York: MacMillan.

*Ellis, A. (1957). *How to live with a neurotic: At home and at work.* New York: Crown. (Rev. ed., 1975, North Hollywood, CA: Wilshire Books).

*Ellis, A. (1962). *Reason and emotion in psychotherapy.* New York: Lyle Stuart. Paperback edition: Secaucus, NJ: Citadel.

*Ellis, A. (1963). Showing the patient that he is not a worthless individual. *Voices, 1*(2), 74–77. (Reprinted and revised, 1985: *Showing clients they are not worthless individuals.* New York: Institute for Rational-Emotive Therapy.

Ellis, A. (1965). *Suppressed: Seven key essays publishers dared not print*. Chicago: New Classics House.

*Ellis, A. (1971a). *Growth through reason*. North Hollywood, CA: Wilshire Books.

*Ellis, A. (1971b). Emotional disturbance and its treatment in a nutshell. *Canadian Counselor*, 5, 168–171. (Revised and reprinted, 1974: New York: Institute for Rational-Emotive Therapy, 1974.

*Ellis, A. (1972). *Executive leadership: The rational-emotive approach*. New York: Institute for Rational-Emotive Therapy.

*Ellis, A. (Speaker). (1973a). *How to stubbornly refuse to be ashamed of anything* (Cassette Recording). New York: Institute for Rational-Emotive Therapy.

*Ellis, A. (1973b). *Humanistic psychotherapy: The rational-emotive approach*. New York: McGraw-Hill.

*Ellis, A. (Speaker). (1973c). *Twenty-one ways to stop worrying* (Cassette Recording). New York: Institute for Rational-Emotive Therapy.

*Ellis, A. (Speaker). (1974a). *Rational living in an irrational world* (Cassette Recording). New York: Institute for Rational-Emotive Therapy.

*Ellis, A. (1974b). *Technique of disputing irrational beliefs (DIBS)*. New York: Institute for Rational-Emotive Therapy.

*Ellis, A. (Speaker). (1975). *RET and assertiveness training* (Cassette Recording). New York: Institute for Rational-Emotive Therapy.

*Ellis, A. (1976a). The biological basis of human irrationality. *Journal of Individual Psychology*, 32, 145–168. (Reprinted: New York: Institute for Rational-Emotive Therapy)

*Ellis, A. (Speaker). (1976b). *Conquering low frustration tolerance* (Cassette Recording). New York: Institute for Rational-Emotive Therapy.

*Ellis, A. (1976c). RET abolishes most of the human ego. *Psychotherapy*, *13*, 343–348. (Reprinted: New York: Institute for Rational-Emotive Therapy)

*Ellis, A. (1976d). *Sex and the liberated man.* Secaucus, NJ: Lyle Stuart.

*Ellis, A. (1977a). *Anger—how to live with and without it.* Secaucus, NJ: Citadel Press.

*Ellis, A. (Speaker). (1977b). *Conquering the dire need for love* (Cassette Recording). New York: Institute for Rational-Emotive Therapy.

*Ellis, A. (1977c). Fun as psychotherapy. *Rational Living, 12*(1), 2–6. (Also: Cassette Recording. New York: Institute for Rational-Emotive Therapy, 1977)

*Ellis, A. (Speaker). (1977d). *A garland of rational humorous songs* (Cassette Recording; Songbook). New York: Institute for Rational-Emotive Therapy.

Ellis, A. (1977e). Skill training in counseling and psychotherapy. *Canadian Counsellor, 12*(1), 30–35.

*Ellis A. (Speaker). (1978). *I'd like to stop, but . . . Dealing with addictions* (Cassette Recording). New York: Institute for Rational-Emotive Therapy.

Ellis, A. (1979a). Discomfort anxiety: A new cognitive-behavioral construct. Part 1. *Rational Living, 14*(2), 3–8.

*Ellis, A. (1979b). *The intelligent woman's guide to dating and mating.* Secaucus, NJ: Lyle Stuart.

Ellis, A. (1979c). Rational-emotive therapy: Research data that support the clinical and personality hypotheses of RET and other modes of cognitive-behavior therapy. In A. Ellis & J. M. Whiteley (Eds.), *Theoretical and empirical foundations of rational-emotive therapy* (pp. 101–173). Monterey, CA: Brooks/Cole.

Ellis, A. (1980a). Discomfort anxiety: A new cognitive-behavioral construct. Part 2. *Rational Living, 15*(1), 25–30.

Ellis, A. (1980b). Rational-emotive therapy and cognitive behaviortherapy: Similarities and differences. *Cognitive Therapy and Research, 4*, 325–340.

*Ellis, A. (Speaker). (1980c). *Twenty-two ways to brighten up your love life* (Cassette Recording). New York: Institute for Rational-Emotive Therapy.

*Ellis, A. (1981). The use of rational humorous songs in psycho-
therapy. *Voices, 16*(4), 29–36.

*Ellis, A. (1983a). *The case against religiosity.* New York: Institute
for Rational-Emotive Therapy.

Ellis, A. (1983b). The philosophic implications and dangers of some
popular behavior therapy techniques. In M. Rosenbaum,
C. M. Franks, & Y. Jaffe (Eds.), *Perspectives in behavior
therapy in the eighties* (pp. 138–151). New York: Springer.

*Ellis, A. (1985a). Intellectual fascism. *Journal of Rational-Emotive
Therapy, 3*(1), 3–12. (Reprinted: New York: Institute for Rational-Emotive Therapy)

*Ellis, A. (1985b). *Overcoming resistance: Rational-emotive thera-
py with difficult clients.* New York: Springer.

Ellis, A. (1986a). Anxiety about anxiety: The use of hypnosis with
rational-emotive therapy. In E. T. Dowd & J. M. Healy
(Eds.), *Case studies in hypnotherapy* (pp. 3–11). New York:
Guilford. (Reprinted in A. Ellis & W. Dryden, *The practice of
rational-emotive therapy.* New York: Springer, 1987)

*Ellis, A. (1986b). Rational-emotive therapy applied to relationship
therapy. *Journal of Rational-Emotive Therapy, 4,* 4–21.

Ellis, A. (1987a). The impossibility of achieving consistently good
mental health. *American Psychologist, 42,* 364–375.

Ellis, A. (1987b). A sadly neglected cognitive element in depression. *Cognitive Therapy and Research, 11,* 121–146.

*Ellis, A. (1987c). The use of rational humorous songs in psycho-
therapy. In W. F. Fry, Jr. & W. A. Salameh (Eds.), *Handbook
of humor and psychotherapy* (pp. 265–288). Sarasota, FL:
Professional Resource Exchange.

Ellis, A. (1988a). *How to stubbornly refuse to make yourself miserable about anything—yes, anything!* Secaucus, NJ: Lyle
Stuart.

*Ellis, A. (Speaker). (1988b). *Unconditionally accepting yourself
and others* (Cassette Recording). New York: Institute for Rational-Emotive Therapy.

Ellis, A. (1989a). *The treatment of psychotic and borderline individuals with RET.* New York: Institute for Rational-Emotive
Therapy. (Original work published in 1965)

Ellis A. (1989b). The history of cognition in psychotherapy. In A. Freeman, K. M. Simon, L. E. Beutler, & H. Arkowitz (Eds.), *Comprehensive handbook of cognitive therapy* (pp. 5–19). New York: Plenum.

*Ellis, A. (Speaker). (1990a). *Albert Ellis live at the Learning Annex* (2 Cassette Recordings). New York: Institute for Rational-Emotive Therapy.

Ellis, A. (1990b). Is rational-emotive therapy (RET) "rationalist" or "constructivist"? In A. Ellis & W. Dryden (Eds.), *The essential Albert Ellis* (pp. 114–141). New York: Springer.

Ellis, A. (1990c). My life in clinical psychology. In C. E. Walker (Ed.), *History of clinical psychology in autobiography.* Homewood, IL: Dorsey.

Ellis, A. (1990d). Rational-emotive therapy. In I. L. Kutash & A. Wolf (Eds.), *The group psychotherapist's handbook* (pp. 298–315). New York: Columbia.

*Ellis, A. (Speaker). (1990e). *Overcoming the influences of the past* (Cassette Recording). New York: Institute for Rational-Emotive Therapy.

Ellis, A. (1990f). Special features of rational-emotive therapy. In W. Dryden & R. DiGiuseppe, *A primer on rational-emotive therapy* (pp. 79–93). Champaign, IL: Research Press.

*Ellis, A. (1991a). Achieving self-actualization. In A. Jones & R. Crandall (Eds.), *Handbook of self-actualization.* Corte Madera, CA: Select Press.

*Ellis, A. (1991b). Foreword to P. Hauck, *Hold your head up high* (pp. 1–4). London: Sheldon.

Ellis, A. (1991c). The philosophical basis of rational-emotive therapy (RET). *Psychotherapy in Private Practice, 8*(4), 97–106.

Ellis, A. (1991d). Rational-emotive family therapy. In A. M. Horne & J. L. Passmore (Eds.), *Family counseling and therapy* (2nd ed.) (pp. 403–434). Itasca, IL: F. E. Peacock.

Ellis, A. (1991e, August 16). *Rational recovery systems: Alternatives to AA and other 12-step programs.* Paper presented at the 99th Annual Convention of the American Psychological Association, San Francisco. Harvard Mental Health Newsletter, 1992.

*Ellis, A. (1991f).The revised ABCs of rational-emotive therapy. In J. Zeig (Ed.), *Evolution of psychotherapy: II.* New York: Brunner/Mazel. (Expanded version: *Journal of Rational-Emotive and Cognitive-Behavior Therapy*, 1992, 9, 139–172).

*Ellis, A. (1991g). Using RET effectively: Reflections and interview. In M. E. Bernard (Ed.), *Using rational-emotive therapy effectively* (pp. 1–33). New York: Plenum.

*Ellis, A. (Speaker). (1991h). *To to refuse to be angry, vindictive, and unforgiving.* (Cassette recording) New York: Institute for Rational-Emotive Therapy.

Ellis, A. (1992). Rational-emotive approaches to peace. *Journal of Cognitive Psychotherapy.*

Ellis, A., & Abrahms, E. (1978). *Brief psychotherapy in medical and health practice.* New York: Springer.

*Ellis, A., & Becker, I. (1982). *A guide to personal happiness.* North Hollywood, CA: Wilshire Books.

Ellis, A., & Bernard, M. E. (Eds.). (1985). *Clinical applications of rational-emotive therapy.* New York: Plenum.

*Ellis, A., & Dryden, W. (1987). *The practice of rational-emotive therapy.* New York: Springer.

*Ellis, A., & Dryden, W. (1990). *The essential Albert Ellis: Seminal writings on psychotherapy.* New York: Springer.

*Ellis, A., & Dryden, W. (1991). *A dialogue with Albert Ellis: Against dogma.* Stony Stratford, Milton Keynes, England: Open University Press.

*Ellis, A., & Grieger, R. (Eds.). (1977). *Handbook of rational-emotive therapy.* (Vol. 1). New York: Springer.

*Ellis, A., & Grieger, R. (Eds.). (1986). *Handbook of rational-emotive therapy.* (Vol. 2). New York: Springer.

*Ellis, A., & Harper, R. A. (1961). *A guide to successful marriage.* North Hollywood, CA: Wilshire Books.

*Ellis, A., & Harper, R. A. (1975). *A new guide to rational living.* North Hollywood, CA: Wilshire Books.

*Ellis, A., & Harper, R. A. (Speakers). (1990). *A guide to rational living* (Cassette Recording). Los Angeles: Audio Renaissance Tapes, Inc.

*Ellis, A., & Hunter, P. (1991). *Why am I always broke? How to be sane about money.* Secaucus, NJ: Lyle Stuart.

*Ellis, A., & Knaus, W. (1977). *Overcoming procrastination.* New York: New American Library.

*Ellis, A., McInerney, J., DiGiuseppe, R., & Yeager, R. (1988). *Rational-emotive therapy with alcoholics and substance abusers.* Elmsford, NY: Pergamon.

Ellis, A., & Schoenfeld, E. (1990). Divine intervention and the treatment of chemical dependency. *Journal of Substance Abuse, 2,* 459–468, 489–494.

*Ellis, A., Sichel, J., Yeager, R., DiMattia, D., & DiGiuseppe, R. (1989). *Rational-emotive couples therapy.* Elmsford, NY: Pergamon.

*Ellis, A., & Vega, G. (1990). *Self-management: Strategies for personal success.* New York: Institute for Rational-Emotive Therapy.

Ellis, A., & Whiteley, J. M. (Eds.). (1979). *Theoretical and empirical foundations of rational-emotive therapy.* Monterey, CA: Brooks/Cole.

*Ellis, A., & Yeager, R. (1989). *Why some therapies don't work: The dangers of transpersonal psychology.* Buffalo, NY: Prometheus.

Ellis, A., Young, J., & Lockwood, G. (1987). Cognitive therapy and rational-emotive therapy: A dialogue. *Journal of Cognitive Psychotherapy, 1*(4), 137–187.

Engels, G. I., & Diekstra, R. F. W. (1986). Meta-analysis of rational-emotive therapy outcome studies. In P. Eelen & O. Fontaine (Eds.), *Behavior therapy: Beyond the conditioning framework* (pp. 121–140). Hillsdale, NJ: Lawrence Erlbaum.

*Epictetus (1890). *The collected works of Epictetus.* Boston: Little, Brown.

Epstein, S. (1990). Cognitive experiential theory. In L. Pervin (Ed.), *Handbook of personality theory and research.* New York: Guilford.

Fillmore, K. M. (1975). Relationships between specific drinking problems in early adulthood and middle age. *Journal of Studies on Alcohol, 36,* 822–907.

Fingarette, H. (1988). *Heavy drinking: The myth of alcholism as a disease*. Berkeley, CA: University of California Press.

Freud, S. (1965). *Standard edition of the complete psychological works of Sigmund Freud*. New York: Basic Books.

*Geis, J. (Speaker). (1972). *Psychology of dieting* (Cassette Recording). New York: Institute for Rational-Emotive Therapy.

Gelles, R. J. (1972). *The violent home*. Beverly Hills, CA: Sage.

Gottheil, E., Alterman, A., Skoloda,T. E., & Murphy, B. F. (1973). Alcoholics' patterns of controlled drinking. *American Journal of Psychiatry, 130*, 418–422.

Grieger, R., & Boyd, J. (1980). *Rational-emotive therapy: A skills-based approach*. New York: Van Nostrand Reinhold.

Haaga, D. A., & Davison, G. C. (1989). Outcome studies of rational-emotive therapy. In M. E. Bernard & R. DiGiuseppe (Eds.), *Inside rational-emotive therapy* (pp. 155–197). San Diego, CA: Academic Press.

*Hauck, P. A. (1973). *Overcoming depression*. Philadelphia: Westminster.

*Hauck, P. A. (1974). *Overcoming frustration and anger*. Philadelphia: Westminster.

*Hauck, P. A. (1977). *Marriage is a loving business*. Philadelphia: Westminster.

*Hauck, P. A. (1991). *Hold your head up high*. London: Sheldon.

Heather, N., & Robertson, I. (1981).*Controlled drinking*. London: Methuen.

Huber, C. H., & Baruth, L. G. (1989). *Rational-emotive and systems family therapy*. New York: Springer.

Jorm, A. P. (1987). *Modifiability of a personality trait which is a risk factor in neurosis*. Paper presented at World Psychiatric Association, Symposium on Epidemiology and the Prevention of Mental Disorder. Reykjavik, Iceland.

Kahneman, D., Slovic, P., & Twersky, A. (Eds.). (1982). *Judgment under uncertainty: Heuristics and biases*. New York: Cambridge University Press.

*Knaus, W. (Speaker). (1976). *Overcoming procrastination.* (Cassette Recording). New York: Institute for Rational-Emotive Therapy.

*Knaus, W. (1982). *How to get out of a rut.* Englewood Cliffs, NJ: Prentice-Hall.

*Knaus, W. (1983). *How to conquer your frustrations.* Englewood Cliffs, NJ: Prentice-Hall.

Knaus, W. (1974). *Rational-emotive education.* New York: Institute for Rational-Emotive Therapy.

*Korzybski, A. (1933). *Science and sanity.* San Francisco: International Society of General Semantics.

Kurtz, W. (1988). *AA: The story.* San Francisco: Harper & Row.

Lakein, A. L. (1973). *How to get control of your time and your life.* New York: Peter Wyden.

Langenbucher, J., & Nathan, P. E. (1983). The 'wet' alcoholic: One drink . . . then what? In W. M. Cox (Ed.), *Identifying and measuring alcoholic personality characteristics.* San Francisco: Jossey-Bass.

Lazarus, A. A. (1990). *The practice of multimodal therapy.* Baltimore: Johns Hopkins.

*Lega, L., et al. (Speakers). (1985). *Thinking and drinking: An RET approach to staying stopped* (Video Cassette). New York: Institute for Rational-Emotive Therapy.

Lester, D. (1988). Genetic theory: An assessment of the heritability of alcoholism. In C. D. Chaudron & D. A. Wilkinson (Eds.), *Theories of alcoholism.* Toronto: Addiction Research Foundation.

*Low, A. A. (1950). *Mental health through will-training.* Glencoe, IL: Willett Publishing Co.

Lyons, L. C., & Woods, P. J. (1991). The efficacy of rational-emotive therapy: A quantitative review of the outcome research. *Clinical Psychology Review, 11,* 357–369.

*Marcus Aurelius (1890). *Meditations.* Boston: Little, Brown.

Marlatt, G. A., Demming, B., & Reid, J. B. (1973). Loss of control drinking in alcoholics: An experimental analogue. *Journal of Abnormal Psychology, 81,* 223–241.

Marlatt, G. A., & Gordon, J. R. (Eds.). (1985). *Relapse prevention: Maintenance strategies in the treatment of addictive behaviors.* New York: Guilford.

Marlatt, G. A., & Rohsenow, D. (1980). Cognitive processes in alcohol use: Expectancy and balanced placebo design. In N. K. Mello (Ed.), *Advances in substance abuse: Behavioral and biological research.* Greenwich, CT: JAI.

Maultsby, M. C., Jr. (1971). Rational-emotive imagery. *Rational Living, 6*(1), 24–27.

*Maultsby, M. C., Jr. (1984). *Rational behavior therapy.* Englewood Cliffs: NJ: Prentice-Hall.

*Maultsby, M. C., Jr., & Ellis, A. (1974). *Technique for using rational-emotive imagery.* New York: Institute for Rational-Emotive Therapy.

Mayer, J. J. (1990). *If you haven't got the time to do it right, when will you find the time to do it over?* New York: Simon and Schuster.

McGovern, T. E., & Silverman, M. S. (1984). A review of outcome studies of rational-emotive therapy from 1977 to 1982. *Journal of Rational-Emotive Therapy, 2*(1), 7–18.

Meichenbaum, D. (1977). *Cognitive-behavior modification.* New York: Plenum.

Mello, N. K., & Mendelson, J. H. (1970). Experimentally induced intoxication in alcoholics: A comparison between programmed and spontaneous drinking. *Journal of Pharmacology and Experimental Therapeutics, 173,* 101–116.

Mello, N. K., & Mendelson, J. H. (1972). Drinking patterns during work-contingent and non-contingent alcohol acquisition. *Psychosomatic Medicine, 34,* 139–164.

Merry, J. (1966). The 'loss of control' myth. *Lancet, 1,* 1257–1258.

Miller, D. (1985). (Ed.). *Popper selections.* Princeton, NJ: Princeton University Press.

Miller, P. M. (1976). *Behavioral treatment of alcoholism.* Elmsford, NY: Pergamon.

Miller, T. (1986). *The unfair advantage*. Manlius, NY: Horsesense, Inc.

Miller, W. R., & Munoz, R. F. (1982). *How to control your drinking: A practical guide to responsible drinking* (rev. ed.). Albuquerque, NM: University of New Mexico Press.

Muran, J. C. (1991). A reformulation of the ABC model in cognitive psychotherapies: Implications for assessment and treatment. *Clinical Psychology Review, 11*, 399–418.

Nagoshi, C. T., & Wilson, J. R. (1987). Influence of family alcoholism history on alcohol metabolism, sensitivity, and tolerance. *Alcoholism: Clinical and Experimental Research, 11*, 392–98.

Pace, N. A., with Cross, W. (1984). *Guidelines to safe drinking*. New York: McGraw-Hill.

Pass it on: Bill Wilson and the A.A. message (1984). New York: AA World Services, Inc.

Peele, S. (1984). The cultural context of psychological approaches to alcoholism: Can we control the effects of alcohol? *American Psychologist, 39*, 1337–1351.

*Peele, S. (1989). *Diseasing of America: Addiction treatment out of control*. Lexington, MA: Lexington Books.

*Peele, S., & Brodsky, A., with Arnold, M. (1991). *The truth about addiction and recovery*. New York: Simon & Schuster.

Persons, J. B., Burns, D. D., & Perloff, J. M. (1989). Predictions of dropout and outcome in cognitive therapy for depression in a private practice setting. *Cognitive Therapy & Research, 12*, 557–575.

Phadke, K. M. (1982). Some innovations in RET theory and practice. *Rational Living, 17*(2), 25–30.

Pittman, B. (1988). *AA: The way it began*. Seattle, WA: Glen Abbey Books.

Popper, K. R. (1962). *Objective knowledge*. London: Oxford.

Roe, A. (1953). A psychological study of eminent psychologists and anthropologists and a comparison with biological and physical scientists. *Psychological Monographs, 67*(352), 1–55.

Robertson, N. (1988). *Getting better*. New York: William Morrow & Co.

Rorer, L. G. (1989). Rational-emotive theory: 1. An integrated psychological and philosophical basis. 2. Explication and evaluation, *Cognitive Therapy and Research. 13*, 475–492, 513–548.

Russell, B. (1965). *The basic writings of Bertrand Russell.* New York: Simon & Schuster.

*Seligman, M. E. P. (1991). *Learned optimism.* New York: Knopf.

*Sichel, J., & Ellis, A. (1984). *RET self-help form.* New York: Institute for Rational-Emotive Therapy.

Siegel, R. K. (1989). *Intoxication: Life in pursuit of artificial paradise.* New York: E. P. Dutton.

Temple, M. T., & Fillmore, K. M. (1986). The variability of drinking patterns and problems among young men, age 16–31. *International Journal of Addictions, 20,* 1595–1620.

*Trimpey, J. (1989). *Rational Recovery from alcoholism: The small book.* Lotus, CA: Lotus Press.

*Trimpey, J., Velten, E., & Dain, R. (1992). Rational recovery from addictions. In W. Dryden & L. Hill (Eds.), *The fundamentals of rational-emotive therapy.* Stony Stratford, England: Open University Press.

*Trimpey, L., & Trimpey, J. (1990). *Rational recovery from fatness: The small book.* Lotus, CA: Lotus Press.

Velten, E. (1986). Withdrawal from heroin and methadone with rational-emotive therapy. In W. Dryden & P. Trower (Eds.), *Rational-emotive therapy: Recent developments in theory and practice* (pp. 228–247). Bristol, England: Institute for RET (UK).

*Velten, E. (Speaker). (1989). *How to be unhappy at work* (Cassette Recording). New York: Institute for Rational-Emotive Therapy.

Vogler, R. E., & Bartz, W. R. (1982). *The better way to drink: Moderation and control of problem drinking.* Oakland, CA: New Harbinger Publications.

*Walen, S. R., DiGiuseppe, R., & Wessler, R. L. (1980). *A practitioner's guide to rational-emotive therapy.* New York: Oxford.

*Warga, C. (1989). Profile of psychologist Albert Ellis. New York: Institute for Rational-Emotive Therapy. (Originally published in *Psychology Today*, Sept., 1989.)

Warren, R., & Zgourides, G. D. (1991). *Anxiety disorders: A rational-emotive perspective*. Elmsford, NY: Pergamon.

Wessler, R. A., & Wessler, R. L. (1980). *The principles and practice of rational-emotive therapy*. San Francisco: Jossey-Bass.

Wiener, D. (1987). *Albert Ellis: Passionate skeptic*. New York: Praeger.

Wilson, B. (1957). *Alcoholics Anonymous comes of age*. New York: AA World Services, Inc.

Wilson, B. (1985). *Alcoholics Anonymous* (3rd ed.). New York: AA World Services, Inc.

*Wolfe, J. L. (Speaker). (1980). *Woman—assert yourself* (Cassette Recording). New York: Institute for Rational-Emotive Therapy.

*Wolfe, J. L., & Brand, E. (Eds.). (1977). *Twenty years of rational therapy*. New York: Institute for Rational-Emotive Therapy.

Wolfe, J. L., & Fodor, I. G. (1975). A cognitive-behavioral approach to modifying assertive behavior in women. *Counseling Psychologist*, 5(4), 45–52.

Wolpe, J. (1982). *The practice of behavior therapy* (3rd ed.). Elmsford, NY: Pergamon.

*Woods, P. J. (1990). *Controlling your smoking*. Roanoke, VA: Scholar's Press.

*Yankura, J., & Dryden, W. (1990). *Doing RET: Albert Ellis in action*. New York: Springer.

*Young, H. S. (1974). *A rational counseling primer*. New York: Institute for Rational-Emotive Therapy.

About the Authors

Albert Ellis, born in Pittsburgh and raised in New York City, holds a bachelor's degree from the City College of New York and M.A. and Ph.D. degrees in clinical psychology from Columbia University. He has been Adjunct Professor of Psychology at Rutgers University, Pittsburg State College, and other universities and has served as Chief Psychologist of the New Jersey State Diagnostic Center and Chief Psychologist of the New Jersey Department of Institutions and Agencies. He is the founder of rational-emotive therapy and the grandfather of cognitive-behavior therapy. He currently is President of the Institute for Rational-Emotive Therapy in New York City, has practiced psychotherapy, marriage and family therapy, as well as sex therapy, for almost fifty years and continues this practice at the Psychological Clinic of the Institute in New York. He is a Board of Advisors member of Rational Recovery Systems.

Dr. Ellis has published over 600 articles in psychological, psychiatric, and sociological journals and anthologies and has authored or edited more than 50 books, including *How to Live With a "Neurotic," Reason and Emotion in Psychotherapy, A New Guide to Rational Living, A Guide to Personal Happiness, The Practice of Rational-Emotive Therapy,* and *How to Stubbornly Refuse to Make Yourself Miserable About Anything—Yes, Anything!*

Emmett Velten was born and raised in Memphis, Tennessee, and holds a bachelor's degree from the University of Chicago and a Ph.D. in psychology from the University of Southern California. His dissertation produced the Velten Mood Induction Procedure, widely used in research on mood states. Dr. Velten has been a clinical school psychologist with the Memphis City Schools, staff psychologist in the Division of Gastroenterology of the University of Alabama School of Medicine, and Chief Psychologist at Yuma County Behavorial Health Services in Arizona. He presently is Clinical Services Director of Bay Area Addiction Research & Treatment (BAART) and California Detoxification Programs, a healthcare system with ten clinics located throughout California. Dr. Velten is a Board of Advisors member of Rational Recovery Systems, an instructor in the Department of Psychiatry at California Pacific Medical Center, and Assistant Clinical Professor at the University of California, San Francisco. Dr. Velten also maintains a private practice in San Francisco. He is a past president of the Association for Behavioral and Cognitive Therapy.

Index